Garden
RESCUE

Garden
RESCUE

First aid for plants and flowers

JO WHITTINGHAM

LONDON, NEW YORK, MUNICH, MELBOURNE, DELHI

Senior Editor Chauney Dunford
Senior Art Editor Alison Shackleton
Illustrator Vanessa Hamilton
Senior Jacket Creative Nicola Powling
Jacket Design Assistant Rosie Levine
Senior producer, Pre-production Tony Phipps
Senior Producer Seyhan Esen
Picture Research Lucy Claxton and Romaine Werblow
Managing Editor Penny Warren
Managing Art Editor Alison Donovan
Publisher Mary Ling
Art Director Jane Bull

DK Publishing
North American Consultants
Lori Spencer and Kate Johnsen
Editor Rebecca Warren

First American Edition, 2013

Published in the United States by DK Publishing,
375 Hudson Street, New York, New York 10014

13 14 15 16 17 10 9 8 7 6 5 4 3 2 1
001—185276—Mar/2013

Published in Great Britain by Dorling Kindersley Limited.

A catalog record for this book is available from the
Library of Congress.

ISBN 978-1-4654-0204-2

DK books are available at special discounts when purchased in bulk
for sales promotions, premiums, fund-raising, or educational use. For
details, contact: DK Publishing Special Markets, 375 Hudson Street,
New York, New York 10014 or SpecialSales@dk.com.

Printed and bound by South China Co. Ltd, China.

Discover more at
www.dk.com

Contents

KNOW YOUR GARDEN

How plants work	10
Know your site and soil	12
Know your trees, shrubs, and climbers	14
Know your perennials and bulbs	16
Know your bedding and lawn	18
How to spot a sick plant	20
How pests and diseases affect plants	22
Growing without chemicals	24
Garden friends and foes	28
What is a weed?	30
Don't Panic!	32

Jo Whittingham is a garden writer with a postgraduate degree in horticulture from the University of Reading, and loves to grow her own crops in a plot bursting with produce. Author of *Grow Something to Eat Every Day*, awarded the Garden Media Guild's Practical Book of the Year 2011, she has also written two books in DK's RHS Simple Steps to Success series; *Fruit and Vegetables in Pots* and *Vegetables in a Small Garden*. She also writes for *Amateur Gardening* magazine and *The Scotsman*.

THE EDIBLE GARDEN

Vegetable Rescue

How to grow vegetables　38
Know your crop types　44
Fruiting crop anatomy　46
What's wrong with my fruiting crops?　48
Fruiting crop clinic　50
Root crop anatomy　52
What's wrong with my root crops?　54
Root crop clinic　56
Leafy salad crop anatomy　58
What's wrong with my leafy salad crops?　60
Leafy salad crop clinic　62
Garden greens anatomy　64
What's wrong with my garden greens?　66
Garden greens clinic　68
Bulb and stem crop anatomy　70
What's wrong with my bulbs and stems?　72
Bulb and stem crop clinic　74
Pod crop anatomy　76
What's wrong with my pod crops?　78
Pod crop clinic　80

Fruit Rescue

How to grow fruit　84
Fruit tree anatomy　90
What's wrong with my fruit tree?　92
Fruit tree clinic　94
Pruning fruit trees　98
Soft fruit anatomy　100
What's wrong with my soft fruit?　102
Soft fruit clinic　104
Pruning fruit bushes　106

THE ORNAMENTAL GARDEN

How to grow ornamentals　110

Tree, shrub, and climber rescue

Garden tree anatomy　120
What's wrong with my garden tree?　122
Garden tree clinic　124
Pruning garden trees　128
Garden shrub anatomy　130
What's wrong with my garden shrub?　132
Garden shrub clinic　134
Pruning garden shrubs　138
Climbing plant anatomy　140
What's wrong with my climber?　142
Climbing plant clinic　144
Pruning climbing plants　146

Perennials, bulbs, and bedding rescue

Perennial plant anatomy　150
What's wrong with my perennials?　152
Perennial plant clinic　154
Patio and bedding plant anatomy　158
What's wrong with my patio plant?　160
Patio and bedding plant clinic　162
Garden bulb anatomy　164
What's wrong with my garden bulbs?　166
Garden bulb clinic　168

Lawn Rescue

Garden lawn anatomy　172
What's wrong with my lawn?　174
Garden lawn clinic　176

A–Z of common pests and diseases　180

Index/Acknowledgments　188

About this book

This book will take you through all the stages necessary to help you diagnose sickly garden plants, including fruit and vegetable crops, and all types of ornamentals. The first step to identifying a problem is to understand how plants grow and what they need. If you know what is normal, it's then far easier to tell when something is wrong. Check your plants for symptoms and use this book to lead you to a solution.

LEARN THE BASICS

The "Know your garden" section explains how plants work and what they need to grow well. It includes summaries of what to expect from all common plant types to help you tell the difference between problems and normal plant behavior. Panels (see right) show common characteristics that can be mistaken for problems. The section also identifies your garden friends and foes, and explains how to garden without chemicals.

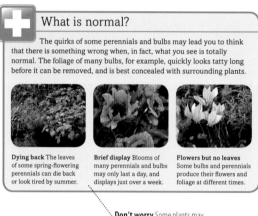

DETAILED ANATOMY

The "Edible garden" and "Ornamental garden" sections feature detailed growing advice to help you avoid plant problems. Anatomy guides (see right) give an overview of the main plant features common to the many plant types, and show where problems can occur. Use this information to help you understand and care for your plants better.

Info panels Learn more about key plant health issues

Plant galleries These show related plants and characteristics

USING THE ICONS
These icons are used throughout the book to help you find the information you are looking for more quickly. Utilize them as a guide.

Normal Check here to see plant characteristics not to worry about.

Diagnosis Look here for plant symptoms and signs of poor health.

Clinic Learn more about plant problems and how to treat them.

Pruning See how to prune your plants to solve or avoid problems.

SOLVING PROBLEMS

As soon as you see signs of poor plant health, first refer to the diagnostic chart (see right) that relates to the plant or crop type. These feature the most common symptoms, and by following the arrows—red for no, green for yes —they will lead to the most likely cause, whether a pest or disease, or poor growing conditions. Follow the page references given to see more about the problem, and finally find out how best to treat it and avoid it in the future.

Diagnosis charts Use these charts to narrow down the likely causes for poor plant health, then refer to the following clinic pages to confirm a diagnosis. Look at the sick plant while reading, or take a sample indoors.

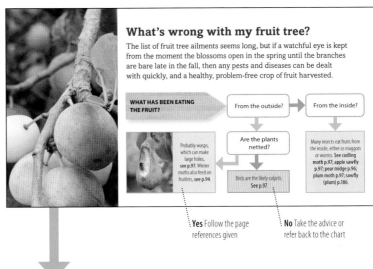

What's wrong with my fruit tree?

The list of fruit tree ailments seems long, but if a watchful eye is kept from the moment the blossoms open in the spring until the branches are bare late in the fall, then any pests and diseases can be dealt with quickly, and a healthy, problem-free crop of fruit harvested.

WHAT HAS BEEN EATING THE FRUIT? → From the outside? → From the inside?

Are the plants netted?

Probably wasps, which can make large holes, see p.97. Winter moths also feed on fruitlets, see p.94.

Birds are the likely culprits. See p.97.

Many insects eat fruits from the inside, either as maggots or worms. See codling moth p.97; apple sawfly p.97; pear midge p.96; plum moth p.97; sawfly (plum) p.186.

Yes Follow the page references given

No Take the advice or refer back to the chart

Notes Use these panels to learn more about plant pests and diseases

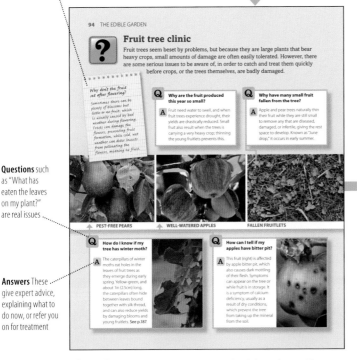

94 THE EDIBLE GARDEN

? Fruit tree clinic

Fruit trees seem beset by problems, but because they are large plants that bear heavy crops, small amounts of damage are often easily tolerated. However, there are some serious issues to be aware of, in order to catch and treat them quickly before crops, or the trees themselves, are badly damaged.

Why don't the fruit set after flowering?
Sometimes there can be plenty of blossoms but little or no fruit, which is usually caused by bad weather during flowering. Frosts can damage the flowers, preventing fruit formation, while cold, wet weather can deter insects from pollinating the flowers, meaning no fruit.

Q Why are the fruit produced this year so small?

A Fruit need water to swell, and when fruit trees experience drought, their yields are drastically reduced. Small fruit also result when the tree is carrying a very heavy crop; thinning the young fruitlets prevents this.

Q Why have many small fruit fallen from the tree?

A Apple and pear trees naturally thin their fruit while they are still small to remove any that are diseased, damaged, or infertile, giving the rest space to develop. Known as "June drop," it occurs in early summer.

PEST-FREE PEARS   WELL-WATERED APPLES   FALLEN FRUITLETS

Q How do I know if my tree has winter moth?

A The caterpillars of winter moths eat holes in the leaves of fruit trees as they emerge during early spring. Yellow-green, and about 1in (2.5cm) long, the caterpillars often hide between leaves bound together with silk thread, and can also reduce yields by damaging blooms and young fruitlets. See p.187.

Q How can I tell if my apples have bitter pit?

A This fruit (right) is affected by apple bitter pit, which also causes dark mottling of their flesh. Symptoms can appear on the tree or while fruit is in storage. It is a symptom of calcium deficiency, usually as a result of dry conditions, which prevent the tree from taking up the mineral from the soil.

Questions such as "What has eaten the leaves on my plant?" are real issues

Answers These give expert advice, explaining what to do now, or refer you on for treatment

Plant clinics The clinic pages give more detail about plant problems to help you determine what is wrong with your plant. How to treat the issue is then explained in the "A–Z of common pests and diseases," pp.180–187.

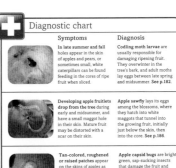

✚ Diagnostic chart

	Symptoms	Diagnosis
	In late summer and fall holes appear in the skin of apples and pears, or sometimes small, white caterpillars can be found feeding in the cores of ripe fruit when sliced.	**Codling moth larvae** are usually responsible for damaging ripening fruit. They overwinter in the tree's bark, and adult moths lay eggs between late spring and midsummer. See p.182.
	Developing apple fruitlets drop from the tree during early and midsummer, and have a small maggot hole in their skin. Mature fruit may be distorted with a scar on their skin.	**Apple sawfly** lays its eggs among the blossoms, where they hatch into white maggots that tunnel toward the growing fruit, initially just below the skin, then into the core. See p.186.
	Tan-colored, roughened or raised patches appear on the skins of apples as they ripen in late summer. Leaves at the shoot tips may also be peppered with small holes.	**Apple capsid bugs** are bright green, sap-sucking insects that damage the fruit and leaves with their toxic saliva. Fortunately, damage is only superficial and fruit can still be eaten. See p.181.
	Ragged holes appear in the skins of ripe fruit, such as peaches, plums, and apples during summer, and gradually increase in size as the sweet flesh beneath is eaten away.	**Wasps** find ripe fruit irresistible and will eat their own way into soft-skinned fruit or feed where birds have already damaged the tougher skins of apples and pears. See p.187.
	Small ripening fruit, such as cherries, vanish altogether, or larger specimens, such as apples, pears, and plums exhibit deep holes where the skin had been pierced.	**Birds** enjoy the taste of ripe fruit and will either eat them whole or peck through the skin with their beaks to take portions of juicy flesh. Larger fruits will often be dislodged from the tree. See p.180.
	Plums ripen prematurely, and when cut open, reveal a brown area around the stone containing maggot excrement or sometimes the culprit; a ⅓in- (1cm-) long, pale pink caterpillar.	**Plum moth caterpillars** hatch in early summer and burrow into developing fruit to feed on their flesh. They eat their way out and overwinter in the bark, ready for next year. See p.185.

Common symptoms To help decide between similar problems, many are grouped together to show the differences between them.

Know **your** garden

Taking time to learn about your plants and plot allows you to choose plants that suit the garden's climate and soil. Settled in the right spot, they will get off to a healthy start, perform well, and shrug off any ailments, while specimens in unsuitable conditions will struggle. This section includes all you need to help understand your garden better, beginning with how plants grow. Use the summary of different plant types—from trees to lawns—to familiarize yourself with what is normal before learning to recognize signs of poor health. Using garden chemicals is covered, along with details of organic methods. Finally, galleries of garden friends and foes, weeds, and symptoms that need not induce panic provide a quick reference to help identify common garden concerns.

How plants work

Each part of a plant has its own important role to perform to promote healthy growth, and ultimately, reproduction. Understanding how plants work helps get the best from edible and ornamental plants, and makes it easier to quickly recognize and help specimens with an ailment or struggling in poor growing conditions.

PLANT BASICS

Just like all other living things, plants have basic needs. They require water, food, light, air, and warmth to grow well, which is where the gardener can often help. Garden plants originate from all over the world, and while many grow in a wide range of conditions, some will suffer in excessive cold or heat. It is therefore best to grow those naturally adapted to suit your local climate.

Plants produce energy for growth using photosynthesis, a process that occurs wherever the green pigment, chlorophyll, is present, mainly in leaves. Exposure to sunlight converts carbon dioxide and water into sugar to fuel cells. Water taken up by the roots is released through pores in the leaves, drawing it upward, and keeping plant tissues healthy. Soil nutrients, dissolved in the water absorbed by the roots, are channeled along the stems to wherever needed.

THE IMPORTANCE OF LEAVES
Plants use the green pigment in their leaves to harness the sun's energy and to power growth. Diseased, damaged, and wilting leaves reduce plant vigor.

THE ROLE OF FLOWERS
Colorful and scented to attract insects, or adapted to scatter pollen in the wind, flowers need to be pollinated for fruit and seeds to form.

REPRODUCTION

Flowering plants produce seed, but many create offspring in other ways, too. Some send up shoots from long, shallow roots, while others cast stems across the soil, allowing plantlets to take root along their length.

PLANT ROOTS

Firmly anchoring plants in the soil, roots also take up all the water and nutrients required. Wilting foliage and stems are often the first indication of root damage caused by pests, diseases, waterlogged soil, or digging.

MALE AND FEMALE PLANTS
Some shrubs bear male and female flowers on separate plants, meaning both must be planted near each other for a good crop of berries on the female plant.

SETTING AND DISPERSING SEEDS
Some fruit bushes and trees are self-pollinating, while others need a pollination partner. Animals feed on the sweet fruit, then disperse the seeds they contain.

PLANT STEMS

At the heart of the plant, the stems provide support, and transport water and food between roots and leaves. The stem's tough outer layer protects against pests and diseases.

Herbaceous stems Unlike trees and shrubs that form permanent growth, herbaceous perennials die back each year. Their temporary stems are usually softer, and taller plants may need support.

Know your site and soil

Every garden plot is unique. Neighboring sites, and even different parts of an average-sized yard, can offer plants quite different growing conditions. This depends on the direction each area faces, the shade and shelter created by surrounding buildings and trees, and the soil type. Spending time getting to know your site will enable you to choose plants that will adapt to the quirks of every corner so they should flourish with minimal attention and few problems.

EXPOSURE

The first important thing to find out about your garden is the direction that it faces, or its exposure. South-facing gardens are usually warm and bright, while those facing north tend to be cool and shady. While some plants crave full sun, others only thrive in shade, so figuring out the exposure of your borders, walls, and patios allows them to be planted well. Take into account shade cast by tall buildings, trees, and hedges.

Providing shelter

Exposure to strong winds can damage plants and prevent pollination of crops. Establish the direction of prevailing winds and diffuse their strength using hedges, trees, and windbreak fabric. Solid walls and buildings provide shelter at their base, but create turbulence on their leeward side, which can be as destructive as the original gusts.

The shelter produced by walls, fences, buildings, hedges, and trees can also cause rain shadows because rainwater often doesn't reach the soil in these areas. This results in very dry conditions and means plants often need watering, in sun and shade.

Winter frost

Knowing when to expect the first and last frost is a useful guide for gardeners, since many plants cannot tolerate freezing conditions. The frost-free growing season shortens the further north and inland your plot.

(above) **Choose plants** that match the site. Ferns, for example, prefer damp shade.

(left) **In a sunny, sheltered** location, tender plants can be grown, but check for frost pockets, where cold air gathers. This can occur in dips or at the base of slopes.

GARDEN SOIL

Too often taken for granted, soil is the lifeblood of the garden, providing the vital moisture and nutrients needed to produce strong, healthy plants. Getting to know your soil is easy and not only allows you to work and improve it effectively, but having an understanding also means that you can choose plants that will naturally grow strongly. As a result, they will be less likely to fall victim to pests and diseases.

Different types of soil

Ideal crumbly garden soil is called loam and does not get too sticky when wet, or dry out too quickly. In reality, most gsrdens have either light or heavy soils. Light, sandy soil is easy to dig, but it drains so freely that it dries out rapidly and nutrients are washed right through it. Heavy, clay soils are much harder to work with, clumping together in big clods that become rock hard when dry. Clay drains slowly after rain, so should not be worked when wet to avoid compaction. Whatever soil type you have, the annual addition of well-rotted organic matter, such as garden compost, will improve it enormously.

TEST YOUR SOIL

Find out the pH of your garden soil using one of the widely available test kits. When mixed with a chemical solution in a small test-tube, soil samples collected from around the garden cause a color change according to the pH, which can then be assessed using a simple color chart.

Acidic or alkaline

Knowing if your soil is acidic or alkaline will affect the plants that you choose to grow. Specialized groups of plants thrive in alkaline soils and acidic soils, but most plants are quite happy in the most common, slightly acidic, garden soils. The range of plants grown locally often gives a good indication of soil pH, but simple testing kits can quickly give a definitive answer (*see above*).

Well-drained or boggy

Water pooling on the soil surface is a sure sign of poor drainage. Many wonderful bog plants will thrive in such wet conditions, but most plants need soil that drains more freely. Break up compacted layers with a garden fork and then work in plenty of grit and organic matter.

IMPROVE YOUR SOIL

The best single way to improve the quality of your soil, and the health of your plants, is to add plenty of organic matter each year. Well-rotted compost or manure can either be dug into new beds and vegetable patches, or applied as a thick mulch on the surface around established plants, avoiding the stems.

SOIL DEFICIENCIES

Discolored foliage can occur when plants are deficient in particular nutrients. Nitrogen and magnesium are easily washed from sandy soils but can be supplemented using fertilizers. Sometimes nutrients are present, but plants are still unable to absorb them, thanks to dry or acidic conditions.

Iron deficiency

Magnesium deficiency

Nitrogen deficiency

Know your trees, shrubs, and climbers

The backbone of your planting, trees and shrubs provide the garden with structure and solidity, while climbers cover, soften, and screen. Their height and shape make them ideal for sheltering the yard from wind and sun, or creating divisions within it. Many also have colorful flowers and berries, attractive foliage, or striking bark.

TREES

Habit Trees produce a single trunk supporting woody branches—some may be multistemmed. So called "fastigiate" trees are tall and slim, while others have a weeping habit.

Grown for Planted for their varied forms, foliage, flowers, fall colors, berries, and bark. They can be used as screens, hedges, and windbreaks.

Where to grow A variety of soils and situations suit most trees, provided they have enough space. Some are not fully hardy, or need specific soil conditions to flourish.

Pruning Young trees need pruning to create the desired shape, but most mature trees only require the removal of dead or damaged wood.

Size Dwarf trees may grow just as tall as your height, while standard trees can tower over 300ft (90m). The rate at which they grow varies tremendously also.

Season of interest Deciduous trees drop their leaves in fall, while evergreens keep their foliage year-round. Spring blossoms, fall-leaf color, and berries, along with winter bark, are all additional features.

Long-term investmant Trees can live for decades, so it's worth choosing one you will enjoy for many years to come, and that suits your yard.

Lifespan Trees can live for centuries, although many popular garden types, such as flowering cherries and crabapples, last for just 50–80 years before gradually dying back.

How sold Can be bought year-round grown in containers, or ordered bare-root from specialty nurseries for fall delivery and planting.

SHRUBS

Habit Shrubs are woody plants with numerous stems arising at soil level. They may be tall or dwarf, bushy or slender, evergreen or deciduous, and many can be trained against a wall.

Grown for Often prized for showy flowers and berries, shrubs can also have attractive foliage, colorful stems, and striking forms. Many are ideal for hedging.

Where to grow Originating from diverse habitats, shrubs grow in a wide range of conditions. Many thrive in fertile soil in full sun, but some prefer shade, specific soil conditions, or are not fully hardy.

Pruning Annual pruning is essential to keep some shrubs in good shape and flowering well. Others only need to have diseased or damaged wood removed in order to thrive.

Size Hugely variable, from low-growing lavenders and heathers, to treelike shrubs up to 20ft (6m) tall. Their size can be controlled by pruning and training.

Season of interest Deciduous and evergreen, shrubs deliver a year-round display. Flowers can be found in every season, while berries and bright bark light up the fall and winter. Plant a variety for prolonged interest in the garden.

Lifespan Large shrubs can last decades, especially if well cared for. Some short-lived and smaller shrubs lose vigor and are best renewed every 5–10 years. Not all shrubs are full hardy and may die sooner, depending on conditions.

How sold Container-grown shrubs are sold in garden centers and nurseries all year, while bare-root specimens are available from nurseries during winter.

(above) **Short-lived color** Lavender often dies off after less than five years.

(right) **Aerial display** Climbers bring color to eye level and can give a fine show.

CLIMBERS

Habit Climbers are vigorous, annual and perennial plants with long herbaceous stems, or perennials with a permanent woody framework.

Grown for Climbers may have bold flowers, attractive foliage, and even fruit. Often grown to cover walls and fences, and to screen unsightly areas.

Where to grow Grow up supports on walls, fences, or pergolas, through other plants, or even along the ground. Some require full sun, while others prefer shade, but most like fertile, moist soil. A few are tender.

Pruning Annual pruning is needed to keep some flowering freely, while most need pruning to keep them neat and within bounds.

Size Varies from 6ft (2m) to 70ft (20m), depending on the climber. Pruning limits size. Be diligent when cutting back fast-growing plants.

Season of interest Most flower from spring to early fall—some in winter and early spring. Evergreen foliage looks good all year; deciduous types can have bold fall tints.

Lifespan A single year for annuals, but decades for some woody climbers, such as wisteria.

How sold Most sold in pots, although annuals, such as sweet peas, are often grown from seed.

What is normal?

Understanding your plants helps you tell which symptoms to worry about and which are normal. Evergreens shedding leaves in summer may look bad, but it is a natural part of foliage renewal. Woody plants can also take time to establish and flower, but it will be worth the wait.

Water shoots Some shrubs produce vigorous stems that never flower. These should be cut out.

Disappearing berries Bright fruit often vanish once ripe because they have been eaten.

Non-stick climbers Even self-clinging climbers need a hand when first planted, so provide support.

Know your perennials and bulbs

These two groups of plants are all about injecting color into the garden. Traditional summer herbaceous borders and spring displays of bulbs make wonderful showcases for perennials and bulbs. Both will mingle happily in mixed plantings, however, and have representatives that flower in every season, so use them to their full potential and don't be afraid to experiment.

PERENNIALS

Habit Hardy perennials generally produce new growth in spring, flower in summer, then die back to the base in fall. The roots and young shoots overwinter, ready to resprout again. Some, like many ferns, are "wintergreen"—keeping their leaves throughout the winter and replacing them every spring.

Grown for Beautiful flowers, colorful foliage, and striking shapes all make perennials great garden plants. Some also bear seed heads and fruit, which are often left to add fall and winter interest. There is a huge range of sizes and shapes, adding year-round spark to mixed borders.

Where to grow There are perennials to suit almost any soil and situation, but most are particular about their growing conditions and will only perform well when planted in the right place. Many do best in full sun and moist, well-drained soil, although some prefer shade or boggy ground. Perennials are often fully hardy, but give tender plants winter protection.

Pruning Cut to the base once old growth has died back in the fall. No further pruning is required, but many perennials benefit from being lifted and divided every 3–5 years. Taller plants may need staking.

Size Perennials vary greatly in size, from low-growing groundcover to upright giants for the back of a border. Most spread to form clumps over several years, which can be divided if they become too big. A few can be invasive.

Season of interest Most perennials flower at different times from spring to fall, some briefly and others for weeks at a time. Plant a selection to give prolonged interest. Many wintergreens have attractive foliage and flower from winter to spring.

Lifespan Well-maintained perennials can live for decades, although they may die out in a few seasons if left undivided and uncared for. Peonies can live for more than 100 years.

How sold Commonly sold in garden centers and nurseries as pot-grown plants, perennials can also be bought bare-root by mail order.

(above) **Wintergreen perennials** Bergenias send up welcome early spring flowers, while the leaves supply year-round colour.

(left) **Enduring colour** Peony plants can thrive for decades with a little care.

BULBS AND TUBERS

Habit Bulb- and tuber-forming plants have underground storage organs evolved from swollen stems, leaves, or roots. The plants grow, flower, then die back, and remain dormant below ground for a period each year.

Grown for The bold flowers of bulbs produce a dramatic, but short-lived display, lasting from as little as a few days to several weeks. They provide seasonal color for borders and pots.

Where to grow Most prefer a well-drained site in full sun, but some species like moist, shady conditions. Many are fully hardy, but some are best lifted or protected over winter.

Pruning Clear away all spent growth when bulbs die back. Allow leaves to die back naturally, because removing them too early weakens the bulb.

Size Bulbs range from small plants, suitable for the front of borders and naturalizing in lawns, to large clump-forming specimens, similar

What is normal?

The quirks of some perennials and bulbs may lead you to think that there is something wrong when, in fact, what you see is totally normal. The foliage of many bulbs, for example, quickly looks old long before it can be removed, and is best concealed with surrounding plants.

Dying back The leaves of some spring-flowering perennials can die back or look tired by summer.

Brief display Blooms of many perennials and bulbs may only last a day, and displays just over a week.

Flowers but no leaves Some bulbs and perennials produce their flowers and foliage at different times.

in stature to many perennials. Dwarf species and cultivars are well suited for growing in containers.

Season of interest Spring is not the only season for bulbs, because different types flower through summer, fall, and even into winter. The majority flower in spring and summer, but plant a selection for year-round color.

Lifespan Given the right conditions, bulbs can flower and spread in the garden for many years, sometimes decades. In poor circumstances, they may only flower for one year.

How sold Dry bulbs are available from garden centers and by mail order. Some are also sold in growth with bare roots "in the green," or growing in pots.

(above) **Naked blooms** *Colchicum* produce flowers before their leaves appear.

(right) **Dramatic heads** Alliums flower in summer – many have attractive seedheads.

Know your bedding and lawn

Fast-growing and vibrant, bedding plants add cheer to the garden and patio pots. Widely available, they are usually treated as annuals, although many will thrive for more than one year if given the correct care. At the heart of most yards, the lawn is often mown then forgotten, but extra attention will be repaid with a greener lawn that wears well and isn't overrun with weeds.

BEDDING

Habit These annual, biennial, or tender perennial plants are often used for a single seasonal display. Some are hardy, but those described as half-hardy or tender should only be planted outdoors when the risk of frost has passed.

Grown for Bedding plants are cultivated for their large or numerous bright flowers, and lush, decorative foliage. Fast growing, they quickly create luxuriant seasonal displays.

Where to grow Ideal for borders, containers, and hanging baskets, most bedding thrives in full sun, although a few, such as impatiens, prefer some shade. They all need fertile, well-drained soil to flower for a prolonged period.

Pruning No pruning is required, but deadhead frequently to encourage more flowers to form. Tender perennials overwintered under cover should be cut back in spring.

Size Generally bushy and compact, most bedding plants don't often grow more than 12in (30cm) tall, particularly in pots, although some types, such as cosmos, are taller.

(above) **Annual color** Short-lived summer annuals give a vivid display for a few months when watered and fed regularly.

(left) **Tender perennial** Protect tender perennials during winter and you will be able to enjoy them year after year.

The stems of those with a trailing habit can reach 24in (60cm) in length, creating dramatic hanging baskets.

Season of interest Bedding plants are usually split into summer and winter/spring bedding. Summer bedding flowers outdoors once nights are frost-free. Winter/spring bedding takes its place in fall, giving color in the colder months.

Lifespan Displays will not usually last in peak condition for more than six months. Many of the plants will grow for longer, but lose their compact form and do not flower as profusely, so are normally discarded. Some tender perennials can look good for several years given winter protection.

How sold Garden centers, nurseries, and mail-order suppliers sell bedding plants at various stages of growth. The smallest are the tiny plug plants, which are best potted and grown on before planting out. Flats of small plants are popular, along with larger specimens in individual pots. Seeds are also widely available.

What is normal?

Bedding plants may not perform as you expect, and lawns can disappoint, but this isn't necessarily due to pests or diseases. Even pristine lawns look unkempt when their edges go untrimmed and grass creeps into borders, while the range of bedding available can easily reveal surprises.

Unusual flowers Bedding plants can be very unusual. If a plant looks odd, check the label for reassurance.

Sticky leaves Some plants, such as petunias, have naturally sticky leaves. They are perfectly healthy.

Lawn weeds All but the best tended lawns contain some weeds. The key is to control the most vigorous.

LAWNS

Habit A continuous carpet of turf, made up of several different grass species, creates a lawn. The roots of the plants are shallow and the leaves are mown short. When cutting the leaves, the central growing point at the base of each plant remains intact, allowing each plant to repeatedly regrow and spread.

Grown for A healthy green lawn to provide a neat foil for beds, or a practical place to sit or play.

Where to grow Lawns do best in a sunny location, on fertile, well-drained soil. Specially formulated mixtures of grass are available for shady and hard-wearing lawns. Improve the soil and drainage well before laying a new lawn.

Pruning Ideally, lawns should be mown weekly when the grass is growing in spring and fall. Most lawns are best cut to a height of about 1in (2.5cm), but should be allowed to grow longer during hot, dry weather to help the grass cope. Avoid removing more than a third of the leaf length with each cut.

Size Lawns can be tiny, or the size of a football field. The bigger the lawn, the longer it will take to maintain.

Season of interest Turf should look good all year round and can be enhanced by planting it with bulbs or wildflowers.

Lifespan Although the lifespan of individual grass plants is relatively short, if well cared for, a lawn can continue to look good for decades.

How sold Different mixes of grass seed are available, depending on the conditions and wear that the lawn will have to withstand. Rolls of sod are also widely available.

(above) **Wildflower lawns** Meadow-style lawns look attractive, and provide an oasis for beneficial insects and wildlife.

(right) **Manicured effects** Achieving the perfect lawn can be a labor of love, but the results are often stunning.

How to spot a sick plant

Recognizing that there is a problem in the garden is the first important step toward diagnosing the cause and finding a remedy. The best way to spot when something isn't right is to become familiar with healthy plants. Take in what surrounds you while you regularly weed, deadhead, and water. Sickly specimens will soon start to stand out clearly.

WHAT TO LOOK FOR

Leaves are the most obvious place to look for trouble. Color changes, wilting, distortion, marks, spots, and holes are all signs that something is wrong. Check both the upper and lower leaf surfaces for small insects, a sticky substance called "honeydew," or moldlike fungal growth.

Flower buds falling or failing to open can indicate poor growing conditions or pest problems, while blooming flowers, and consequently fruit set, can be spoiled by pests or bad weather. Check ripening fruit for marks, splits, holes, and rot.

Stem damage is a prime site for infection and should be cut back promptly. Watch for weak, floppy herbaceous stems, dark, wet-looking or weeping marks, and fungus growing from woody plants. Root problems are often betrayed by weak growth and wilting foliage.

A general lack of vigor and poor performance suggest a problem with the growing conditions, perhaps soil that is too dry or a site that is too shady. Plants in the wrong place are particularly susceptible to pests and diseases in their weakened state.

CHEWED LEAVES
Different pests eat holes, nibble notches, strip entire leaves, or munch them from within. Growth can be stunted and young plants killed by heavy attacks.

WILTING STEMS
Lack of water in the leaves and stems causes plants to wilt. This can, however, be caused by waterlogging and root problems as well as dry soil.

A sickly specimen The yellowing, marked leaves are a sure sign that this plant is sick. A quick glance suggests it's too big for its pot, leaving it dry and malnourished.

DISCOLORED LEAVES

Foliage that takes on shades of yellow, brown, red, or purple in the growing season shows a plant in distress. Take it is an early warning sign and act.

SIGNS OF DECAY

Dark patches, spots, fungal growth, and rotting on any part of a plant are usually the symptoms of disease. Old or weak plants are most at risk of infection.

WEAK GROWTH

Poor growth and pale or yellowing foliage can indicate a lack of nutrients, unsuitable growing conditions, root problems, or pest infestation.

Some things are normal

Although many symptoms of poor plant health are obvious, a number of quite normal characteristics can cause alarm, particularly for new gardeners. Stepping back to take a look at the general condition of the plant, or the rest of the garden, can help you decide what is normal and what might be a cause for concern. Avoid assuming the worst.

Bold leaf colors Many garden plants have been bred with unusually colored, variegated, and patterned foliage, which may be mistaken for a problem.

Imperfect fruit Strangely shaped fruit can occur for no obvious reason. However, they still taste great, and are part of the fun of growing your own crops.

Bump on the trunk Many ornamental and fruit trees are grafted onto rootstocks. A harmless bump sometimes forms low on the trunk where the graft took place.

Older leaves yellowing Evergreen plants naturally drop a portion of their older leaves during the growing season. Where the plant is otherwise healthy, this is fine.

Plantlets and bulbils Most plants reproduce as seed, but some also produce offsets, plantlets, and bulbils, which can appear at the roots, stems, or flowers.

Natural dieback The lower leaves of some plants, such as palms and some evergreens, die back as they grow, eventually leaving a bare stem.

How pests and diseases affect plants

It is often easy to see that there is something wrong with a plant, but difficult, even for experienced gardeners, to diagnose exactly what the problem is. A little knowledge of how pests and diseases attack plants, and the symptoms they cause, can really help to reveal what is wrong. Even if the exact culprit remains unknown, the diagnosis at least allows some sensible remedial action to be taken.

SPOTTING SYMPTOMS

Plants attacked by pests and diseases often exhibit wounds or points of infection, can grow less vigorously, and perhaps produce fewer flowers or smaller yields of fruit than healthy specimens. Nutrient deficiencies and poor growing conditions similarly affect plants and those subject to these stresses are vulnerable to infection. Wounds and weakness created by attacks can also leave plants open to further problems.

Pinpointing pests

Pests affect plants in a variety of ways. Some of the easiest to identify are those that eat large holes in leaves. The culprits may still be present and patterns of damage are distinctive. These pests spoil the appearance of plants, can reduce vigor, and even kill seedlings. Sap-feeding insects feed on leaves and stems, often causing distortion, discoloration, and stunting of young

(above top) **Currant blister aphid** causes raised areas on currant leaves. See p.182.

(above) **Peach leaf curl** results in distorted pink-red foliage on peach trees. See p.184.

(left) **Virus** on a blueberry bush produces yellow and coral pink mottling on foliage.

Garden greens are targeted by pigeons, which rapidly strip foliage to the stems, leaving sharp beak marks.

growth. Look under leaves and on bark to find and name the pest.

It may be hard to tell what has caused leaves to wilt and die unless you can find the soil-dwelling pest responsible for root damage. Pests can ruin fruit by feeding on them from the inside or outside, but rarely affect the rest of the plant and are often easy to identify.

Distinguishing disease

Fungal infections are common and usually create dusty markings or spots on foliage, causing leaves to die back in severe cases. Fungi can also kill seedlings, rot fruit, and cause root and stem decay, which can kill even large plants. Toadstools or bracket fungi can sometimes be seen at the base or on branches of infected woody plants.

There are many symptoms for viruses, such as distorted and stunted growth, yellow leaf patterns, or stripes of unwanted color on flowers. Bacterial infections are less common, but spread rapidly resulting in softening of tissue, oozing liquid, and an unpleasant smell.

USING GARDEN CHEMICALS

Even dedicated organic gardeners may sometimes use permitted garden chemicals to help control difficult pests and diseases. Although all garden chemicals being sold have been tested to minimize risks to the user and environment, they should only be used against their intended target when really necessary, and exactly as directed on the label.

Safety Wear rubber gloves and avoid inhaling droplets or dust by standing upwind of the treated area. Only use recommended products on edible plants and store out of the reach of children.

Insecticides Some work on contact with the insect and are sprayed all over leaves. Others are absorbed by plants to kill insects that feed on them. Spray in the evening to avoid killing bees.

Fungicides Most are available as sprays with a systemic action and can treat infection in all areas once absorbed by the plant. Others are available as powders to mix with water for spraying or used as a dust.

Weed killers Contact sprays or liquids painted onto leaves quickly kill annual weeds; those with a systemic action are absorbed into the plant to kill the roots of persistent perennials.

Growing without chemicals

Whether or not you choose to use pesticides and inorganic fertilizers on your plot, many valuable lessons can be learned from the principles of organic gardening. The central idea is to create conditions that foster plants bursting with health. Strong growth enables plants to more readily resist pests and diseases, although plenty of options remain open to organic gardeners when problems do arise.

NATURAL GROWTH

The promise of fresh, organically produced fruit and vegetables is frequently the motivation for growing your own. Those gardeners concerned about the effects of chemicals on children, pets, wildlife, and the wider environment, however, are often enthusiastic to grow ornamental plants organically too.

Organic gardening encourages an understanding of local growing conditions and the way plants work. In turn, this helps prevent many difficulties and is becoming increasingly valuable as the range of pesticides available to amateur gardeners decreases.

Create a healthy balance

Successful organic gardening relies on establishing a balance where plants flourish in fertile soil improved with lots of organic matter and pest numbers are kept in check by beneficial wildlife. Achieving this takes time, as can the change in

mindset required for gardeners used to reaching for the sprayer at the first sign of trouble. Even in successful organic plots a low level of damage has to be tolerated, and there will be occasions when pests and diseases get the upper hand. There is, however, something deeply satisfying about learning from these incidents, and finding ways to keep them from recurring in future.

Feed the soil not the plant

Improving garden soil by adding substantial quantities of bulky organic matter every year is the most effective way to boost the health of

Mingling edible and ornamental plants in containers and all around the garden can create fabulous, colorful combinations, and help to distract pests from cropping plants.

PLANTS TO ATTRACT BENEFICIAL INSECTS

Many insects help gardeners by pollinating crops or feeding on troublesome plant pests. To help attract these allies, provide them with nectar and pollen by growing a range of plants that flower throughout the year.

Trees and shrubs are especially good food sources when they are in flower. Avoid plants that have double blooms because they often produce no nectar.

Gaillardias Daisylike flowers are a favorite with insects because their flat surface is easy to land on. Their many tiny central florets are filled with sweet nectar, which gives insects a good feed from each flower.

your plants. Organic matter improves the structure of the soil, helps retain moisture, slowly releases valuable nutrients, and feeds the underground creatures that keep soil healthy.

Well-rotted garden compost and barnyard manure are two of the best materials for digging in to new beds or laying as a thick mulch on the soil around established plants. In fact, some organic gardeners practice the appealing "no-dig" method. Once a mulch is applied, it is left for worms to work it into the soil, almost entirely removing the need for a spade.

No garden should be without a compost heap to convert spent plant material, grass clippings, most weeds, and even kitchen waste into a source of free, top-quality soil improver. Turn the heap with a fork, keep it covered to exclude weed seeds, and crumbly compost is ready in a few months.

Encourage beneficial wildlife

Providing suitable food and shelter helps attract a variety of wildlife into the garden. Many visitors, such as

Gardens bursting with flowers all year are magnets for pollinating insects, vital for good fruit crops, and other insects, like the hoverfly, that prey on plant pests.

birds, hedgehogs, ladybugs, and frogs, will repay your kindness by feeding on pests that are troubling your plants. Where they find infestations to feast on, these beneficial creatures will often return repeatedly or even breed, taking full advantage of the plentiful food source, controlling the pests.

Although good garden hygiene is important to prevent disease, leave fallen leaves, wood piles, and old perennial growth in a few areas, as cover for wildlife during winter.

Foxgloves A long flowering season makes this a valuable plant for insects. Not all insects can access nectar from the tubular flowers, but bumblebees disappear right inside to feed with their long tongues.

Poached egg plant The carpet of yellow-centered, white flowers produced by easy-to-grow *Limnanthes douglasii* is a magnet for beneficial insects. They can hop from one flower to the next.

Frothy flower heads Showy heads with many flowers, particularly those of umbellifers like sweet Cicely, are attractive to insects because they can move from one tiny flower to the next without much effort.

Even a small source of water will attract frogs and toads as well as birds and mammals. Bring insect allies into the garden to pollinate and prey on pests by planting nectar-rich flowers year-round.

Preventing problems

Prevention is always better than cure, and organic gardeners can adopt many strategies to keep pests and diseases at bay. Where they exist, grow cultivars bred with resistance to a particular problem. Disease-resistant forms of edible crops are common, but some ornamental plants also have this useful quality.

Crop rotation has long been practiced to help prevent pests and diseases from building up in the soil. Related edible crops, such as root crops, are grown together and moved to a new bed each year. This means it is several years before a crop returns to the same site, which is longer than most pests and diseases can survive in the soil. Apply the same principle in the ornamental garden by not replacing plants that have experienced problems with anything closely related.

Barriers are an effective way to keep pests and plants apart. Fine

Old plastic bottles can be put to good use. Cut them in half and place them over young plants to protect against slugs and snails. They can also act as watering funnels.

insect mesh, horticultural fabric, and various gauges of netting work well at keeping small insects, butterflies, and birds away from crops. Low-flying carrot rust flies will be thwarted by a 24in- (60cm-) high barrier around beds of carrots, and cabbage collars stop cabbage root flies from laying their eggs in the soil near young plants. Try to prevent slugs and snails from reaching vulnerable plants. Barriers include eggshells, copper tape, and pine needles.

Pests are often attracted by the strong scent of their host plants and can be distracted by mixing them with other highly aromatic plants, such as French marigolds. This is known as "companion planting" and has the added benefit of extra color, particularly in the vegetable plot.

Combat pests and diseases

If these methods fail to stop the spread of pests and diseases, there are other effective organic ways to tackle them. Traps are useful for reducing the prevalence of insect pests and can also provide an indication of their numbers. Beer

BIRD SCARERS

Though beneficial when eating pests, birds can attack crops. Every gardener has a favorite bird-scaring method to protect vulnerable plants. The light reflected from rows of CDs or shiny baubles, suspended from a string, can deter them. Decoy birds may convince them that your garden is already taken.

CDs and DVDs

Bird decoy

Shiny baubles

A simple compost heap turns unwanted garden waste into valuable soil improver.

traps sunk into the soil attract and drown slugs and snails. Hung in the branches of a tree, they trap wasps, while sticky yellow sheets ensnare greenhouse pests. Pheromone traps can also be used to lure fruit tree pests to a sticky end before mating.

Predatory mites, along with parasitic wasps and nematode worms, are available as biological controls capable of reducing the numbers of many common pests. They are effective used in the correct conditions, but it is important to remember that the pest must already be present for them to feed on, and many only work well in warm weather or in greenhouses.

Some natural chemicals can be used as pesticides to kill insects and treat fungal diseases in organic gardens. You can control some insect pests by using insecticidal soap and plant extracts, such as pyrethrum. These must be applied frequently since they kill pests on contact, and remember that they may harm beneficial insects too.

Use a variety of organic techniques to keep away pests and diseases. Here, a scarecrow and vibrant companion planting add color and a certain quirky style to this vegetable plot.

Garden friends and foes

Sometimes it may be hard to believe, but not every creature in the garden is out to eat your plants for breakfast. Many come to feast on the pests themselves, stop by to pollinate flowers, or move into the soil or compost heap to break down decaying material. Learn to distinguish these allies from your gardening foes to keep them safe, and to encourage more of them in to help.

STRIKE A BALANCE

Gardens are hard work to create, so when pests spoil a crop or prized plant, it is easy to take it personally and reach for the nearest pesticide. Like all visitors though, they're just looking for somewhere to eat or rest, and whichever friends and foes make

a home in your garden, remember that one often cannot exist without the other being present.

Without a steady supply of pests to eat, the gardener's friends will go elsewhere. There is clearly a balance to be struck here, where beneficial creatures keep pests at a manageable level, which organic growers will tell you sometimes works better than others. One thing guaranteed to upset this balance however, is the use of pesticides in the garden. Often extremely effective, they quickly wipe out their target, and sometimes other insects too, leaving nothing for the pest predators to eat.

Good beetle bad beetle Many beetle species cause gardeners problems, including the bright red lily beetle (*left*). Identify pests carefully however, because numerous beetles play useful roles, too.

Always consider their use carefully. Plants have their own defense mechanisms, and can often easily sustain a certain level of attack, without the need for intervention.

Identify the enemy

Damage to plants is often more noticeable than the pest itself. Take a look at the casualties and you will often find that if adult insects or their larvae are responsible, they will still be present, feeding away. Slugs and snails will only be found during the day in wet weather, but you can most likely catch them after dark if you use a flashlight.

Many insect larvae and slugs lurk underground, only to be seen when plants become sickly, root crops are lifted, or soil is turned. Birds and mammals, such as rabbits and deer,

THE BAD BUGS

Most gardens have a few common pests that recur every year, which vary depending on the range of plants cultivated and the location. You will quickly come to recognize those that inhabit your own plot, find out which plants they favor, and learn the best ways to deal with them.

Slugs and snails

Sawfly larvae

Caterpillars

Fallen fruit and decaying plant material can tempt pests into the garden. Keep it neat, while leaving a few hiding places for beneficial wildlife.

may never be caught while feeding, but can munch their way through borders rapidly. Look for distinctive beak and bite marks, along with droppings and footprints, to help identify the culprits.

Look out for your friends

Birds are the most obvious beneficial creatures, and encouraging them into the garden helps keep a lid on insect pest, slug, and snail numbers. Frogs, toads, newts, and bats are just some of the larger animals that visit or take up residence to feed on many of the commonest foes.

Insects are the gardener's allies, too. Ladybugs and lacewings are renowned for their prodigious aphid eating, but hoverfly larvae, ground beetles, and centipedes are among many more that view garden pests as lunch. Pollinating insects, including the much maligned wasp, visit flowers and transfer pollen between both edible and ornamental plants, ensuring viable seeds and juicy fruit. An array of worms, beetles, and microscopic organisms also works hard to keep soil in good condition.

THE GOOD GUYS

Beneficial creatures come in all shapes and sizes. Enticing as many into the garden as possible helps keep pest numbers in check, improves pollination, and provides you with a fascinating place to work and relax.

Bees Honeybees, bumblebees, and other species are crucial for pollinating flowers. Blooms rich in nectar will help attract them.

Ladybugs The adults and their fierce larvae prey on aphids in large numbers. Evergreen shrubs and dry leaves make ideal winter homes.

Frogs and toads Two of the few creatures with an appetite for slugs, they often go unnoticed. Attract them by digging a small pond.

Lacewings The delicate adults feed on pollen and nectar, while their voracious larvae devour countless aphids and other small insects.

Thrushes Beautiful garden birds, song thrushes use large, flat stones to break snail shells, enabling them to eat the creature inside.

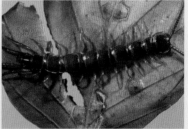

Centipedes Copper-colored, many-legged, and fast moving, centipedes live in fallen leaves and prey on small soil-dwelling pests.

What is a weed?

A weed is simply a plant growing where it is not wanted. They can be wild species that pop up from wind-blown seeds, or cultivated plants that have spread too rapidly or self-seeded too successfully. Weeding is an inescapable part of gardening, but understanding the plants you are dealing with and taking steps to control them can greatly reduce the work involved.

CONTROLLING WEEDS

The obvious question is "why bother weeding?" It is often said that an untidy garden is best for beneficial wildlife, so why can't we just tolerate weeds and save ourselves some work? The trouble with this approach is that the most vigorous weed plants quickly take over, which may work well in a meadow or wildlife garden. But, in most gardens, it is often not practical simply to let them flourish.

Most ornamental plants, fruit, and vegetables, particularly when they are young or newly planted, cannot cope with the competition from fast-growing weeds for water, light, and nutrients. Their growth and flowering will be adversely affected, and without help they will be weakened and may die. Weeds can also harbor many of the pests and diseases that trouble garden plants, so they are also best removed to reduce the risk of infection spreading.

Weeding by hand

Digging is what comes to mind when most people think of weeding, but

COMMON GARDEN WEEDS

When tackling weeds, understanding the way they spread is the key to success. They fall into two groups: annuals and perennials. Annuals can germinate and produce hundreds of seeds in a matter of weeks, allowing them to spread like wildfire. Luckily, as long as weeds are hoed or lifted before they scatter their seeds, they are easy to control. Perennials have fleshy roots that plunge deep into soil or spread just below the surface. Caught young, their removal is simple, but the large roots of established plants break easily and must be dug out entirely to keep the plant from spreading.

Dandelion Spread by wind-blown seeds, remove all of the deep taproot or the dandelion will simply reshoot.

Groundsel Each fast-growing annual plant can produce thousands of fluffy seeds from yellow flower heads.

Creeping thistle A clump-forming perennial with spreading roots, purple flowers, and airborne seeds.

Nettles Small annual nettles spread by seed. Large clumps of perennial nettles grow from fleshy roots.

AVOIDING PROBLEMS

To keep weeding to a minimum, don't dig. Most soil is full of weed seeds, which germinate in the surface layer. Turning the soil just brings a fresh batch of seeds to the surface, so use a hoe instead. To prevent weed growth use mulches, such as shredded bark or porous landscape fabric.

Many weeds are attractive plants that are really beneficial to wildlife. Make use of the flowers of thistles and clover, which feed pollinating insects.

this heavy work is only required to bring rough ground into cultivation or remove deep roots.

Hoeing is the quicker and easier option, best done on a hot, dry day, so severed weeds wilt and die rapidly, and you don't have to worry about picking them up from the ground. Groundcover plants suppress weeds in borders, while green manures fill bare soil in vegetable plots. As for keeping a lawn weed-free, regular mowing is the most effective method.

Using weed killers

Weed killer sprays can be particularly helpful for keeping paths neat and treating lawns, but be careful to use the correct chemical for the job, and don't let the spray drift onto plants.

Buttercups The creeping stems of this perennial spread rapidly, but its shallow roots make it easy to remove.

Annual meadow grass Short tufts of grass with feathery flower heads seed and reroot rampantly if not removed.

Bindweed twines around other plant stems. Dig out its perennial root system or it regenerates.

Bittercress Annual rosettes of lobed leaves and white flowers produce seed pods that pop when touched.

Docks Large leaves and tall flower spikes are fed by a deep perennial taproot, which is hard to remove.

Ragwort Uproot the feathery leaves and yellow, late-summer flowers—they are poisonous to livestock.

Don't panic!

When you start to discover all of the things that can go wrong in the garden, it's easy to imagine that every spot, mark, fallen leaf, misshapen growth, or creepy crawly is sinister. Thankfully, this is not the case, and what you see may be a natural part of the plant's cycle of growth, a pest or disease that is of little consequence to a healthy plant, or simply part of the fascinating diversity of life in the garden.

Yellowing leaves Older leaves of evergreen shrubs fall during spring and summer. Don't worry. It's normal, as long as new leaves are produced.

KEEP CALM

It is important not to panic when you spot what might be a problem. In order to keep a clear head, identify what has been seen and decide if any action is required. A useful first step is to take a look at the whole plant to see if it shows any obvious signs of trouble. If not, what you've seen may be a harmless bug or normal leaf fall. However, if things don't look right, be careful where you lay the blame.

Mistaken identity

The presence of pests often attracts other creatures onto plants, and it's wise to remember that beneficial creatures also share our gardens.

What you have seen may have arrived to feed on the sweet, sticky honeydew excreted by sap-sucking insects, or to prey on the pests themselves. Don't squash or spray insects at first sight; look further and they may lead to the real problem.

The mark of good fruit

Learning to tolerate nibbles and marks of homegrown crops can be a challenge when only blemish-free, store-bought produce has been your experience. Surface spots rarely affect eating quality, and most damage can be easily sliced off. Rather than panicking about every blotch, enjoy the satisfaction and fresh flavors of your own homegrown produce.

Rose leaf-rolling sawflies Roses tolerate a few leaves being curled tightly and eaten from the inside by these small caterpillars. Just ignore it.

REMEMBER TO RELAX

All this talk of plants under attack could stress a gardener out, but be sure to unwind outside after all your hard work. Lounging in a deck chair, while tolerating low levels of pest damage, gives beneficial wildlife a free rein, and keeps you among your plants, ready to spot any problems as they arise.

Ants Often seen collecting sticky honeydew excreted by sap-sucking insects, ants rarely harm plants and are easily tolerated. Let them be.

Cuckoo spit Blobs of white foam in early summer hide small, sap-sucking froghoppers. They cause little damage and are easily tolerated.

Shield bugs Although these striking insects are relatively large and feed on sap, they do not cause garden plants any serious problems.

June drop Just as the crop on apple and pear trees looks promising in early summer, trees shed diseased and excess fruit. This is normal.

Lichens Growing on branches and stems, lichens are not parasitic and are totally harmless to plants. In fact, lichens indicate clean air.

Fasciation Strange, flattened, or curled shoots and flowering stems can occur if the young growing point is damaged. It's odd but harmless.

Pollen beetles These small beetles feed on pollen from spring into summer. Harmless to the plants, they are only a nuisance in cut flowers.

Tomato ghost spot Fungal spores cause pale orange, circular marks on tomato skins. Marks are only skin-deep and fruits are perfectly edible.

Ladybug larvae More vicious-looking than most pests, ladybug larvae are great allies. Leave them alone to feed on aphids.

Slow-release fertilizer granules These small pale brown beads, found among roots of pot-grown plants, are often mistaken for pest eggs.

The **edible** garden

Homegrown fruit and vegetables are one of the greatest rewards in the garden, but delicious leaves, roots, pods, and fruit need good conditions to grow well and, unfortunately, are just as tempting to pests and diseases as they are to us. Bumper harvests are not produced by chance, and depend on thorough soil preparation, good timing, and the right care. This section explains how to give your crops the best start, with tips for avoiding problems as they grow. Similar crops are grouped together, and useful anatomy guides illustrate their main features and how they affect growing and harvesting. These are followed by flowcharts and illustrated question-and-answer pages to help diagnose common problems for each crop type and direct you to a practical solution.

RESCUE

Vegetables

Identifying what is chewing holes in cabbage leaves, causing onion bulbs to rot, or stopping runner beans from setting is the first vital step toward rescuing your crop. Fruiting crops, roots, leafy salads, garden greens, bulbs and stems, and pods are covered separately to help pinpoint pests and diseases specific to each crop type, as well as symptoms resulting from poor growing conditions. Follow the advice given promptly, and it will often be possible to save your crop.

How to grow vegetables

Most vegetables are fast-growing annual plants that produce tasty crops in a matter of months. Growing from seed is satisfying and cheap, but knowing where, when, and how to sow is vital. If time and space are limited, buy young vegetable plants to grow on. Either way, a healthy start will produce strong, vigorous plants that will taste delicious.

Choosing the right site

Vegetables produce their best crops when given a good location, ideally in full sun, in rich, well-drained soil, and sheltered from the wind. Trying to grow crops in the shade of hedges and trees will never be a great success, not only since light is limited, but also because hedges and trees prevent rain from reaching the soil, and absorb moisture with their extensive roots. Buildings also create shade and rain shadows—consider this before planting near the house.

Choose the best site you can for cultivating vegetables. Avoid soil where water collects after rain, does not seep away rapidly, and is poorly drained. This is unsuitable for crops. Drains can be installed where the problem is serious, but digging compacted soil and working in grit can improve conditions considerably, or raised beds can be constructed.

Strong winds batter delicate plants and deter pollinating insects, so some shelter from the prevailing wind is vital, particularly in exposed spots. Barriers that filter the wind, such as hedges and windbreak fabric, are better than solid walls, which create damaging air turbulence on their leeward side.

Sowing under cover or outside

The simplest place to sow or plant vegetables is directly into the soil, where they can be left to put down roots and grow to maturity. This easy method works well for many crops, such as root vegetables and salads, and requires relatively little effort,

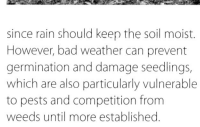

since rain should keep the soil moist. However, bad weather can prevent germination and damage seedlings, which are also particularly vulnerable to pests and competition from weeds until more established.

Seed can also be sown under cover in a greenhouse, cold frame, or on a sunny windowsill. This gives heat-loving crops, such as tomatoes and peppers, the warmth they need in order to germinate, and allows all crops a head start in early spring, ready to be planted out later.

Strong, indoor-raised young plants cope better with minor pest damage than seedlings sown directly into the soil. However, growing under cover requires more equipment and time than sowing directly outside, so the advantages have to outweigh the extra expense and effort involved.

AVOIDING PROBLEMS

Don't waste seed on recklessly early sowings. They won't germinate when it is cold outside, and those that do will often disappoint by running to seed quickly. Heat-loving vegetables, such as green beans and zucchini, cannot tolerate frost and won't grow in cold weather, so are often sown under cover. Avoid sowing these too early and running out of space indoors for rapidly growing plants.

(above) **Growing bags** If you have limited space for growing crops, use growing bags, positioned in the sun as temporary beds. They are ideal for many types of crops.

(left) **Raised beds** If your soil is poor or unsuitable for the crops you want to grow, consider using raised beds to provide the perfect growing conditions.

Preparing the soil

Once your site is selected, allow time to improve the soil for your crops. Dig plenty of organic matter, such as garden compost or manure, into the soil in fall or spring to improve its structure and fertility. It is always best to dig in manure well in advance of planting, but do not add it to beds where you plan to grow root crops, because it causes the roots to fork.

If you have acidic soil and plan to grow salad greens, add lime to the soil in fall to raise the pH and reduce the risk of clubroot disease (see p.182). However, never add lime at the same time as applying fertilizers or manure.

Before sowing or planting remove all weeds and any large stones. Use a rake to level the surface of the bed and break down any lumps of soil.

If sowing small seeds, keep raking until the soil has a lightly crumbly texture, known as a "fine tilth."

When to sow and plant

Of course, the right time to sow and plant varies among crops, but for almost all vegetables that can be sown outdoors, wait until the soil begins to warm in spring. When this happens will depend on your local climate and the weather conditions each year, but a good indication is when the weeds begin to germinate rapidly. This is your cue to get into the garden and start sowing, although it is always a good idea to sow small quantities of seeds every few weeks in case the fickle spring weather changes, causing some to fail, and to prevent gluts if all your sowings are successful. Keeping a

simple record of when crops were sown, planted, and harvested each year can help you to work out the best times to get vegetables started in future years.

Some crops, such as broad beans and garlic, are hardy enough to be sown and planted in fall or late winter, and will reward you by growing through the cold months to mature in late spring and summer. It is also possible to sow and plant other crops earlier outdoors by warming the soil under cloches or garden fabric for a week or two in early spring. This is also a helpful way to dry out sodden soil that would otherwise be too wet for sowing, and to protect late summer sowings of many vegetables from cooler fall nights as they mature and become ready to harvest.

Deciding what to grow

There is such a huge range of vegetable seeds and young plants available that it can be difficult to choose what to grow. For the best harvest, consider what will grow well in your climate and soil, as well as what you have space for and time to look after. Importantly, don't forget to grow the crops you enjoy eating.

Heat-loving crops, such as peppers and squashes, will only thrive and ripen outdoors in a warm, sunny summer, while many leafy crops, such as lettuce, don't perform well in areas with hot, dry weather. Cultivars are often bred with characteristics that suit particular conditions, for example, dwarf runner beans for windy areas or fast-ripening cherry tomatoes for cooler regions, so choose those best for your garden. Some crops are almost trouble-free and produce good harvests with little effort, while others, like garden greens and carrots, are particularly prone to pests and diseases, and frequently need protection or treatment. Stick with easy crops if you lack time to deal with problems, and choose disease-resistant varieties.

How to sow seeds

Whether sowing outdoors in the soil or under cover in containers, it is important that the soil or potting mix is moist, and that seeds are sown thinly and at the correct depth. The most common method for sowing into a seedbed outside is to mark rows with a string line and create narrow furrows using the tip of a trowel. The depth of the furrow depends on the type and size of seed sown, but usually ranges from 1/2–2in (1–5cm) deep. Water the furrow thoroughly before sowing. Pour seeds into your hand and carefully sprinkle them thinly and evenly along the trench. Larger seeds can simply be placed at the desired spacing. Some gardeners prefer to "station sow" seeds, sowing several together in clusters and leaving good spaces between them. This works well for large vegetables sown in their final positions, such as broccoli and parsnips, which are then thinned to a single plant per station. After sowing, the furrow should be covered with soil and labeled.

When sowing in pots, cell packs, or seed flats, choose a good potting mix. Fill your containers, firm the mix gently, and water, either using a watering can with a fine nozzle or by soaking in a shallow tray of water. Sprinkle seeds thinly over the surface, cover with about twice their depth of

SOWING SMALL BATCHES OF SEEDS

Some plants, like peppers and tomatoes, are very productive, which means you don't need many to enjoy a good harvest. Rather than waste time and seed growing more plants than you need, decide how many plants you actually want, and sow just a few seeds more for safe measure. Sow the seeds into individual pots to avoid the need to prick them out later.

1 Use small pots Fill small pots, measuring about 2in (5cm) across, with multi-purpose potting mix or propagation mix. Water them well and leave them to drain until the mix is just moist to touch.

2 Sow seed Make a small indent in the potting mix with your finger and sow one or two seeds in each pot. Cover the seeds lightly with more mix and put the pots on a warm windowsill or in a propagator.

3 Grow on As the seeds germinate, thin the seedlings to leave one per pot and grow them on. Repot the seedlings as they grow into larger pots until they are big enough to plant in their final location.

sifted potting mix, and firm gently. Large seed can be planted deeper into individual holes—drop in the seeds and cover with potting mix.

Water the sown seeds again if necessary and place in a propagator, or cover with a clear plastic bag to prevent the surface from drying out.

Caring for seedlings

Once seeds have germinated, those growing in the soil need little care apart from regular weeding, which can be done quickly by running a hoe between rows on a sunny day. Seedlings will also need protection from slugs and snails, but should only need watering in hot, dry weather.

Seedlings under cover definitely need more attention. As soon as they germinate, remove any coverings over the flats or pots to allow air to circulate, reduce the risk of damping off, and avoid hindering their rapid growth. They need bright light but should be protected from damage by direct sunlight in their early days using shading. Turn seedlings on the windowsill daily to avoid them leaning in one direction toward the light. Never let the mix dry out; water gently from above using a fine nozzle or allow it to soak up water from a flat. Take care not to overwater.

Thinning and pricking out

Wherever they are grown, seedlings need space to spread their leaves and roots rapidly without competition. Those in rows or seed flats will quickly begin to suffer without prompt thinning or pricking out. These jobs are usually done when plants are large enough to handle, or have developed their first "true" leaves, like those of the mature plant.

Planting outside Seedlings raised under cover can be planted outside once they have been hardened off. If planting them in rows, use a string guide or a long garden stake to ensure they are straight and spaced at a suitable distance apart.

Thinning out Seedlings growing outdoors in rows, or under cover in cell packs, usually require thinning. The aim here is to remove weaker plants and leave evenly spaced, strong plants to grow. Thinning to the final spacing required for each crop can be done in stages in case some plants are lost to pests or disease. Seedlings in cell packs are usually thinned to a single plant.

Minimizing disturbance to the remaining plants while thinning is important, so work when the ground is moist and pinch back the plants at soil level, rather than uprooting them.

Pricking out Seedlings growing together in pots or flats will need pricking out into new containers to give them space to develop. Water the seedlings and prepare seed flats or pots to receive them—as for sowing. Tease each seedling from the potting mix using a dibber or pencil, holding it by the leaves, never the stem or roots. Make a small hole in the mix surface, lower the roots in, firm the seedling in, and water.

Hardening off

Plants grown under cover become used to their warm, still conditions and need the chance to toughen up gradually before being planted outside, where the weather can be wet and windy, and the nights cold. It is best to allow about two weeks

for this acclimatizing process. Begin by increasing the ventilation in the greenhouse or on the windowsill, then move the plants outdoors into a cold frame or sheltered location for a short time each day. This time outdoors can be extended until they are ready to stay out overnight, either covered in a cold frame or with fabric over them. They are then ready to be planted out into their final locations, although some more tender crops may still need protection on cold nights. It is wise to harden off young plants bought from the garden center or by mail order before planting out too. Transfer them into larger pots if required, give them a day or two under cover to settle, then begin the same process as for plants you have raised yourself.

Easy planting To help avoid disturbing their roots when planting out, plants can be raised in biodegradable pots that break down naturally in the soil.

How to plant out

When the time comes to plant out, make the effort to do things right and improve the chances of your vegetable garden being healthy and productive. Don't delay—get plants out of their pots and into the soil as soon as they have a good root system that holds the potting mix together when they are gently knocked from their pot.

Before planting, check the recommended final spacing for each crop to make sure that every plant has room to grow to its full potential. Plants that are too close together compete with each other for water, food, and light; can be difficult to weed between; and are at greater risk from pests and diseases. Planting distances are usually printed on seed packets. To make planting out easier and more accurate, mark the required distance on a stake to use as a guide.

Water plants thoroughly before planting them out, ensuring they are fully hardened off first. Prepare the soil, then use a trowel to dig a hole to the right depth, so that the soil will be level with the potting mix surface —or slightly deeper for tomatoes and garden greens, which benefit from extra support. Carefully tip the plant from its pot, supporting the stem at the same time. Place the plant in the hole, ensuring it is upright, and firm the soil around the roots. Carefully water the plant in well using a watering can fitted with a fine nozzle to avoid washing the soil from around the roots.

Problems to watch out for

Numerous in almost every garden, slugs and snails (p.186) will target any crop, particularly when the weather

AVOIDING PROBLEMS

Waiting for warmer weather
Heat-loving crops like zucchini and tomatoes will be killed by frost and can be damaged by cold, wet weather. In bad conditions in late spring, these plants can get stuck under cover, waiting for some suitable warmth before planting out. If this happens, don't let plants become pot-bound and stunt their growth. Pot them into progressively larger containers to keep them healthy until conditions improve.

has been wet, or you have recently watered. Wireworms (p.187) move through the soil, munching through the stems of seedlings, leaving them lying wilting on the surface. Tiny flea beetles (p.183) nibble damaging little round holes in the leaves of salad greens and related crops, such as radishes and arugula, weakening plants. Bean seed flies (p.180) cause distortion in bean seedlings, and mice love to feast on recently germinated peas and beans. Birds (p.180) will quickly destroy rows of garden greens, peas, and beans.

Seedlings under cover are less prone to pests, but are often not out of reach of slugs and snails, or mice (p.183). Damping off (p.182) is a common fungal disease where the air is moist and ventilation poor.

ROUTINE CARE

There are plenty of steps that every gardener can take to avoid potential problems and keep the plants growing in their vegetable plot strong and healthy until they are ready to harvest.

Watering How much to water depends on rainfall, soil type, and each individual crop. Never allow the soil to dry out because wilting plants are vulnerable to disease and will eventually die of thirst. Recently transplanted plants need the most frequent watering, and in dry conditions, crops with large leaves, along with those that have swelling fruits and roots, will need a steady supply of moisture. Water plants in containers regularly, probably at least once a day in summer, especially those growing under cover.

Fertilizing Plants growing in well-prepared soil should be able to obtain all the nutrients they require without the need for extra fertilizing. Be sparing in the use of fertilizers, because the soft growth they promote is appealing to pests and prone to cold damage. Overwintered crops often benefit from a general fertilizer to boost spring growth.

   Plants grown in containers will need regular feeding—nutrients in potting mix soon become depleted.

Weeding Remove and discard weeds as soon as possible because they not only compete with your crops for essential water, nutrients, light, and space, but also harbor pests and diseases. Ensure you remove the roots of perennial

Best results Routine care is essential for keeping plants healthy and ensuring the best crops. Even brief periods spent providing support, weeding, watering, and fertilizing early in the season will be rewarded by stronger plants that are less prone to problems.

weeds, such as dandelions, while annual weeds can simply be cut off at the base using a hoe.

Supports Providing the right supports for plants keeps them neat and easier to harvest. It also helps protect their stems in windy weather and enables them to bear the weight of heavy crops. Another advantage is that fruit and pod crops are kept off the ground, where they are prone to pests or fungal diseases

Vigilance Keep a close eye on your vegetable plot so that if a problem develops, you can tackle it early, before plants are badly damaged and when you have the best chance of success. Squash any aphids (p.180) you see; remove any leaves, stems, or plants that show signs of disease; and put up sticky traps to alert you to insect pests in the greenhouse. Check plants regularly and if you spot any unexpected changes, look more closely for pests or diseases.

AVOIDING PROBLEMS

Crop rotation Pests and diseases can build up in the soil over time if the same crops are always grown in the same place. To help prevent this, grow closely related crops together in the same bed and move them to a new plot each year. Rotate root crops, peas and beans, and garden greens from the cabbage family in a simple three-year cycle.

Know your crop types

Edible plants can be divided into six main crop types, according to the part of the plant that is harvested. Categorizing them like this is useful because many of the crops in each group are related, thriving in similar conditions and vulnerable to the same problems. Knowing your crop types helps develop an understanding of each group's needs, making it the easy route to successful vegetable growing.

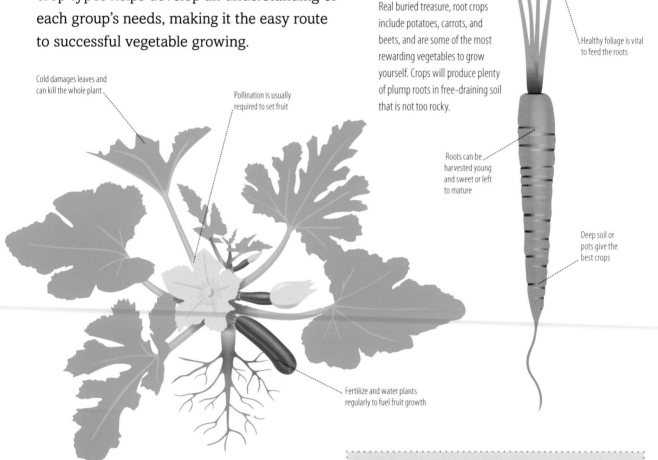

ROOT CROPS

Real buried treasure, root crops include potatoes, carrots, and beets, and are some of the most rewarding vegetables to grow yourself. Crops will produce plenty of plump roots in free-draining soil that is not too rocky.

Healthy foliage is vital to feed the roots

Cold damages leaves and can kill the whole plant

Pollination is usually required to set fruit

Roots can be harvested young and sweet or left to mature

Deep soil or pots give the best crops

Fertilize and water plants regularly to fuel fruit growth

FRUITING CROPS

These heat-loving crops, including tomatoes, peppers, and zucchini, produce fruit through summer into fall. Grown from seed each year, they need a warm sunny site or a greenhouse to grow rapidly and yield ripe fruit.

MULTI-PURPOSE CROPS

Most crops are grown to harvest a specific part, whether it's their roots, leaves, or fruit. However, some can also be harvested in other ways, providing a second feast. Young pea shoots are delicious, so are the baby leaves of beets, while male zucchini flowers are ideal for stuffing and frying.

Freshly picked leaves are
packed with flavor

Watch out for common
pests and diseases that
affect all garden greens

SALAD GREENS

Grown for their delicious, fresh
foliage, salad greens, such as lettuce,
arugula, and Swiss chard, are quick
to grow. Many can be harvested
repeatedly by leaving the central
growing point intact when picking.

GARDEN GREENS

Garden greens flourish given a cool
climate and fertile soil. Some, like
cabbage and kale, are grown for their
sturdy leaves, while others, such as
broccoli, produce delicious flower heads.

Only once pollinated,
the attractive flowers
develop into pods

Strong foliage keeps
growing bulbs and
stems well fed

Bulbs and stems
come in diverse
colors and shapes

BULB AND STEM CROPS

This group produces aromatic
bulbs, like onions and garlic,
and fine-flavored stems, such
as asparagus and celery. They
taste wonderful straight from
the soil, but some are easy to
dry and store well.

POD CROPS

Edible in their entirety or shelled
for just their succulent seeds, pods
are so superior freshly picked that
they deserve a place in every
garden. Often tall or climbing
plants, peas and beans benefit
from supports.

Pod crops all enjoy
moist, well-drained soils

Fruiting crop anatomy

Although commonly regarded as vegetables, the plants in this group are technically fruit, since the seed-bearing part is what we eat. All are heat-loving and fast growing, and need to be sown indoors in early spring to be ready to plant in a sunny spot outside, once the risk of frost has passed.

TOMATO FAMILY

These plants come in all shapes and sizes, so choose those that suit your growing space. While cordon tomatoes can grow very tall, eggplant and peppers are ideal for patio pots, and many chiles and cherry tomatoes thrive on windowsills.

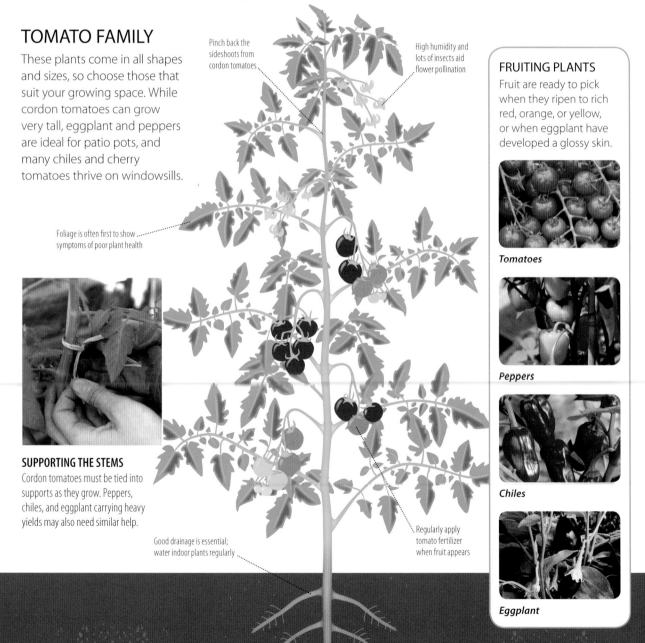

Pinch back the sideshoots from cordon tomatoes

High humidity and lots of insects aid flower pollination

Foliage is often first to show symptoms of poor plant health

Good drainage is essential; water indoor plants regularly

Regularly apply tomato fertilizer when fruit appears

SUPPORTING THE STEMS
Cordon tomatoes must be tied into supports as they grow. Peppers, chiles, and eggplant carrying heavy yields may also need similar help.

FRUITING PLANTS
Fruit are ready to pick when they ripen to rich red, orange, or yellow, or when eggplant have developed a glossy skin.

Tomatoes

Peppers

Chiles

Eggplant

CUCUMBER FAMILY

Such fun to grow, these large-leaved plants take the form of ground-hugging bushes or trailing vines that can be grown up supports. Cool weather at any stage stops these heat lovers in their tracks, and a constant supply of water and nutrients is essential for their rapid growth.

SWEET CORN

A tall, elegant plant, sweet corn will not survive cold and is best sown in pots under cover to plant out in early summer. Planting in blocks, not rows, allows the pollen from the plume of male flowers at the top of each plant to fall onto the silky tassels of the female flowers below, creating cobs filled with kernels.

SUPPORTS
Training cucumbers, trailing zucchini, and small winter squashes up supports saves space and keeps fruit off the soil.

HARVEST YOUNG
Zucchini and summer squashes swell incredibly quickly, soon becoming overly large and watery, so pick when young.

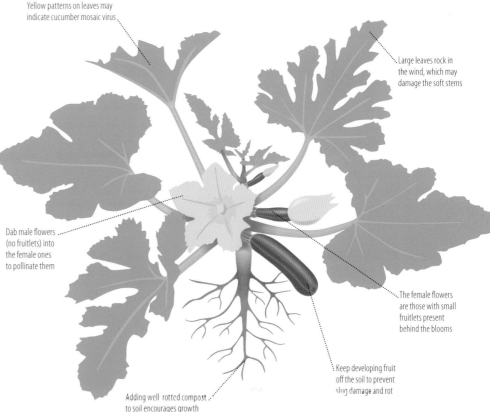

Yellow patterns on leaves may indicate cucumber mosaic virus

Large leaves rock in the wind, which may damage the soft stems

Dab male flowers (no fruitlets) into the female ones to pollinate them

The female flowers are those with small fruitlets present behind the blooms

Keep developing fruit off the soil to prevent slug damage and rot

Adding well rotted compost to soil encourages growth

FRUITING CROPS
The diverse colors and shapes of these fruit look good in the garden. Leave winter squashes to ripen in the sun for the best flavor.

Cucumbers

Zucchini

Summer squashes

Winter squashes

What's wrong with my fruiting crops?

Cool spells can slow the growth of these summer crops, from germination to fruiting, and maintaining the temperature, especially at night, helps keep them healthy. Checking leaves and fruits for signs of pests, diseases, and nutrient deficiencies nips problems in the bud.

LEAVES ARE STICKY TO TOUCH AND HAVE INSECTS ON THEM.

Do white insects fly up when the plants are disturbed?

Aphids are often found on the young growth at the shoot tips. **See p.180.**

Whiteflies are sap-sucking insects that usually hide under the leaves. **See p.187.**

THE SEEDS I PLANTED AREN'T GROWING, WHY?

Did they germinate?

These crops needs warmth to germinate. **See How to sow seeds p.40.**

This is probably damping off disease. **See p.182.**

MY PLANTS AREN'T FLOWERING OR SETTING FRUIT. WHY IS THAT?

Has the weather been cold or wet?

These are heat-loving crops and won't flower or set fruit in cold conditions. Try growing them under cover or hope the weather improves.

Have they been watered well?

Fruit will not set if the plant is thirsty. **See p.50.**

Have you been feeding with a high potassium tomato feed?

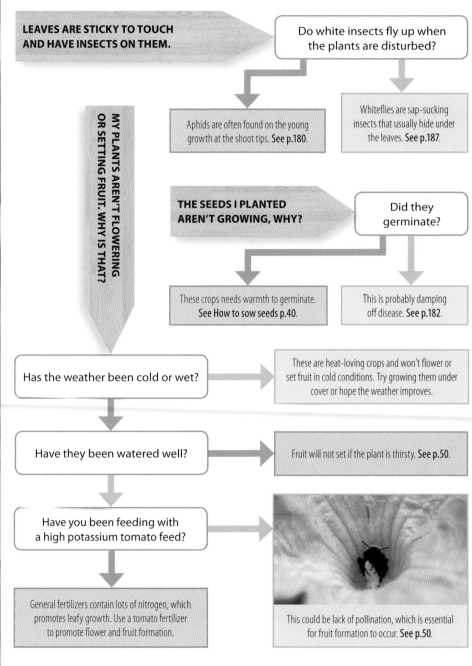

General fertilizers contain lots of nitrogen, which promotes leafy growth. Use a tomato fertilizer to promote flower and fruit formation.

This could be lack of pollination, which is essential for fruit formation to occur. **See p.50.**

THE LEAVES HAVE CHANGED COLOR AND DON'T LOOK RIGHT.

Have plants been protected from cold weather?

Protect plants from cold and harden them off fully before planting outside. **See p.51.**

Have plants been regularly fertilized and watered?

These crops need lots of water and nutrients. **See Routine care p.43.** Could be magnesium deficiency. **See p.50.**

Are plants exposed to intense sunlight?

Leaves can be scorched by strong light, especially under cover. **See p.51.**

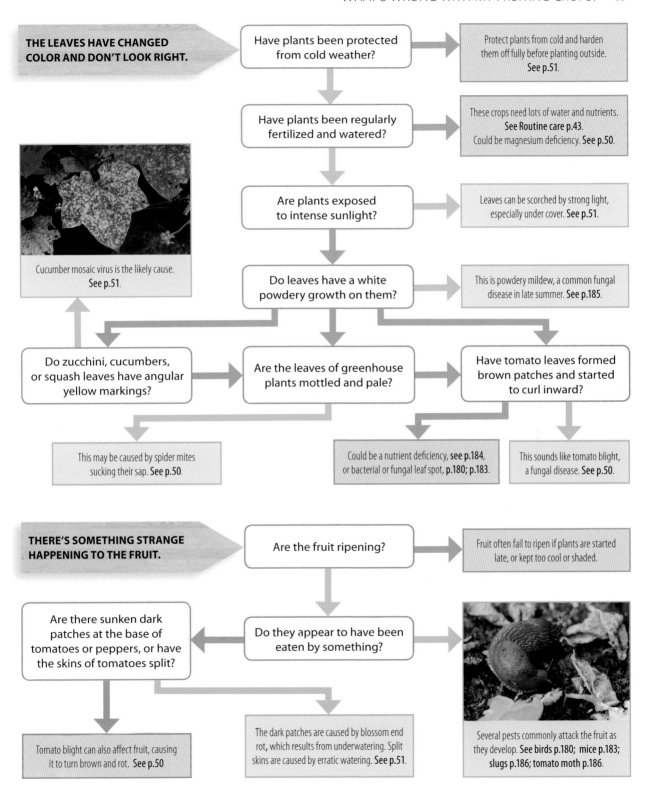

Cucumber mosaic virus is the likely cause. **See p.51.**

Do leaves have a white powdery growth on them?

This is powdery mildew, a common fungal disease in late summer. **See p.185.**

Do zucchini, cucumbers, or squash leaves have angular yellow markings?

Are the leaves of greenhouse plants mottled and pale?

Have tomato leaves formed brown patches and started to curl inward?

This may be caused by spider mites sucking their sap. **See p.50.**

Could be a nutrient deficiency, **see p.184,** or bacterial or fungal leaf spot, **p.180; p.183.**

This sounds like tomato blight, a fungal disease. **See p.50.**

THERE'S SOMETHING STRANGE HAPPENING TO THE FRUIT.

Are the fruit ripening?

Fruit often fail to ripen if plants are started late, or kept too cool or shaded.

Are there sunken dark patches at the base of tomatoes or peppers, or have the skins of tomatoes split?

Do they appear to have been eaten by something?

Several pests commonly attack the fruit as they develop. **See birds p.180; mice p.183; slugs p.186; tomato moth p.186.**

Tomato blight can also affect fruit, causing it to turn brown and rot. **See p.50**

The dark patches are caused by blossom end rot, which results from underwatering. Split skins are caused by erratic watering. **See p.51.**

Fruiting crop clinic

Although fruiting crops are prolific when healthy, harvests can be badly affected by pests, diseases, and poor growing conditions. Plants grown in greenhouses are particularly vulnerable to insect pests and incorrect care. Recognizing these common problems early often means they can be resolved quickly.

Why aren't the flowers producing fruit?

Flowers need to be pollinated for fruit to form. During bad weather pollinating insects may not be able to visit the flowers. Dry conditions also inhibit pollination. Keep plants well watered and mist flowers or wet down the greenhouse to encourage fruit to set.

Q **Are yellowing leaves caused by nutrient deficiency?**

A Fruiting crops grown in containers are prone to magnesium deficiency in summer. Older leaves turn yellow at the edges and between the veins, then gradually darken to red, purple, or brown. **See p.184**.

Q **How do I identify spider mite damage on my plants?**

A Tiny spider mites suck the sap of many greenhouse plants during summer. They cause leaves to look dull and mottled, which then dry up and fall off, severely weakening the plants. **See p.186**.

HEALTHY TOMATOES

RIPENING SWEET CORN

SPIDER MITE DAMAGE

Q **Is this caused by tomato blight?**

A Tomato blight is a fungal disease that most commonly affects outdoor crops in late summer, but can occur under cover too. Leaves develop brown patches and curl up, dark blotches form on the stems, and fruit turns sickly brown and rots. **See p.185**.

Q **What's eaten my sweet corn cobs?**

A The sugary kernels of ripening sweet corn are irresistible to many pests, and whole crops can be stripped very quickly. Birds pull the protective leaves aside to access the cob, mice will nibble their way inside, and hungry rodents may flatten the entire plant. **See birds p.180 and mice p.183**.

Diagnostic chart

Symptoms	Diagnosis
 **Plants recently moved** outdoors or exposed to cold show damage to young growth. Leaves are pale and wilt, or where damage is serious, shoot tips turn brown and die.	**Cold damage** affects all fruiting crops because they are tender plants from warm climates and so they can't tolerate cold. They will suffer or even die if moved outdoors too early in spring.
 **Leaves develop patches** of pale, bleached tissue following bright, sunny weather. These patches dry out and do not recover, and may becoming moldy in damp conditions.	**Scorch** by intense sunlight causes this type of damage and can be worse where the sun's rays are magnified when the plant is under cover or by droplets of water lying on the surface of the leaf.

Q How can I stop zucchini from becoming too large?

A In warm weather zucchini and summer squashes grow very quickly. To enjoy them small and sweet, check plants and pick small fruit daily—look for fruit hiding among the large leaves.

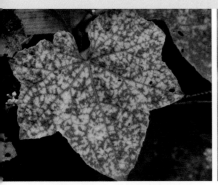

 CUCUMBER MOSAIC VIRUS

 WATER TOMATOES REGULARLY

Why are plants wilting even though they are watered every day?

Shoots wilting even when the soil is moist are a sign of excess water. If drainage is poor, roots and stems decay, and water doesn't reach the leaves. Water the plants less often.

Q Do my plants have cucumber mosaic virus?

A Strange yellow patterns on the leaves of cucumbers, zucchini, and squashes, along with distorted fruit, are an unmistakable sign that they are infected with cucumber mosaic virus. This disease is spread by aphids and can occur at any time in summer on plants grown under cover or outside. See viruses p.187.

Q What's wrong with my tomatoes?

A Poor growing conditions cause a number of tomato problems. Dark, tough patches at the base of fruit are blossom end rot, a sign of calcium deficiency due to dry conditions—water plants more. Split skins result from irregular watering—don't let plants dry out. Fruit fails to ripen when temperatures and light levels are low.

Blossom end rot

Splitting tomato skins

Unripe fruit

Root crop anatomy

These hearty crops are the underground storage saved by plants to give them energy to grow and flower the following year. Many can be picked young for sweet summer salads or left to mature, and they keep well for winter, either in the ground or lifted and stored under cover.

TUBERS

Certain root crops produce clusters of swollen roots, known as tubers. Potatoes are planted each year from special "seed potatoes," while Jerusalem artichokes can be grown and harvested as a clump year after year.

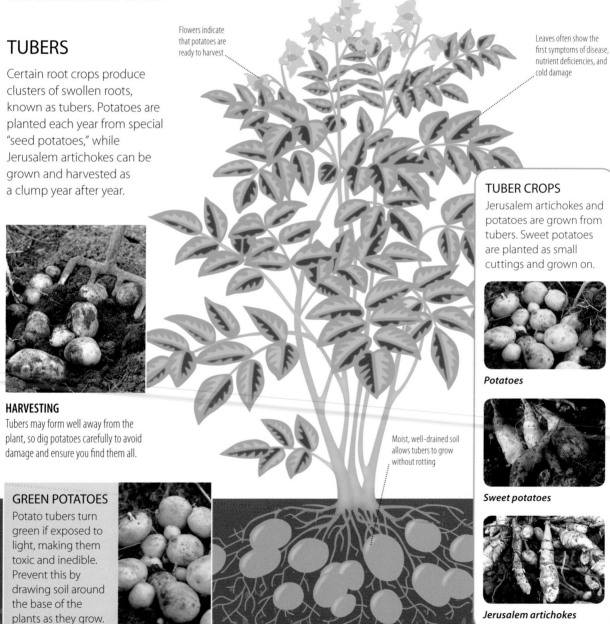

Flowers indicate that potatoes are ready to harvest

Leaves often show the first symptoms of disease, nutrient deficiencies, and cold damage

Moist, well-drained soil allows tubers to grow without rotting

HARVESTING
Tubers may form well away from the plant, so dig potatoes carefully to avoid damage and ensure you find them all.

GREEN POTATOES
Potato tubers turn green if exposed to light, making them toxic and inedible. Prevent this by drawing soil around the base of the plants as they grow.

TUBER CROPS
Jerusalem artichokes and potatoes are grown from tubers. Sweet potatoes are planted as small cuttings and grown on.

Potatoes

Sweet potatoes

Jerusalem artichokes

TAPROOTS

Single, vertical roots are known as taproots, and can be long and tapering, cylindrical, or round. Plants are grown from seed, produce plump roots, then flower. Some mature in as little as six weeks, others over many months.

Many root crops are best grown under fabric or netting to avoid pests

If the top growth flowers, the roots will be tough

Upright foliage doesn't cover the soil, so regular weeding is essential

Long roots need deep, rock-free, well-drained soil

Breaking the root causes misshapen crops. Never transplant root crops

HARVESTING

Rounded roots can often be pulled up by their leaves, but use a hand fork to loosen soil around longer roots to avoid damage.

FORKED ROOTS

Prepare soil carefully for carrot and parsnip crops; their roots may fork if they hit a rock, or if manure was applied before sowing.

MAKING THE MOST OF TAPROOTS

These versatile vegetables take up little space, can be picked quickly to enjoy as sweet, baby roots in salads, and flourish when kept well watered in deep pots.

Tasty leaves As well as their roots, beets, turnips, and radishes can be picked for their leaves.

Interim crop Sow fast-growing root crops between slower crops to make full use of your space.

CROPS WITH TAPROOTS

These crops can be harvested when young and tender, or left to grow and reach maturity. Fully grown roots have thicker skins, and many keep well in the soil during fall and winter until needed.

Carrots

Parsnips

Rutabagas

Turnips

Beets

Radishes

What's wrong with my root crops?

The obvious trouble with roots is that they are underground, making damage difficult to detect. Leaves can show telltale signs of problems below the soil during spring and summer, or damage may just be limited to the foliage. Either way, the roots are often still edible and delicious.

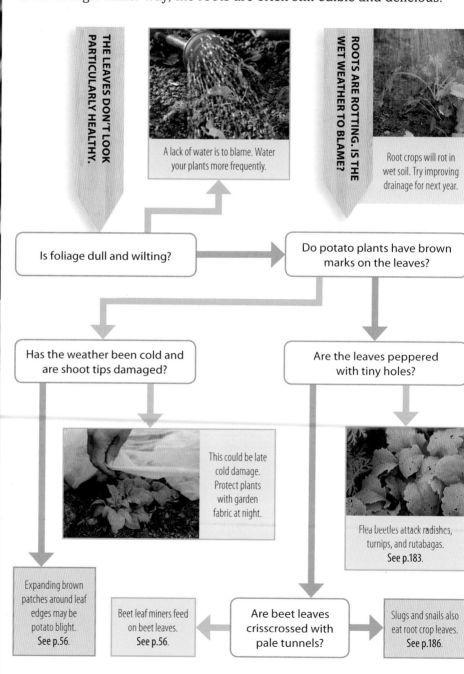

THE LEAVES DON'T LOOK PARTICULARLY HEALTHY.

A lack of water is to blame. Water your plants more frequently.

ROOTS ARE ROTTING. IS THE WET WEATHER TO BLAME?

Root crops will rot in wet soil. Try improving drainage for next year.

Is foliage dull and wilting?

Do potato plants have brown marks on the leaves?

Has the weather been cold and are shoot tips damaged?

Are the leaves peppered with tiny holes?

This could be late cold damage. Protect plants with garden fabric at night.

Flea beetles attack radishes, turnips, and rutabagas. See p.183.

Expanding brown patches around leaf edges may be potato blight. See p.56.

Beet leaf miners feed on beet leaves. See p.56.

Are beet leaves crisscrossed with pale tunnels?

Slugs and snails also eat root crop leaves. See p.186.

THE ROOTS ARE MARKED AND AREN'T APPETIZING. WHY?

Are your potatoes the problem?

Do the skins have raised, rough, dark patches?

This is common potato scab See p.57.

Forked roots are caused by rocky or recently manured soil. **See p.57.** Roots with split skins are caused by erratic watering. Water more often.

Are your root vegetables misshapen?

Are some tubers all or partially green?

Greening happens when tubers are exposed to light. **See p.52.**

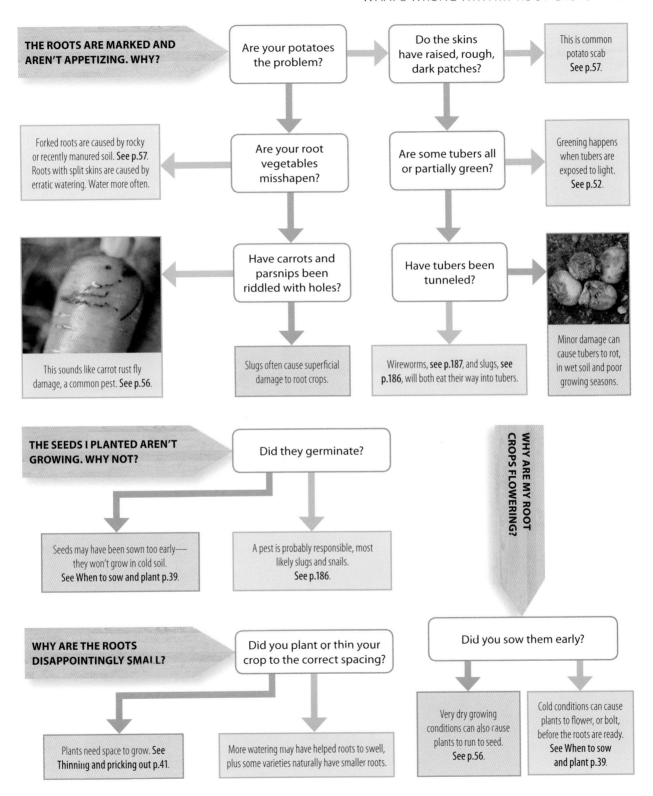

This sounds like carrot rust fly damage, a common pest. See p.56.

Have carrots and parsnips been riddled with holes?

Have tubers been tunneled?

Minor damage can cause tubers to rot, in wet soil and poor growing seasons.

Slugs often cause superficial damage to root crops.

Wireworms, **see p.187**, and slugs, **see p.186**, will both eat their way into tubers.

THE SEEDS I PLANTED AREN'T GROWING. WHY NOT?

Did they germinate?

WHY ARE MY ROOT CROPS FLOWERING?

Seeds may have been sown too early— they won't grow in cold soil. **See When to sow and plant p.39.**

A pest is probably responsible, most likely slugs and snails. See p.186.

WHY ARE THE ROOTS DISAPPOINTINGLY SMALL?

Did you plant or thin your crop to the correct spacing?

Did you sow them early?

Plants need space to grow. See **Thinning and pricking out p.41.**

More watering may have helped roots to swell, plus some varieties naturally have smaller roots.

Very dry growing conditions can also cause plants to run to seed. **See p.56.**

Cold conditions can cause plants to flower, or bolt, before the roots are ready. **See When to sow and plant p.39.**

Root crop clinic

With lush foliage above ground and swollen roots in the soil, these crops are doubly attractive to pests and diseases. It is, however, easy to minimize damage by preparing the soil correctly and using simple growing techniques, such as crop rotation and pest barriers, which are very effective.

Why are my parsnip roots so badly scarred?
Parsnips are prone to parsnip canker, a fungal disease that causes rough, orange-brown areas to form, often around the top of roots. Most common in poorly drained soils, the disease enters roots via damage caused during cultivation or by carrot rust fly larvae. See p.184.

Q Why have my root crops suddenly bolted?

A Crops grown from seed may run to seed, or "bolt," in unfavorable conditions, producing flowers rather than roots. Early spring sowings may bolt after exposure to cold, but later dry conditions can also be to blame.

Q Will beet leaf miners harm my beet plants?

A Beet leaf miner fly larvae eat their way through the internal tissues of the leaves during summer, leaving ugly brown trails. Light damage is harmless, but heavy infestations can cause leaves to die – pick them off.

▲ **CARROT RUST FLY NETTING** ▲ **HEALTHY POTATO LEAVES** **BEET LEAF MINER DAMAGE**

Q Are plants being eaten by carrot rust flies?

A Thin, brown tunnels and slim, cream maggots in the roots of carrots and parsnips are a sure sign of carrot rust flies. Several generations of flies lay eggs on the roots from late spring to early fall. Their holes also allow fungal infections into the roots causing them to rot. See p.181.

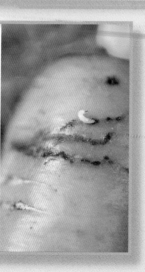

Q Are these symptoms of potato blight?

A Potato blight starts with brown patches on the edges and tips of the leaves, which quickly spread and cause whole stems to collapse and die. Carried in the air and in water droplets, this fungal disease is worst in warm, humid summers; water can carry spores down to infect tubers. See p.185.

Q **Why are potato leaves curled and yellowing?**

A Many viruses affect potatoes, causing various leaf symptoms, including yellow patterning, brown spots, stiffening, and distortion. Aphids can spread viruses. **See Viruses, p.187.**

Q **Why have the potato tubers become green in the soil?**

A Tubers turn green when exposed to light, making them poisonous and inedible. To prevent this, mound soil around the plants as they grow, or grow them through black plastic. **See p.52.**

Q **Why are my carrot roots misshaped or forked?**

A Long, straight carrots tend to fork if they meet a rock or if grown in recently manured soil. Apply manure several months before sowing, and grow your carrots in raised beds if the soil is rocky.

 FLEA BEETLES IN ACTION

 PROBLEM-FREE POTATOES

Why are potato plants popping up everywhere?

Even tiny tubers left in the soil may sprout the following year, and carry the risk of spreading diseases to new crops. Avoid this by being careful to lift every tuber when harvesting.

Q **Should I worry about flea beetles?**

A Small, shiny, black flea beetles eat many little round holes in the upper surfaces of radish, turnip, and rutabaga leaves in late spring and summer. They are most noticeable jumping from disturbed leaves. A few holes will not trouble plants, but serious damage can kill seedlings and reduce crops. **See p.183.**

Q **What's wrong with my potato tubers?**

A Dark, flaky patches on the skin are a sign of common potato scab, which causes superficial damage. Narrow tunnels made by rusty brown wireworms can render tubers inedible by late summer. Some potato viruses cause light brown marks in the flesh, called "spraing". **See Common potato scab p.182; Wireworms p.187.**

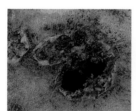

Potato scab

Potato wireworm

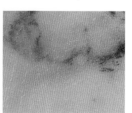

Potato spraing

Leafy salad crop anatomy

Their profusion of tender, flavor-packed leaves makes these fast and easy-to-grow crops vulnerable to drought, and a favorite with pests as well as gardeners. Grown as annuals from seed each year, many are highly productive for a short period, and are best sown in small quantities every few weeks for a continuous supply.

HEARTING

Many lettuces, chicories, and endives form dense heads of leaves, known as hearts, as they mature. After about 12 weeks the whole plant is usually cut at the base for a single, large crop of salad.

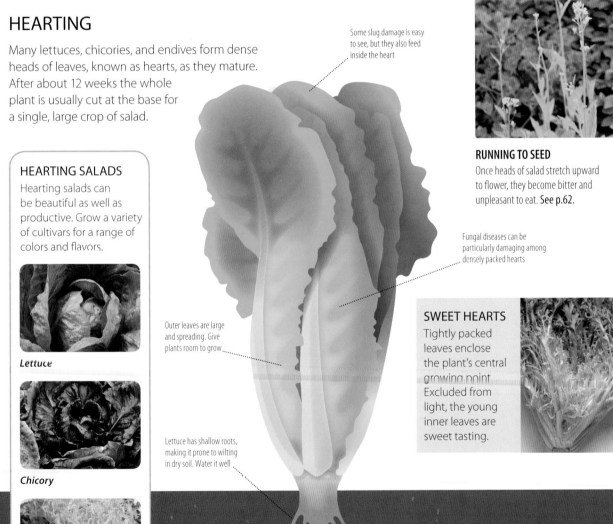

Some slug damage is easy to see, but they also feed inside the heart

RUNNING TO SEED
Once heads of salad stretch upward to flower, they become bitter and unpleasant to eat. **See p.62.**

Fungal diseases can be particularly damaging among densely packed hearts

HEARTING SALADS
Hearting salads can be beautiful as well as productive. Grow a variety of cultivars for a range of colors and flavors.

Lettuce

Chicory

Endive

Outer leaves are large and spreading. Give plants room to grow

Lettuce has shallow roots, making it prone to wilting in dry soil. Water it well

SWEET HEARTS
Tightly packed leaves enclose the plant's central growing point. Excluded from light, the young inner leaves are sweet tasting.

LOOSE-LEAF SALAD

Often fast-growing and compact, this diverse range of crops is perfect for smaller gardens. Leaves can be picked as required over several weeks, either singly or by cutting above the base, leaving the plants to regrow. Their open shape makes them less disease-prone than hearting crops.

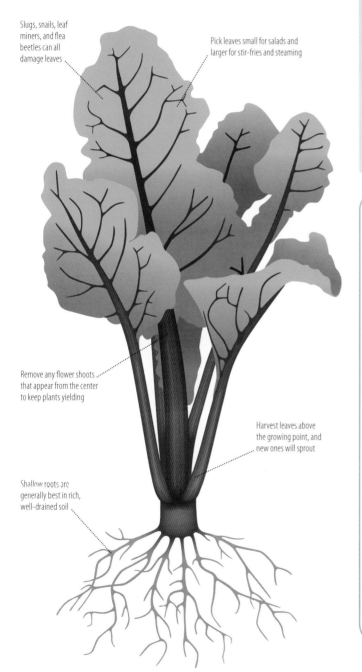

Slugs, snails, leaf miners, and flea beetles can all damage leaves

Pick leaves small for salads and larger for stir-fries and steaming

Remove any flower shoots that appear from the center to keep plants yielding

Harvest leaves above the growing point, and new ones will sprout

Shallow roots are generally best in rich, well-drained soil

MICROGREENS

These delicious garnishes are an easy crop to grow on a windowsill or in a greenhouse. Try a whole range of herbs and leafy salad crops for color and flavor.

Sow Fill a flat with propagation mix, sow seed thinly, and cover lightly with mix. Water and stand the seeds in a warm, light place.

Harvest Cut with scissors as soon as two weeks after sowing, when the seedlings have their first true leaves. Then sow a new batch.

LOOSE-LEAF SALAD CROPS

Loose-leaf salad can be sown densely and cut as small leaves, 1¼in (3cm) above the soil, then left to regrow. They can also be spaced farther apart to provide repeated crops of larger leaves over longer periods.

Lettuce   *Arugula*

Mizuna   *Swiss chard*

Spinach   *Herbs*

What's wrong with my leafy salad crops?

Pests and diseases love the soft leaves of salad crops, and can wreak destruction incredibly quickly. Control slugs and snails during wet spring and summer conditions. Be alert for symptoms of fungal diseases year-round; protected winter crops can be lost if ventilation is poor.

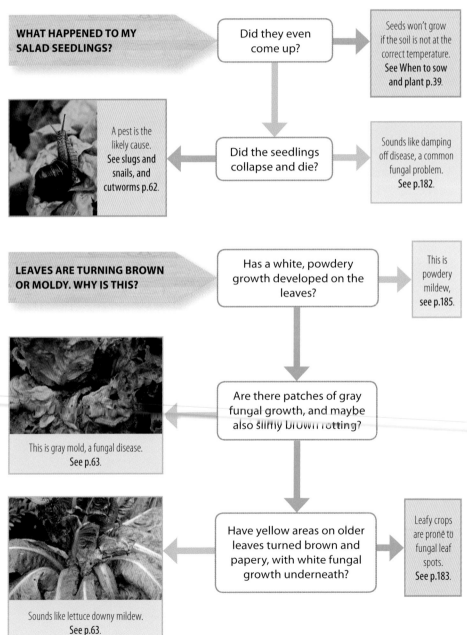

WHAT HAPPENED TO MY SALAD SEEDLINGS?

Did they even come up?

→ Seeds won't grow if the soil is not at the correct temperature. **See When to sow and plant p.39.**

Did the seedlings collapse and die?

→ Sounds like damping off disease, a common fungal problem. **See p.182.**

← A pest is the likely cause. **See slugs and snails, and cutworms p.62.**

LEAVES ARE TURNING BROWN OR MOLDY. WHY IS THIS?

Has a white, powdery growth developed on the leaves?

→ This is powdery mildew, **see p.185.**

Are there patches of gray fungal growth, and maybe also slimy brown rotting?

← This is gray mold, a fungal disease. **See p.63.**

Have yellow areas on older leaves turned brown and papery, with white fungal growth underneath?

→ Leafy crops are prone to fungal leaf spots. **See p.183.**

← Sounds like lettuce downy mildew. **See p.63.**

SOMETHING IS EATING THE LEAVES. WHAT COULD IT BE?

Are there large ragged holes and slimy trails?

This means it's slugs and snails. **See p.62.**

Are there many tiny, round holes?

Beet leaf miners tunnel through the leaves of Swiss chard and perpetual spinach. **See p.62.**

This is most likely to be flea beetle damage. **See p.63.**

WHY ARE THE LEAVES WILTING?

Have you kept the plants well watered and fertilized?

Salad crops need plenty of water and feeding to grow well.

Check the roots for sap-sucking lettuce root aphid. **See p.62.**

Are plants growing in full summer sun?

Even in moist soil some crops wilt in hot sun. Try growing summer salads in a shadier spot.

LEAVES ARE SMALL AND TASTE BITTER. WHAT CAUSES THIS?

Are the plants becoming tall and producing flowers?

Flowering is the end of the plant's productive life for leaves. Resow a new batch of seeds and grow a fresh crop. **See p.62.**

Lack of water can lead to slow growth, and tough and bitter leaves. Water your plants more often. **See p.63.**

WHOLE PLANTS ARE ROTTING OFF AT THE BASE. WHY?

This is common if the weather has been very wet or the soil has poor drainage. Try improving the soil, to prepare it for next year.

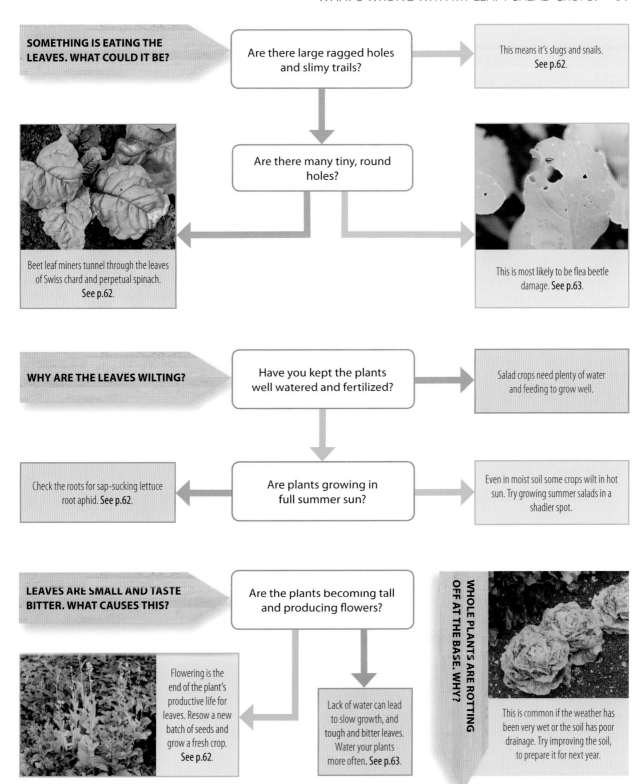

Leafy salad crop clinic

Although quick and simple to grow, the succulent foliage of leafy salad crops is a frustratingly soft target for pests and diseases. Preventive measures are necessary in most gardens to keep slugs, snails, and fungal infections at bay, because by the time a problem is spotted, much of the crop may be lost.

Are my plants being attacked by cutworms?

Where individual plants suddenly collapse, and damage progresses along the rows over several days, large, brown caterpillars called cutworms may be responsible. They live in the soil, feeding on roots, which can kill seedlings. Check the soil near plants and remove the pests.

Q How do I recognize the signs of lettuce root aphids?

A Check around the roots and you are likely to find a white, waxy substance along with clusters of pale cream lettuce root aphids. These insects feed on the sap from roots during summer, reducing yields. **See p.185**.

Q Are slugs and snails damaging my growing crops?

A Ragged holes in leafy salad crops, along with decimated rows of seedlings, are the work of slugs and snails. Slugs also often make their way into lettuce hearts. Problems are worst in wet weather. **See p.186**.

▲ **BOLTING CHARD**

▲ **HEALTHY SPINACH LEAVES**

SLUG-EATEN LETTUCE

Q Why are the plants tall and flowering?

A Known as bolting, all leafy plants flower when mature, and the leaves become small, tough, and bitter. Harvest leaves early, while still at their best. Keep all crops except lettuce productive by cutting back the flowering stems. Dry conditions and sowing at the wrong time promote bolting.

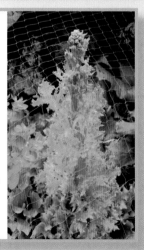

Q Should I worry about beet leaf miners?

A Perpetual spinach and Swiss chard are related to beetroot and can be attacked by beet leaf miner. The small, white maggots feed inside leaves, creating pale brown trails. Growth of young plants is particularly vulnerable. Pick off and destroy affected leaves as soon as possible.

Q Should I worry if plants wilt during summer?

A Soft salad leaves wilt quickly in hot weather, sometimes even in moist soil, because the large leaves lose water rapidly. Don't worry—water them well and try growing them in light shade.

Diagnostic chart

Symptoms	Diagnosis
 **Yellow patches appear and expand** on older leaves first, quickly making them unappealing. Look under the leaves to find a bloom of white fungal growth on these patches.	**Downy mildew** is a fungal disease that thrives in wet and humid conditions, and can affect seedlings as well as fully grown plants. Remove infected leaves from plants quickly. **See p.182.**
 **Lettuce leaves develop fluffy,** gray fungal growth, and affected tissues turn yellow-brown and slimy. This often happens around the main stem, where rot sets in, killing the plant.	**Gray mold** is a fungal disease that can affect plants at any stage. It is most prevalent in moist growing conditions and infects plants through injuries or can be carried on seeds. **See p.183.**

FLEA BEETLE DAMAGE

COLORFUL HERBS

Why do the leaves taste bitter and unpleasant?

Some crops, such as chicory, taste bitter, but others lose their sweetness if they experience dry spells and then begin to bolt. This also tends to make their leaves smaller and tough to eat.

Q Do flea beetles do much damage to salad crops?

A Shiny, black flea beetles are hard to see until foliage is disturbed and they all jump to the ground. These small beetles pepper the leaves of arugula and pak choi with tiny holes in summer. Light damage can easily be tolerated if plants are well watered, but a serious infestation can slow growth and kill seedlings. **See p.183.**

Q What's wrong with my herb plants?

A Mint rust is a fungal disease that causes distorted and yellowing leaves and stems on mint plants. Herbs in pots, even drought-tolerant thyme, need regular watering to prevent unsightly dieback. Pale mottling on leaves of sage and other herbs is caused by sap-sucking thrips. **See Rust (mint) p.185; Dieback p.182; Thrips p.186.**

Signs of mint rust

Dieback on thyme

Thrips on sage

Garden greens anatomy

All members of the cabbage family, garden greens are large plants, grown for their leaves or tightly packed flower heads. Slow-growing, they require plenty of space and moist, fertile soil to fuel development. Planting them together and moving their bed each year helps protect crops from pests and soilborne diseases.

LEAF CROPS

Winter cabbage, kale, and Brussels sprouts are all hardy winter crops, and kale and some cultivars of cabbage can be harvested year-round. Grown from seed or bought as small plants, they are attractive enough to look good in a flower bed if you don't have a vegetable patch.

Spring cabbage cultivars are picked as loose leaves, not full heads

All crops will run to seed, so harvest them promptly when they are ready

Protect leaves from birds and egg-laying butterflies by covering plants with netting

Older, lower leaves naturally yellow and fall. Don't worry. Just remove and compost them

Their shallow roots make the plants prone to falling over

CLUB ROOT

This disease causes swollen roots and kills plants. To help avoid it, rotate crops, improve drainage, and add lime to acidic soils. See p.69.

INSECT COLLARS

Use collars to prevent cabbage root flies from laying their eggs at the base of young plants. See p.69.

LEAFY GREENS

Leafy greens look and taste different from each other. Harvest cabbage heads whole, and pick kale leaves and Brussels sprouts individually.

Summer cabbage

Winter cabbage

Kale

Brussels sprouts

FLOWER HEADS

Grown for their dense heads of unopened flower buds, broccoli and cauliflower can be harvested year-round if the right cultivars are planted. Broccoli is relatively compact and ready to harvest in as little as four months; larger, overwintering crops can be in the ground for up to a year.

WRAP CAULIFLOWER
Protect cauliflower heads from sunlight and cold by bending and tying the leaves over to cover the flower head.

HARVEST BROCCOLI
Cut the main head of broccoli while still compact. Leave the plants to bear smaller heads farther down the stem.

The tight flower heads soon loosen, so harvest them promptly

Purple sprouting broccoli bears flower heads down the length of the main stem

Check the underside of leaves for aphids and caterpillar eggs

Space plants well apart to allow air to flow between the large leaves

Plant into firm soil that has not been broken up to keep plants from falling over

FLOWERING CROPS

Cauliflower needs good growing conditions so many gardeners begin by growing more easygoing broccoli.

Purple sprouting broccoli

Cauliflower

Broccoli

What's wrong with my garden greens?

Popular with pests, the cabbage family will need protection with netting in many gardens to keep birds away in winter and spring, and butterflies at bay during summer. They are also hungry plants, their large leaves quickly showing root damage or a shortage of nutrients.

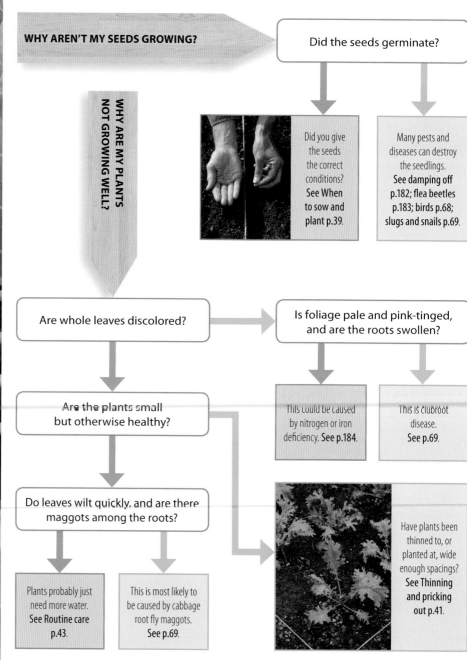

WHY AREN'T MY SEEDS GROWING?

Did the seeds germinate?

Did you give the seeds the correct conditions? **See When to sow and plant p.39.**

Many pests and diseases can destroy the seedlings. **See damping off p.182; flea beetles p.183; birds p.68; slugs and snails p.69.**

WHY ARE MY PLANTS NOT GROWING WELL?

Are whole leaves discolored?

Is foliage pale and pink-tinged, and are the roots swollen?

Are the plants small but otherwise healthy?

This could be caused by nitrogen or iron deficiency. **See p.184.**

This is clubroot disease. **See p.69.**

Do leaves wilt quickly, and are there maggots among the roots?

Plants probably just need more water. **See Routine care p.43.**

This is most likely to be caused by cabbage root fly maggots. **See p.69.**

Have plants been thinned to, or planted at, wide enough spacings? **See Thinning and pricking out p.41.**

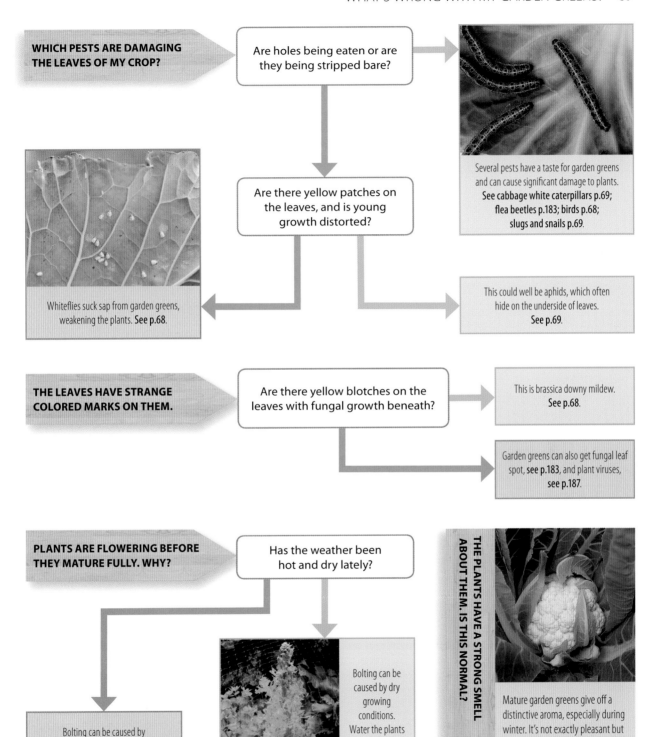

WHICH PESTS ARE DAMAGING THE LEAVES OF MY CROP?

Are holes being eaten or are they being stripped bare?

Several pests have a taste for garden greens and can cause significant damage to plants. **See cabbage white caterpillars p.69; flea beetles p.183; birds p.68; slugs and snails p.69.**

Are there yellow patches on the leaves, and is young growth distorted?

Whiteflies suck sap from garden greens, weakening the plants. **See p.68.**

This could well be aphids, which often hide on the underside of leaves. **See p.69.**

THE LEAVES HAVE STRANGE COLORED MARKS ON THEM.

Are there yellow blotches on the leaves with fungal growth beneath?

This is brassica downy mildew. **See p.68.**

Garden greens can also get fungal leaf spot, **see p.183**, and plant viruses, **see p.187**.

PLANTS ARE FLOWERING BEFORE THEY MATURE FULLY. WHY?

Has the weather been hot and dry lately?

Bolting can be caused by dry growing conditions. Water the plants more frequently.

Bolting can be caused by low spring temperatures. **See When to sow and plant p.39.**

THE PLANTS HAVE A STRONG SMELL ABOUT THEM. IS THIS NORMAL?

Mature garden greens give off a distinctive aroma, especially during winter. It's not exactly pleasant but it's nothing to worry about. Removing fallen leaves may help.

Garden greens clinic

All garden greens belong to the cabbage family, sharing a need for fertile soil and a susceptibility to the same pests and diseases. Giving them a good start is key, so prepare the soil well, look after them when newly planted out, protect with bird netting as they grow, and keep a close eye out for signs of problems.

What causes yellow patches on the leaves?

Brassica downy mildew is a fungal disease, spread in water droplets, and causes pale yellow patches on leaf surfaces, with distinctive pale, fluffy fungal growth below. Soft young growth is most at risk, especially in moist conditions. Leaves fall off. See Downy mildew p.182.

Q Why aren't my cauliflower plants forming heads?

A These demanding plants need well-improved, nutrient-rich soil, and may not initiate flower heads if the soil is poor or there is insufficient moisture. Cold conditions when planting out can also prevent head formation.

Q Are my greens under attack from cabbage whiteflies?

A Cabbage whiteflies suck sap from under the leaves and only appear when disturbed. Large infestations weaken plants and encourage sooty mold to develop. **See Whiteflies p.187; Sooty mold p.186.**

DISCOLORED LEAVES   **BIRD NETTING IN PLACE**

WHITEFLIES UNDER A LEAF

Q Why are the lower leaves turning yellow?

A Most garden greens tend to drop their lower, older leaves as they mature, and as long as the plant is healthy and growing well, this is not a problem. Remove and compost any fallen, discolored, or yellowing leaves to keep them from attracting or harboring pests and diseases in the garden.

Q Has my crop been attacked by birds?

A All garden greens are a favorite food of birds, which will quickly peck leaves of mature plants down to the stalks and graze seedlings off at ground level. Examination of damaged plants will often reveal some tearing and sharp beak marks that would not be caused by caterpillars. See p.180.

Diagnostic chart

Symptoms	Diagnosis
 **Foliage becomes pale**, wilts readily, resulting in a poor crop and plants that collapse and die. When lifted from the soil, the roots are drastically swollen and distorted.	**Club root** is a soil-borne disease that affects all garden greens, the spores of which can remain viable in the soil for 20 years. Plants grown in acidic and waterlogged soil are most at risk. **See p.182.**
 **Growth slows and plants wilt** on excessively sunny days from mid-spring into early fall. Young plants may wilt and die soon after being transplanted from a seed bed or planted out.	**Cabbage root flies** lay their eggs at the base of plants. The resulting maggots eat the roots, until eventually plants cannot take up enough water, causing them to wilt and even die. **See p.181.**

 Are slugs and snails a threat to my garden greens?

 Leaves are a favorite of slugs and snails. Some damage is easily tolerated on established plants, but seedlings and transplants can quickly be destroyed during damp weather. **See p.186.**

APHID INFESTATION

 CATERPILLAR DAMAGE

Why do my Brussels sprouts and kale plants fall over during winter?

Garden greens have shallow roots, and taller crops, such as Brussels sprouts, kale, and sprouting broccoli can be toppled by winter weather. Insert stakes in fall for extra support.

 What damage can aphids do to my crop?

Aphids feed on garden greens during spring and summer. Colonies can become large, and are most often found under the leaves or on stems, where they can cause leaves to pucker and even stunt growth. Gray and waxy mealy aphids are also common during summer. See p.180.

How can I quickly recognize cabbage white caterpillars?

The caterpillars of cabbage white butterflies can seriously damage crops between early summer and early fall by eating holes in the leaves. Watch out for groups of tiny yellow eggs underneath leaves from late spring, pick off any yellow and black spotted caterpillars, and keep butterflies away from plants with netting. **See p.181.**

Clusters of yellow eggs

Feeding caterpillars

Adult butterfly

Bulb and stem crop anatomy

This diverse group encompasses the onion family, along with a range of other plants grown for delicious fat bulbs or tender stems. Most are grown each year as annuals, but asparagus and rhubarb are both usually bought as young plants, and grown as perennials that will be productive for many years.

THE ONION FAMILY

These plants are grown either for their bulbs or their edible stems of densely packed leaves. Often sown as seed, onions and shallots can be raised from small bulbs called "sets," while garlic is grown from cloves.

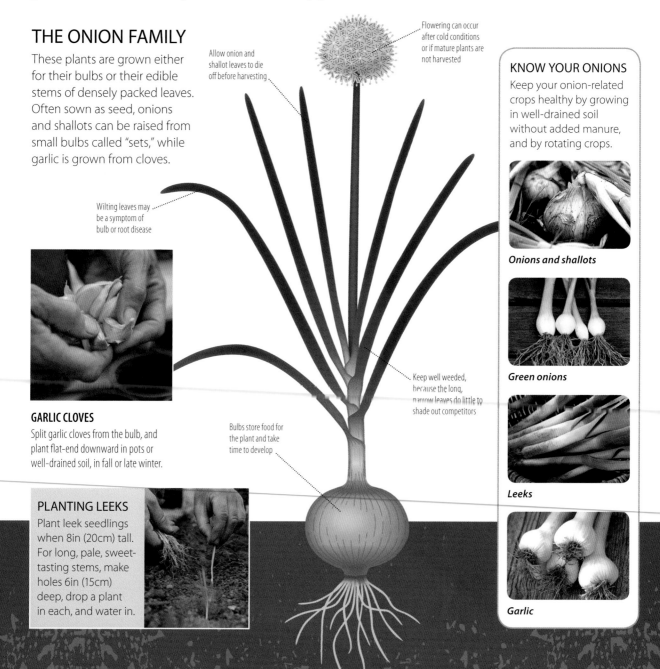

Allow onion and shallot leaves to die off before harvesting

Flowering can occur after cold conditions or if mature plants are not harvested

Wilting leaves may be a symptom of bulb or root disease

Keep well weeded, because the long, narrow leaves do little to shade out competitors

Bulbs store food for the plant and take time to develop

GARLIC CLOVES
Split garlic cloves from the bulb, and plant flat-end downward in pots or well-drained soil, in fall or late winter.

PLANTING LEEKS
Plant leek seedlings when 8in (20cm) tall. For long, pale, sweet-tasting stems, make holes 6in (15cm) deep, drop a plant in each, and water in.

KNOW YOUR ONIONS
Keep your onion-related crops healthy by growing in well-drained soil without added manure, and by rotating crops.

Onions and shallots

Green onions

Leeks

Garlic

WEIRD AND WONDERFUL

The bulbs formed by this collection of plants are swollen roots, stems, or leaf bases, which plants use as a way of storing food to fuel flowering. Some are also grown for their stems, which are best harvested young, and can be blanched by excluding light to keep them tender and sweet.

SWEET SUMMER RHUBARB

Although the pale pink stems of forced rhubarb are a delicacy, it is easy to grow your own. Cover dormant plants with dry straw in late winter or early spring, and exclude light by covering with a terra-cotta forcing pot, or any tall pot. Cut the sweet stems about one month later.

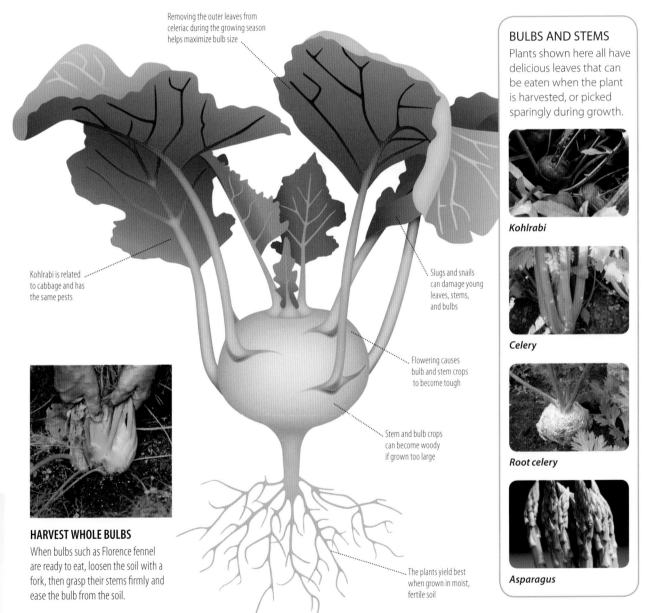

Removing the outer leaves from celeriac during the growing season helps maximize bulb size

Kohlrabi is related to cabbage and has the same pests

Slugs and snails can damage young leaves, stems, and bulbs

Flowering causes bulb and stem crops to become tough

Stem and bulb crops can become woody if grown too large

The plants yield best when grown in moist, fertile soil

HARVEST WHOLE BULBS

When bulbs such as Florence fennel are ready to eat, loosen the soil with a fork, then grasp their stems firmly and ease the bulb from the soil.

BULBS AND STEMS

Plants shown here all have delicious leaves that can be eaten when the plant is harvested, or picked sparingly during growth.

Kohlrabi

Celery

Root celery

Asparagus

What's wrong with my bulbs or stems?

This diverse group of crops needs vigilance during spring and summer, the main growing season, when a range of crop-specific insect pests can cause problems if not controlled. Watch for rapid, tall growth, which indicates bolting, along with wilting, which can be a sign of root rots.

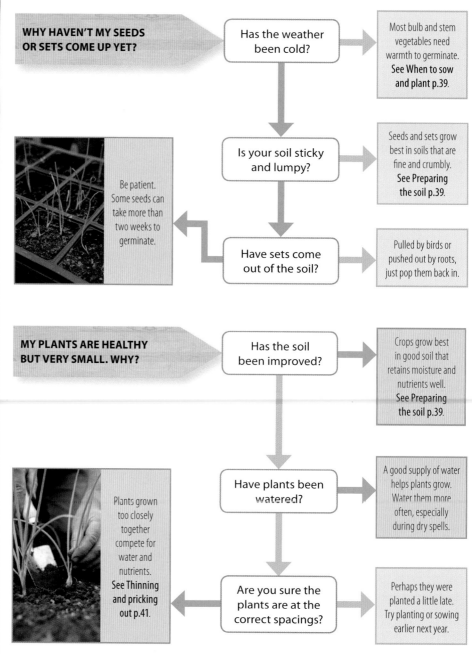

WHY HAVEN'T MY SEEDS OR SETS COME UP YET?

Has the weather been cold?

Most bulb and stem vegetables need warmth to germinate. **See When to sow and plant p.39.**

Is your soil sticky and lumpy?

Seeds and sets grow best in soils that are fine and crumbly. **See Preparing the soil p.39.**

Be patient. Some seeds can take more than two weeks to germinate.

Have sets come out of the soil?

Pulled by birds or pushed out by roots, just pop them back in.

MY PLANTS ARE HEALTHY BUT VERY SMALL. WHY?

Has the soil been improved?

Crops grow best in good soil that retains moisture and nutrients well. **See Preparing the soil p.39.**

Plants grown too closely together compete for water and nutrients. **See Thinning and pricking out p.41.**

Have plants been watered?

A good supply of water helps plants grow. Water them more often, especially during dry spells.

Are you sure the plants are at the correct spacings?

Perhaps they were planted a little late. Try planting or sowing earlier next year.

**WHAT'S WRONG WITH
THE LEAVES ON MY PLANTS?**

Have the leaves of onions
wilted and yellowed
before maturity?

Check the base of bulbs and roots for
signs of onion white rot. **See p.74.**

Do the leaves have spots
with fungal growth?

The leaves of onions, shallots, and garlic
yellow and die down naturally when they
mature. It's nothing to worry about.

This could be one of a few diseases.
**See onion downy mildew p.75; leek
rust p.75; fungal leaf spot p.183.**

**YOUNG PLANTS HAVE BEEN
DAMAGED OR DESTROYED.**

Are there white maggots
around the roots of onion,
leek, or garlic plants?

**SHOULD MY GARLIC
PLANTS FLOWER?**

Other pests that attack young plants
include slugs and snails, **see p.186,** and
flea beetles, **see p.183.**

These are onion fly larvae.
See p.74.

Are you growing a "hardneck"
variety of garlic?

**WHAT PESTS ARE EATING THE
LEAVES, BULBS, AND STEMS?**

Slugs and snails will damage all bulb and
stem crops. **See p.186.** Other pests are specific to certain
crops only. **See asparagus beetle p.75; leek moth p.74;
onion fly p.74; onion thrips p.184.**

Cold conditions usually
trigger bulb and stems to
flower early, or bolt.
Dry conditions can
also contribute.
See p.75.

These varieties always produce
flowers—just cut them off.

Bulb and stem crop clinic

These varied crops are generally easy to grow, but there are a few significant pests, diseases, and problems to watch out for. A number of these can be avoided by growing related plants together and rotating them to a new bed each year, which prevents pests and diseases from accumulating in the soil.

Why won't my garlic split into cloves?

The reason you have one large bulb instead of many individual cloves is that most cultivars require exposure to cool temperatures below 50°F (10°C) for at least 30 days to initiate splitting. This is why garlic is planted in well-drained soil in fall or late winter.

Q My crop is wilting. Has it been attacked by onion flies?

A In early summer the white maggots of onion flies eat the roots of young onions, shallots, garlic, and leeks, causing plants to wilt and even die. Later attacks are rarely fatal, but the damage may start to rot. **See p.184.**

Q How do I recognize the symptoms of onion white rot?

A Thick white fungal growth at the roots and base of the bulb indicates onion white rot. This fungus produces spores that remain viable in the soil and can reinfect onion crops for seven years. **See p.184.**

LEEK MOTH CATERPILLARS   **HARVESTED ONIONS**   **INFECTED ONION BULBS**

Q Is the damage caused by leek moths?

A Leeks and onions can be attacked by leek moth caterpillars. During summer and early fall, pale patches appear where they have been feeding as leaf miners on the internal tissue of the leaf. Caterpillars can bore into the center of leeks where they eat the young leaves and prevent new growth. **See p.183.**

Q How can I store a bumper harvest of garlic and onions?

A Large garlic and onion crops can easily be stored for fall and winter use by lifting them carefully and drying them. Simply lay them on wire racks in the sun or indoors until the skins are crisp and totally dry. Try plaiting the dried stalks to hang in bunches indoors or store them in net bags. Keep them dry and well ventilated.

Drying racks   *Plaited onions*   *Stored garlic*

Q **Why has my celery bolted and started to flower?**

A Young plants do not like the cold and may run to seed, or bolt, if the temperature falls below 50°F (10°C). Onions, shallots, leeks, garlic, fennel, and kohlrabi also bolt. Don't sow or plant too early.

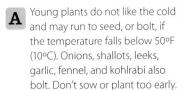

 ## Diagnostic chart

Symptoms	Diagnosis
 **Pale yellow patches** develop on the upper leaf surfaces and gradually turn brown. Fuzzy gray fungal growth also appears at the same points on the underside of the leaf.	**Downy mildew** is a fungal disease that affects many plants, including rhubarb (below), and is problematic for young plants and onions. It often occurs in moist conditions. **See p.182.**
 **Orange lumps develop on the leaves** of leeks, garlic, onions, and shallots, then burst to produce many bright orange spores. Infected leaves often turn yellow and can die back.	**Leek rust** is a fungal disease that is most common during wet or humid weather. Although unsightly, it rarely has a serious impact on the growth of plants and doesn't require treatment.

 *Why do the bulbs I store after harvesting go rotten?*

Any damage, along with moisture in the skin, leaves bulbs at risk of decay. Only store clean, dry, healthy bulbs. Keep them in a cool, dry place and check them regularly for rot.

 HEALTHY RHUBARB LEAVES   **UNDAMAGED ASPARAGUS**

Q **What has happened to my rhubarb plant?**

A Orange-brown, tissuelike patches on the upper surface of rhubarb leaves, with gray-white fungal growth below, are typical signs of downy mildew disease. It is most common after damp conditions in late spring and summer. Remove infected leaves as soon as possible. **See p.182.**

Q **How can I identify asparagus beetles?**

A These beetles are easy to spot, with their red body and yellow-spotted back. The ½in- (1cm-) long larvae strip the leaves and bark from asparagus stems, causing them to yellow and dry. They overwinter in the soil and emerge in late spring, feeding and laying eggs on plants until fall. **See p.180.**

Pod crop anatomy

Peas and beans come in a range of shapes and sizes, but are all legumes, meaning they have bacteria-filled root nodules that absorb nitrogen from the atmosphere to feed the plants. Grown annually from seed for their pods or the seeds inside, they yield best in soil that retains moisture in summer.

PEAS

A quick and easy crop to grow, as long as seeds are not sown into cold soil or eaten by mice, peas are usually removed from their shells, but some cultivars have tender pods that can be eaten whole.

TYPES OF PEAS

Traditional peas need to be shelled before eating, while snow peas and sugar snap varieties are eaten pod and all.

Shelling peas

Snow peas

Sugar snaps

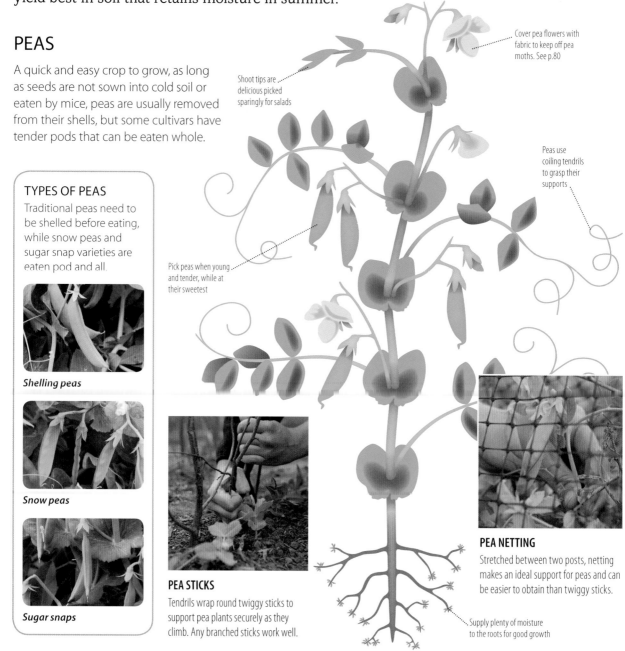

Cover pea flowers with fabric to keep off pea moths. See p.80

Shoot tips are delicious picked sparingly for salads

Peas use coiling tendrils to grasp their supports

Pick peas when young and tender, while at their sweetest

PEA STICKS

Tendrils wrap round twiggy sticks to support pea plants securely as they climb. Any branched sticks work well.

PEA NETTING

Stretched between two posts, netting makes an ideal support for peas and can be easier to obtain than twiggy sticks.

Supply plenty of moisture to the roots for good growth

BEANS

Dwarf and climbing, hardy and tender, there is a bean to suit every garden and season. Broad beans are hardy and germinate at low temperatures, so can be sown in fall or early spring. Green and runner beans need mild conditions, so don't plant them outside until the risk of cold has passed.

Pinch back shoot tips when they reach the top of supports

Keep flowering plants well watered for the best harvest

Slugs and snails damage pods, especially on low-growing dwarf green beans

Climbing bean leaves can be damaged by cold or shredded by strong winds

Climbing beans twist their stems around supports as they grow

PICK YOUNG

All beans are best picked when small and sweet to encourage further crops, and to avoid old, stringy pods.

TIE IN STEMS

Carefully tie young stems to their supports using soft twine, to start them climbing and to prevent wind damage.

TRANSPLANTING

Beans dislike root disturbance, so sow them under cover into deep pots or toilet paper rolls. Plant them outside once the risk of cold and frost has passed.

TYPES OF BEANS

Dwarf green and runner beans, and shorter broad beans, are the best for smaller or windy gardens, although yields are lower.

Runner beans

Green beans

Broad beans

What's wrong with my pod crops?

Generally resilient, peas and beans are most vulnerable as seeds and seedlings, when green and runner beans need warmth to grow well. Watch foliage for signs of fungal diseases during spring and summer, and give plants sturdy supports from the start to prevent wind damage.

WHY AREN'T THERE MANY PODS ON MY PLANTS?

Did the plants have many flowers?

Overwatering or excess rain can cause leaves to grow at the expense of flowers.

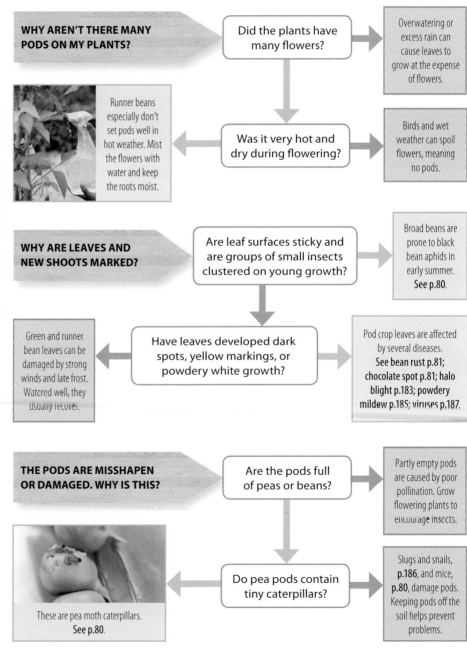

Runner beans especially don't set pods well in hot weather. Mist the flowers with water and keep the roots moist.

Was it very hot and dry during flowering?

Birds and wet weather can spoil flowers, meaning no pods.

WHY ARE LEAVES AND NEW SHOOTS MARKED?

Are leaf surfaces sticky and are groups of small insects clustered on young growth?

Broad beans are prone to black bean aphids in early summer. **See p.80.**

Green and runner bean leaves can be damaged by strong winds and late frost. Watered well, they usually recover.

Have leaves developed dark spots, yellow markings, or powdery white growth?

Pod crop leaves are affected by several diseases. **See bean rust p.81; chocolate spot p.81; halo blight p.183; powdery mildew p.185; viruses p.187.**

THE PODS ARE MISSHAPEN OR DAMAGED. WHY IS THIS?

Are the pods full of peas or beans?

Partly empty pods are caused by poor pollination. Grow flowering plants to encourage insects.

These are pea moth caterpillars. See p.80.

Do pea pods contain tiny caterpillars?

Slugs and snails, p.186, and mice, p.80, damage pods. Keeping pods off the soil helps prevent problems.

SEEDLINGS ARE DAMAGED AND NOT GROWING WELL.

Have conditions been cold?

Growth will slow or stop in the cold, leaving seedlings vulnerable to pests. Better weather will help.

This damage is caused by bean seed flies. **See p.80.**

Did seedlings emerge with ragged leaves and stems?

Have the seedlings been damaged or destroyed since they germinated?

This could be slugs and snails, **see p.186**, or mice, **p.80.**

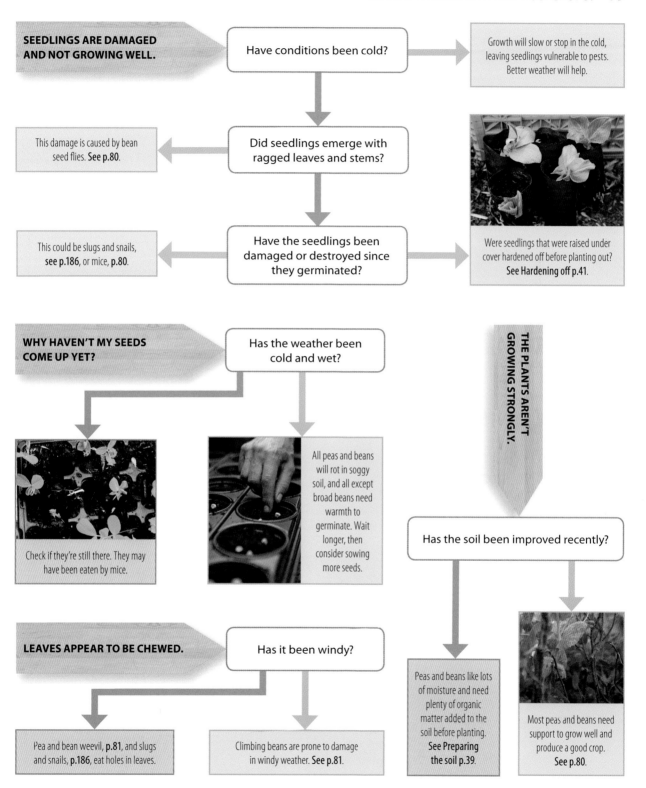

Were seedlings that were raised under cover hardened off before planting out? **See Hardening off p.41.**

WHY HAVEN'T MY SEEDS COME UP YET?

Has the weather been cold and wet?

THE PLANTS AREN'T GROWING STRONGLY.

Has the soil been improved recently?

Check if they're still there. They may have been eaten by mice.

All peas and beans will rot in soggy soil, and all except broad beans need warmth to germinate. Wait longer, then consider sowing more seeds.

LEAVES APPEAR TO BE CHEWED.

Has it been windy?

Peas and beans like lots of moisture and need plenty of organic matter added to the soil before planting. **See Preparing the soil p.39**.

Most peas and beans need support to grow well and produce a good crop. **See p.80.**

Pea and bean weevil, **p.81**, and slugs and snails, **p.186**, eat holes in leaves.

Climbing beans are prone to damage in windy weather. **See p.81**.

Pod crop clinic

Once established in good growing conditions, pod crops are resilient, and although they are affected by a number of pests, will often grow on regardless and produce a respectable crop. It is at the seedling stage that they really need protecting from cold, wet weather, and a few voracious pests.

Have mice attacked my peas and beans?

Shoots chewed off at ground level and small holes left where seeds were planted are sure signs that hungry mice have been feasting on the peas and beans you sowed or planted out. They love the fat seeds and shoots, and can destroy whole rows overnight. **See p.183.**

Q Have my plants been attacked by bean seed flies?

A Seedlings of green and runner beans emerge looking brown and tatty, or may not germinate. The tiny white larvae of bean seed flies feed on them underground, causing plants to grow slowly or die. **See p.180.**

Q Are black bean aphids on broad beans a problem?

A Black bean aphids infest the tips of broad beans in summer. They suck sap, weakening plants, and stop pods from forming. Pinching back the young growth once the first pods have set deters aphids. **See p.180.**

PERFECT PEA PODS

UNSUPPORTED PEA PLANTS

BLACK BEAN APHIDS

Q How do I spot pea moth caterpillars?

A Small cream-colored caterpillars with black heads can often be found inside pea pods, feeding on the peas. These are the young of the pea moth, which lays its eggs on the flowers in summer. Early and late sowings that do not flower during this period will escape this pest. **See p.184.**

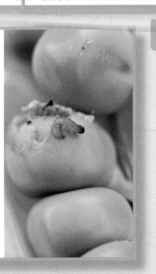

Q How can I stop my peas from collapsing?

A Whether they are dwarf cultivars that grow to just knee-high, or tall climbing varieties, almost all peas need supports to keep them upright. Their clinging tendrils need plenty of places to attach, so choose twiggy sticks or netting pulled taut between posts, rather than smooth stakes.

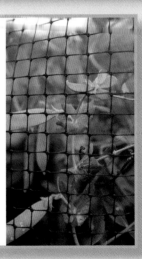

Diagnostic chart

Symptoms	Diagnosis
 **Round, brown spots on the leaves** of broad beans. They may grow or join to form large patches. Stems, pods, and flowers can also show similar symptoms.	**Bean chocolate spot** is a fungal disease that can reduce yields or even kill plants and whole crops. It is worst in moist conditions, where drainage is poor or the weather is wet. **See p.181.**
 **Orange or brown pustules develop on the foliage** of broad, green, and runner beans, sometimes producing visible clusters of spores. Stems and pods may also be infected.	**Rust** is a common fungal disease during warm, wet summers, and often affects beans planted close together. Severe infection can cause leaves to die and result in poor harvests. **See p.185.**

 Q **Bean leaves look tattered and stems are broken**

A Wind can seriously damage the leaves of climbing green and runner beans, and unsupported peas and broad beans. Tie plants in regularly and use temporary windbreaks in exposed areas.

DAMAGED BEAN LEAVES

HEALTHY BORLOTTI BEANS

How can I protect bean seedlings from cold once planted outside?

To protect frost-tender green and runner beans outdoors, make simple cloches using tall, clear plastic bottles with their bases cut off. Remove the caps to provide ventilation.

 Q **Have my plants been attacked by weevils?**

A Adult pea and bean weevils are responsible for the U-shaped notches, often found nibbled into the margins of peas and broad beans. Although this damage looks worrisome, it rarely affects the health of established plants. Young plants can suffer after heavy attack but should recover if watered and fed well.

 Q **How can I ensure the flowers on my beans form pods?**

A Birds can damage red runner bean flowers and stop pods from forming, but white-flowered cultivars are usually left alone. Hot, dry weather prevents runner beans from setting pods, so water plants and mist flowers well to minimize problems. Empty pods are often due to patchy pollination caused by bad weather.

White-flowered variety

Water crops well

Misting the flowers

RESCUE

Fruit

Both tree and bush fruit can bear heavy crops for many years, so it is well worth making an effort with their planting and care. Follow the general advice given regarding site preparation, planting, supports, and pest protection for all new plants. Refer to the separate tree fruit and soft fruit sections for help identifying and dealing with the cause of any symptoms. Both also feature advice on when and how to prune different crops, a task essential to encourage good plant health and plentiful fruit.

How to grow fruit

Most fruit trees and bushes are long-lived, and crop reliably for years. Take time to choose the right cultivars, and pick a good site to give them the best chance of success. Fruit bushes and trees can grow large, so consider their final size before planting. If space is limited, try training them against a wall or fence, or growing in them in containers.

Choosing the right fruit

It is useful to buy fruit trees and bushes from a specialty fruit nursery, not only because they offer a huge selection of healthy, well-pruned plants, but also because they can provide you with reliable advice. This can be particularly helpful when faced with the enormous range of fruit tree cultivars available.

Look for cultivars that have been bred locally to cope well in your climate and choose those that are most suitable. Some will only ripen their fruit fully given a good summer, while others bear their blossoms late, helping them to avoid damaging late frost in cooler regions. Many cultivars offer some resistance to common diseases, which can help to keep them productive longer.

Most fruit trees are sold grafted onto rootstocks in order to limit their eventual size and make them more manageable trees for the garden. There are many rootstocks available that each influences tree growth in different ways—from very dwarfing to vigorous—so it is vital to choose the right one for the space available. Check if your chosen tree is "self-compatible," meaning it can pollinate its own flowers, or whether it needs a partner tree that flowers at the same time, to aid pollination.

Soft fruit bushes are much simpler, because they are self-compatible, so can be planted singly, although blueberries set more fruit when cross-pollinated. Many modern cultivars produce much larger fruit on more compact plants and offer good disease resistance, so are well worth seeking out. Plant a mix of early and late cultivars to extend the yielding period.

AVOIDING PROBLEMS

Certified plants Many countries have regulations to inspect certain fruit trees and bushes at nurseries for disease, and to certify those that are healthy. In the US, for example, black currants are checked for a range of problems. It makes good sense to buy certified plants where possible.

When to plant

Fruit trees and bushes are sold growing in containers or "bare-root," which simply means they have been field grown and dug out just before sale. This has a direct bearing on when they should be planted.

Bare-root plants are only sold during the dormant season, between late fall and early spring. This is the best period to plant trees and shrubs, providing the ground is not frozen, because it gives their roots the chance to gain a foothold before they come into leaf in the spring.

Although container-grown fruit is available year round, it should also ideally be planted while dormant. Avoid planting in summer, when hot, dry conditions can stress newly planted trees and shrubs. Any that are planted in summer should be kept very well watered.

Avoid disappointment Cherries are very tempting to grow but need the right conditions to yield well. Check your site before buying any fruit plants to determine what will grow well there, and what won't.

If there has been a pest or disease problem before, don't replant any susceptible fruit in the same soil. To avoid the buildup of viruses and other diseases, which reduce yields, move strawberries to a fresh site every three or four years.

Preparing soil for planting

Soft fruit bushes can stay productive for around ten years, and fruit trees for decades more, so it's well worth spending time improving the soil properly. This is best done in fall. Weed the area well, ensuring all perennial weeds are removed. For each tree dig over an area about 3ft (1m) square, slightly less for each fruit bush, breaking up any compacted layers that could impede drainage. Then dig in well-rotted organic matter to improve the soil structure.

Most fruit prefers slightly acidic soil, but blueberries must have soil with a low pH, between 4.0–5.5. Add acidic potting mix before planting. If you don't have acidic soil, grow blueberries in containers.

Choosing the right site

All fruit trees and bushes should be planted in full sun, and will produce earlier, sweeter fruit as a result. However, most fruit, especially soft fruit, will still set and ripen well in partial shade. What is vital is that they are not planted in a low-lying spot where frost lingers, known as a "frost pocket." Here, the early spring blossoms can be damaged by the cold, and will then fail to set fruit.

It is also important to avoid planting in poorly drained soil, where water pools after heavy rain. If soil drainage isn't good, improve it before planting by digging plenty of sharp grit and potting mix into the soil, or by installing a drainage system.

Freestanding fruit trees can be too large for many gardens, but most can be trained against walls in space-saving fans, cordons, and espaliers.

These restricted trees look very attractive and crop well. Planted against south- or west-facing walls, they benefit from the extra warmth, which enables fruit to ripen in cooler areas. Another advantage is that training trees makes it easier for you to protect the blossoms from frost by draping the tree with garden fabric. This particularly useful for peaches, which flower very early.

AVOIDING PROBLEMS

Plant a fruit patch Traditionally, fruit was planted in its own patch in the garden, which still makes sense when growing soft fruit that needs to be protected from hungry birds. When planting, consider enclosing all your fruit bushes under one large, netted fruit cage. This is simpler and more effective than trying to cover individual plants with nets. It also makes picking easier.

How to plant fruit crops

Prepare the soil for planting well in advance, so that your fruit trees and bushes can be planted as soon as possible. Unwrap bare-root plants, trim any long or broken roots back with pruners, and soak the plants in a bucket of water for an hour. Cover the roots at all times when they are exposed to the air. Plants in containers should also be watered thoroughly, so the root ball is moist.

Fruit trees When planting fruit trees, first drive a stake into the ground in the chosen planting location, then dig a hole large enough to take the roots. Fruit trees are commonly bought container-grown, and it is important they are planted so the surface of the potting mix sets at soil level, (see How to plant a bare-root tree, below). Tease the roots gently from the edge of the root ball and position the trunk close to the stake. Ensure that any scar on the trunk where the tree was grafted onto the rootstock is above soil level. Backfill the hole with soil, firming it in stages with your foot as you do, and keep the tree straight. Once this is done, firm the soil again, tie the tree to the stake, water well, and apply a thick mulch of well-rotted manure or compost, keeping it clear of the bark.

Fruit bushes Fruit bushes are planted in the same way as trees, although their smaller root balls need correspondingly smaller holes, and they do not need a supporting stake. Cane fruits, such as raspberries and blackberries, have shallow root systems, and are often sold bare-root, so ensure their planting holes are wide enough to spread out the roots fully, and that the canes are planted at the same depth as they were at the nursery. To encourage black currants to produce plenty of strong stems from ground level, they are usually planted about 2in (5cm) deeper than they were before.

Strawberry plants Strawberries thrive in fertile soil, improved with well-rotted garden compost or manure before planting. Plants are available in containers or bare-root. Whichever you are planting, take care to position the crown of the plant— the point from which the leaves sprout—level with the soil surface. Too deep and the crown may rot, while too shallow and the plant may dry out and die. Dig a hole for each plant with a trowel, spread out the roots, gently firm the soil back around the plant, and water in well.

HOW TO PLANT A BARE-ROOT FRUIT TREE

Bare-root fruit trees are planted slightly differently from container-grown trees and should be planted as soon as possible after purchase to prevent the roots from deteriorating. The same basic technique can also be used when planting bare-root fruit bushes, as well as bare-root ornamental trees and shrubs. Planting should be done between fall and spring.

1 Correct level Mound soil at the base of the planting hole and set the roots on top. The aim is to ensure the tree is planted to the same depth it was growing at the nursery. Add more soil if needed.

2 Backfill Carefully fill the hole with soil, taking care not to leave air pockets between the roots. Ease the soil between the roots with your fingers and firm it down repeatedly using your foot as you fill the hole.

3 Support Secure the tree to its stake using an adjustable tree tie and water it in well. Bare-root trees are prone to drying out, so keep them well watered throughout their first year.

(right) **Supporting fruit** Some fruit bushes crop so heavily that their branches sag under the weight. Providing extra support prevents them from snapping.

(far right) **Staking trees** Most tree stakes are used as a temporary measure to support the tree while its roots establish and the trunk develops. Check ties annually.

Staking trees

All fruit trees need additional support when first planted to prevent them from rocking in the wind or blowing over while their roots become established. Choose a sturdy, pointed, wooden stake that has been pressure-treated with preservative to extend its useful life. The length of the stake depends on the length of clear trunk the tree will have when mature, because it needs to reach just below the lowest branches to ensure it does not rub against them. Allow an extra 20in (50cm) to drive into the ground.

Attach the tree to the stake using a tree tie with soft material to act as a cushion between the trunk and stake, which prevents chafing. Large trees benefit from the support of two stakes, driven in about 20in (50cm) apart, with a crossbar attached just below their tops, to which the tree is tied. This method can also be used where large root balls make positioning a single stake awkward.

Trees grafted onto very dwarfing rootstocks should always be staked, all others should have their stakes removed after four or five years.

Support for fruit trees and bushes

Training fruit trees to cover walls and fences makes them easier to fit into smaller gardens, and given a sunny exposure, can help ripen the fruit.

Stone fruits, such as cherries and plums, can be trained as fans, while apples and pears are most commonly grown as cordons and espaliers. The elegant shapes of these restricted forms of fruit trees are created by training them onto strong horizontal wires, securely attached to the wall or fence at regular intervals. Wires for cordons should be spaced about 24in (60cm) apart, for espaliers about 16in (40cm) apart, and for fan-trained trees about 6in (15cm) apart. Wires can be hard work to put up, but they allow the new growth to be tied into the desired position easily. Wires will support the trees throughout their long life, so it is worth doing well.

Gooseberries, along with red and white currants, can also be trained as cordons, and are a good choice for lower walls and fences—they don't grow as tall as fruit trees. They only require a single cane for support.

The growth of cane fruits, like raspberries and blackberries, is usually long and unwieldy, and is best trained onto supports to help keep plants tidy and aid fruit picking. Raspberries can simply be tied to posts around 6ft (1.8m) tall, but the

canes are more often tied onto horizontal galvanized wires stretched between strong wooden posts. This system suits the extremely long canes of vigorous blackberries best. Wires attached to walls or fences can also be used to train cane fruits where space in the garden is limited.

Growing fruit in containers

Most fruit grows well in containers and, since pot-grown plants never reach the size of those in open soil, this is the perfect way to include them in a small garden. While their smaller stature means that the harvests will never be huge, pot-grown plants are easier to cover or move to protect them from frost and birds, or to position them in a favorable sunny spot, sheltered from the wind. Select compact, modern soft-fruit cultivars where available.

Containers Your choice of container is important because trees and bushes should only be planted in a pot no more than 4in (10cm) wider than their root ball. Repot them into a slightly larger pot each year until the plant has reached its final size. If you want to invest in a beautiful, expensive pot, this is the stage to

do so. Containers must have good drainage holes in their base. Where only one or two have been made, add a layer of broken clay pots or coarse gravel to the bottom of the pot to ensure that the potting mix doesn't become waterlogged.

Potting mix Growing in pots allows you to provide plants preferred soil conditions easily. Choose good-quality, soil-based mixes for fruit trees and bushes, which holds nutrients and moisture better than soil-less equivalents. They are also heavier, which makes tall plants less likely to blow over. Soil-based potting mix is a good option for fruit bushes, while trees will do best planted in heavier mix. Blueberries need acidic soil to thrive and should be given an lime-free potting mix with a pH of 4.0–5.5. Strawberries will only be productive for a short time, so they can simply be grown in any good multi-purpose potting mix.

Planting Make sure that pot-grown plants have been well watered, or bare-root plants soaked before planting. Add gravel to the bottom of the pot to improve drainage, then cover with potting mix to a depth

Water well Crops in pots are especially sensitive to dry spells when they are in flower or fruit. A lack of water at this stage can result in a very disappointing harvest.

that allows the plant to set in the pot at the same level as it was before. Fill around the roots with more mix, firming well as you go, and fill the pot to about 2in (5cm) below the rim to allow for easy watering. Place the pot in its final spot and water well.

All fruit growing in containers will need watering regularly and feeding with a high-potassium liquid tomato fertilizer every two weeks during the growing season until the fruit is ripening. Regular repotting, or replacement of the top layer of old potting mix for mature plants, is essential to keep plants healthy.

Trees and shrubs will also require pruning, although less so than those grown directly in the soil.

AVOIDING PROBLEMS

Rootstocks for pots Although you might expect the smallest trees to be best for pots, this actually isn't the case. Most very dwarfing rootstocks, such as G64 for apples, need extremely good growing conditions to flourish, which is difficult to provide in containers. It is far better to choose a rootstock like G11 with more vigor that will cope well in a pot, while its overall size will be constrained by the dimensions of your container.

What to watch out for

Once plants produce fruit, particularly soft fruit, birds (p.180) are often a major problem. Whole crops can be eaten unless they are netted before they begin to ripen. Damage to tree fruit caused by birds also allows wasps (p.187) and brown rot (p.181) to move in, so check fruit ripeness regularly and pick quickly.

Most fruit plants flower while there is still a risk of late frost, which will damage flowers and prevent fruit from setting. Protect plants where possible with fabric. Wet weather can also prevent pollination and encourage gray mold (p.183).

All fruit are bothered to some degree by problems but fungal and bacterial diseases that infect fruit trees are the main cause for concern. See Fruit tree clinic pp.94–97; Soft fruit clinic pp.104–105.

ROUTINE CARE

Fruit trees and bushes are easy to grow as long as their needs are met. In gardens where many types of fruit are grown, it is a good idea to establish a maintenance routine.

Watering

Water newly planted trees and bushes whenever the weather is dry during the growing season. A really good soak, allowing water to permeate deeply into the soil, helps roots establish. In dry areas, improve harvests with occasional heavy watering during summer.

Feeding and mulching

A balanced fertilizer can be applied, at the recommended rate, around trees and bushes of fruiting age in early spring. Young plants also benefit from a mulch of well-rotted manure or compost around their base in early spring, ensuring it doesn't touch the stem or trunk.

Weeding and garden hygiene

Controlling weeds reduces competition and removes sources of pests and diseases. Keep surrounding soil clear of grass for the first four years while young trees become established in lawns. Raking up and disposing of fallen fruit and leaves removes sources of reinfection for the following year. Any unharvested fruit remaining on the tree should also be removed.

Pruning

Correct pruning, carried out at the right time of year, using clean, sharp tools, removes dead and diseased wood from fruit trees and bushes, allows air and light to penetrate among their branches, and keeps plants yielding heathily.

Barriers

Protect soft fruit with netting before it starts to ripen to keep out hungry birds. Cover fan-trained peaches with clear plastic, held away from the branches, from early winter until late spring, to prevent peach leaf curl infection (p.184). Fixing sticky grease bands to tree trunks prevents winter moths (p.187) from climbing into trees and laying their eggs. Pest traps hung in apple and plum trees during late spring and summer attract and trap male codling moths (p.182) and plum moths (p.185), preventing them from reproducing.

Moving strawberries

Viruses and other diseases can build up in the soil, and old strawberry plants become less productive over time. Plants are best dug up and replaced in a new part of the garden.

AVOIDING PROBLEMS

Regular care Providing fruit crops with regular care and attention, little and often, will help to keep them healthy and better able to resist attacks by pests and diseases. It is also a good opportunity to check your plants for the first signs of problems.

Fruit tree anatomy

Fruit trees may be large, but their shapely forms, spring blossoms, and colorful fruit make them attractive as well as productive. Best planted in winter or early spring, healthy trees crop heavily and can easily be incorporated into small yards by choosing those on dwarf rootstocks, training them up walls, or growing in containers.

STONE FRUIT

These fruit, with a hard central stone, have succulent, sweet flesh that requires plenty of sun to ripen fully, and do well trained as fans on south-facing walls. Many self-pollinating cultivars are available, which allow a lone tree to set ample crops of fruit.

Soft-skinned fruit are prone to pest damage, so pick soon once ripe

For larger fruit, thin out fruitlets on plums, peaches, and nectarines

Blossoms can be killed by late frosts

Fruit is ripe when it comes away with a lift and gentle twist

Prune stone fruit in summer to avoid silver leaf disease. See p.186

Pests and diseases overwinter in fallen leaves. Always rake them up

An appropriate rootstock will limit the growth of these vigorous trees

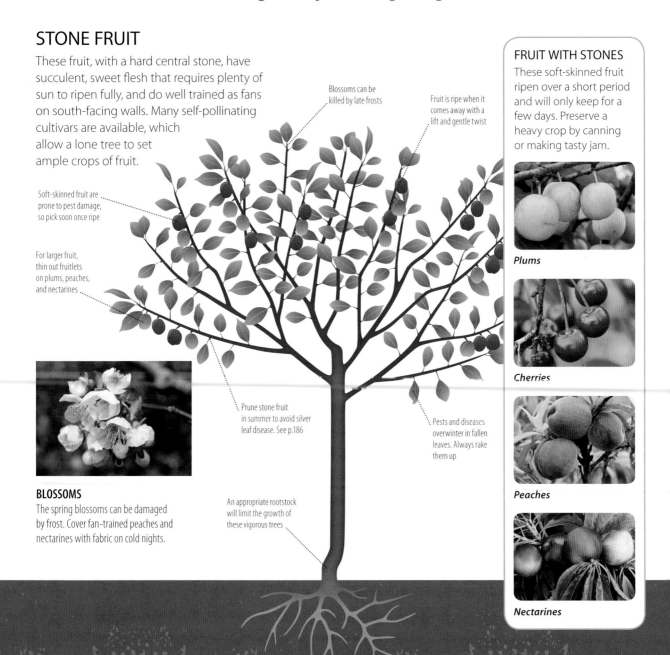

FRUIT WITH STONES
These soft-skinned fruit ripen over a short period and will only keep for a few days. Preserve a heavy crop by canning or making tasty jam.

Plums

Cherries

Peaches

Nectarines

BLOSSOMS
The spring blossoms can be damaged by frost. Cover fan-trained peaches and nectarines with fabric on cold nights.

PIP FRUIT

Apples and pears have pip-filled cores, and firm flesh with a protective outer skin. Most should be planted with a compatible cultivar that flowers at the same time to act as a pollination partner. They are available grafted onto various rootstocks that limit the final size of the tree.

GROWING FIGS

Heat-loving figs are often trained as fans against south-facing walls, and may bear slow-ripening fruit in late summer. To encourage fruiting, plant into large containers or line the planting hole with slabs. Protect tiny overwintering fruit with fabric or by moving potted plants indoors.

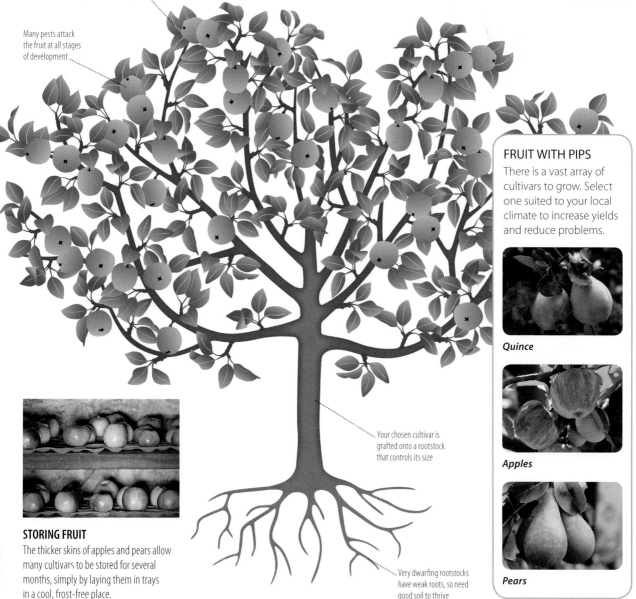

New growth can be prone to aphid attack. See p.180

Many pests attack the fruit at all stages of development

FRUIT WITH PIPS

There is a vast array of cultivars to grow. Select one suited to your local climate to increase yields and reduce problems.

Quince

Apples

Pears

Your chosen cultivar is grafted onto a rootstock that controls its size

Very dwarfing rootstocks have weak roots, so need good soil to thrive

STORING FRUIT

The thicker skins of apples and pears allow many cultivars to be stored for several months, simply by laying them in trays in a cool, frost-free place.

What's wrong with my fruit tree?

The list of fruit tree ailments seems long, but if a watchful eye is kept from the moment the blossoms open in the spring until the branches are bare late in the fall, then any pests and diseases can be dealt with quickly, and a healthy, problem-free crop of fruit harvested.

WHAT HAS BEEN EATING THE FRUIT?

From the outside? → **From the inside?**

From the outside? ↓

Are the plants netted?

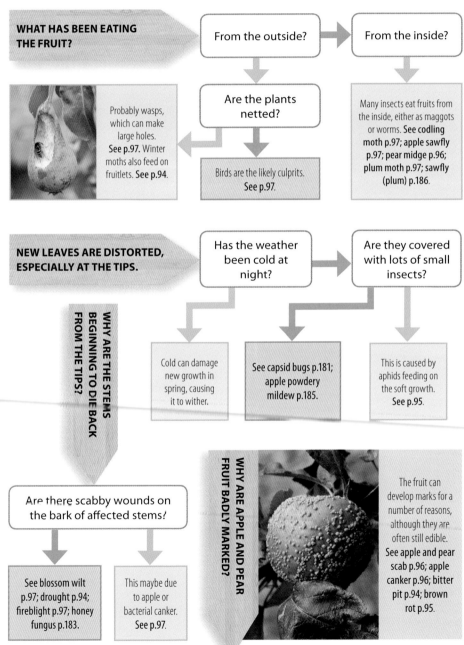

Probably wasps, which can make large holes. **See p.97.** Winter moths also feed on fruitlets. **See p.94.**

Are the plants netted? ↓

Birds are the likely culprits. **See p.97.**

From the inside? ↓

Many insects eat fruits from the inside, either as maggots or worms. **See codling moth p.97; apple sawfly p.97; pear midge p.96; plum moth p.97; sawfly (plum) p.186.**

NEW LEAVES ARE DISTORTED, ESPECIALLY AT THE TIPS.

Has the weather been cold at night? → **Are they covered with lots of small insects?**

WHY ARE THE STEMS BEGINNING TO DIE BACK FROM THE TIPS?

Cold can damage new growth in spring, causing it to wither.

See capsid bugs p.181; apple powdery mildew p.185.

This is caused by aphids feeding on the soft growth. See p.95.

Are there scabby wounds on the bark of affected stems?

See blossom wilt p.97; drought p.94; fireblight p.97; honey fungus p.183.

This maybe due to apple or bacterial canker. See p.97.

WHY ARE APPLE AND PEAR FRUIT BADLY MARKED?

The fruit can develop marks for a number of reasons, although they are often still edible. See apple and pear scab p.96; apple canker p.96; bitter pit p.94; brown rot p.95.

THE TREE DOESN'T FRUIT WELL, IF AT ALL. WHY?

Have you planted it recently?

It will need time to establish. Check that you planted it correctly. **See How to plant fruit crops p.86.**

Have you kept it well watered and fed?

Keep it well watered while in flower. Dry spells prevent fruit from forming.

Are you sure it's growing in the right spot?

Check the plant's preferred growing conditions. **See Choosing the right site p.85.**

Are you sure you pruned it correctly?

Check the tree for signs of pests and diseases. **See Fruit tree clinic pp.94–97.**

Good pruning promotes healthy growth, flowering, and fruiting. **See Pruning fruit trees pp.98–99.**

Do you water and feed your tree regularly?

Fertilizing and watering promotes healthy growth and encourages the tree to produce a better crop.

Are there pollinator varieties growing nearby?

Check the tree for signs of pests and diseases. **See Fruit tree clinic pp.94–97.**

THE LEAVES ON MY PEACH ARE DISCOLORED AND TWISTED.

This could only be peach leaf curl, which only affects peaches and closely related fruit. **See p.96.**

THE FRUIT DON'T RIPEN FULLY, OR TAKE A LONG TIME. WHY?

Most fruit need sun in order to ripen properly, which can be delayed by poor weather or if planted in the wrong place. Ensure your tree isn't shaded, and keep it well watered.

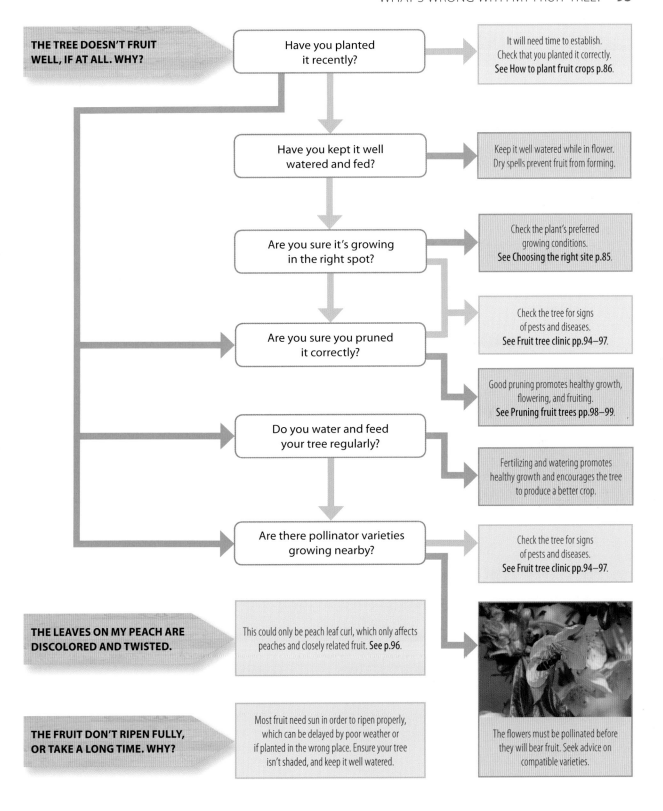

The flowers must be pollinated before they will bear fruit. Seek advice on compatible varieties.

? Fruit tree clinic

Fruit trees seem beset by problems, but because they are large plants that bear heavy crops, small amounts of damage are often easily tolerated. However, there are some serious issues to be aware of, in order to catch and treat them quickly before crops, or the trees themselves, are badly damaged.

Why don't the fruit set after flowering?

Sometimes there can be plenty of blossoms but little or no fruit, which is usually caused by bad weather during flowering. Frosts can damage the flowers, preventing fruit formation, while cold, wet weather can deter insects from pollinating the flowers, meaning no fruit.

Q Why are the fruit produced this year so small?

A Fruit need water to swell, and when fruit trees experience drought, their yields are drastically reduced. Small fruit also result when the trees is carrying a very heavy crop; thinning the young fruitlets prevents this.

Q Why have many small fruit fallen from the tree?

A Apple and pear trees naturally thin their fruit while they are still small to remove any that are diseased, damaged, or infertile, giving the rest space to develop. Known as "June drop," it occurs in early summer.

PEST-FREE PEARS

WELL-WATERED APPLES

FALLEN FRUITLETS

Q How do I know if my tree has winter moth?

A The caterpillars of winter moths eat holes in the leaves of fruit trees as they emerge during early spring. Yellow-green, and about 1in (2.5cm) long, the caterpillars often hide between leaves bound together with silk thread, and can also reduce yields by damaging blooms and young fruitlets. See p.187.

Q How can I tell if my apples have bitter pit?

A This fruit (right) is affected by apple bitter pit, which also causes dark mottling of their flesh. Symptoms can appear on the tree or while fruit is in storage. It is a symptom of calcium deficiency, usually as a result of dry conditions, which prevent the tree from taking up the mineral from the soil.

Can aphids cause much damage to fruit trees?

A Aphids suck sap from the new growth, weakening the tree and causing distorted leaves. The pests also attract sooty mold. **See Aphids, p.180; Sooty mold, p.186.**

Q **What's wrong with the leaves of my cherry tree?**

A Brown spots on the leaves that fall away to create small holes during spring and summer are due to a condition called shothole, caused by a number of fungi and bacteria. Silver leaf disease gives leaves of plums and cherries a silvery surface. It enters the tree via wounds or pruning cuts, most commonly in spring. Affected branches often die back, and whole trees can be killed if seriously infected. **See Shothole, p.186; Silver leaf, p.186.**

Shothole

Silver leaf

▲ **BROWN ROT ON FRUIT**

HEALTHY CHERRY LEAVES

What's eating tunnels in the leaves of my apple and cherry trees?

Apple leaf miners are small green caterpillars that feed on the tissues inside apple and cherry leaves in late summer. They also weave white cocoons. Damage is only superficial.

 Is the fruit on my tree affected by brown rot?

A Brown rot is an aptly named fungal condition that causes expanding squishy, brown patches to develop on fruit. Infection is spread by water splash and usually occurs if the fruit skin is damaged, such as by insect or bird attack. The rotten fruit will either drop from the tree or shrivel up and remain in place. **See p.181.**

 What are the orange spots on the bark of some stems?

A These bright pustules are caused by a fungal disease, coral spot, which infects dead stems and branches, and can spread into healthy growth. **See p.182.**

 Why does my fruit tree look so sickly?

A Key nutrients are easily washed from the soil by heavy rain or watering, or are sometimes difficult for plants to absorb because of drought or an unfavorable soil pH. Symptoms to watch for include yellowing leaves, poor flowering, small fruit, and weak growth. Plants in pots are most affected. **See Nutrient deficiencies, p.184**

Q Are my pears being eaten by pear midge?

A In late spring and early summer, pear fruitlets infected with the maggots of pear midge become black at their base and fall from the tree. Large numbers of fruit can be affected, even whole crops. The tiny maggots live in the center of the fruitlets, feeding on the flesh, then migrate into the soil when the fruit fall to the ground, ready to infect next year's crop. **See p.184.**

Q How do I recognize apple and pear scab?

A These fungal diseases cause dark blotches to form on fruit, which may be distorted or crack, and allow in rot. Infected leaves also develop similar dark patches and may fall early. **See p.180.**

Q What sort of canker has infected my tree?

A Fungal apple and pear canker causes distorted, sunken areas of bark on these trees. Cherries and plums with holey leaves and weeping infected areas have bacterial canker. **See p.180.**

HEALTHY NECTARINES

DISEASE-FREE APPLE LEAVES

APPLE CANKER ON A BRANCH

Q Are these symptoms of peach leaf curl?

A Leaves of peaches and nectarines that have become twisted, blistered, and turned vivid shades of red and purple have been infected with peach leaf curl. This fungal disease infects leaves in early spring and will eventually cause them to drop prematurely, weakening the plant. **See p.184.**

Q Why do some apple leaves look white?

A In spring, new growth on apple trees can appear white, thanks to a covering of powdery fungal growth. This is caused by apple powdery mildew, which also affects pear trees, although less seriously. Infected shoots often grow weakly, can be misshapen, and may die back early. **See p.185.**

Q **How can I tell if blossom wilt has caused dieback?**

A The blossom wilt fungus infects apples, plums, cherries, pears, and peaches, causing the blossoms to wither and nearby leaves to turn brown and die, but persist on the tree. **See p.181.**

SYMPTOMS OF FIREBLIGHT

Q **How do I identify if a fruit tree has fireblight?**

A Apple and pear blossoms that have died, quickly followed by neighboring leaves and stems during spring and early summer, could be a symptom of the bacterial disease, fireblight. Similar to blossom wilt, fireblight causes areas of bark to sink, the wood underneath to turn orange-red, and sometimes bacterial ooze may seep from infected areas. **See p.182.**

Diagnostic chart

Symptoms	Diagnosis
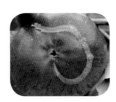 **In late summer and fall** holes appear in the skin of apples and pears, or sometimes small, white caterpillars can be found feeding in the cores of ripe fruit when sliced.	**Codling moth larvae** are usually responsible for damaging ripening fruit. They overwinter in the tree's bark, and adult moths lay eggs between late spring and midsummer. **See p.182.**
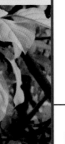 **Developing apple fruitlets drop from the tree** during early and midsummer, and have a small maggot hole in their skin. Mature fruit may be distorted with a scar on their skin.	**Apple sawfly** lays its eggs among the blossoms, where they hatch into white maggots that tunnel into the growing fruit, initially just below the skin, then into the core. **See p.186.**
Tan-colored, roughened or raised patches appear on the skins of apples as they ripen in late summer. Leaves at the shoot tips may also be peppered with small holes.	**Apple capsid bugs** are bright green, sap-sucking insects that damage the fruit and leaves with their toxic saliva. Fortunately, damage is only superficial and fruit can still be eaten. **See p.181.**
 **Ragged holes appear in the skins** of ripe fruit, such as peaches, plums, and apples during summer, and gradually increase in size as the sweet flesh beneath is eaten away.	**Wasps** find ripe fruit irresistible and will eat their own way into soft-skinned fruit or feed where birds have already damaged the tougher skins of apples and pears. **See p.187.**
Small ripening fruit, such as cherries, vanish altogether, or larger specimens, such as apples, pears, and plums exhibit deep holes where the skin had been pierced.	**Birds** enjoy the taste of ripe fruit and will either eat them whole or peck through the skin with their beaks to take portions of juicy flesh. Larger fruits will often be dislodged from the tree. **See p.180.**
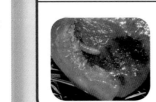 **Plums ripen prematurely,** and when cut open, reveal a brown area around the stone containing maggot excrement or sometimes the culprit; a ½in- (1cm-) long, pale pink caterpillar.	**Plum moth caterpillars** hatch in early summer and burrow into developing fruit to feed on their flesh. They then eat their way out and overwinter in the bark, ready for next year. **See p.185.**

Pruning fruit trees

Don't be intimidated by pruning established fruit trees. It is more straightforward than you might think, and is vital to keep a tree healthy, cropping well, and in an attractive shape. Choosing the right time of year to prune and using clean, sharp tools promotes quick healing and helps prevent infection. Excessive pruning encourages leaves, not fruit, so don't overdo it.

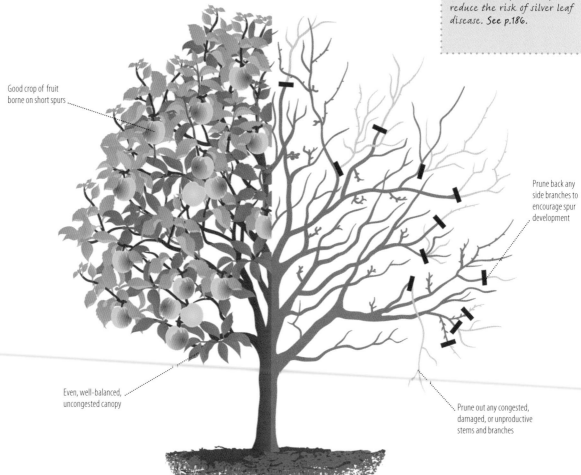

Good crop of fruit borne on short spurs

Prune back any side branches to encourage spur development

Even, well-balanced, uncongested canopy

Prune out any congested, damaged, or unproductive stems and branches

APPLE AND PEAR TREES

Both pears and apples should be pruned during winter, while their branches are bare. First remove any dead, diseased, or damaged wood, and crossing or congested branches that prevent air and light from getting into the canopy. Most apples and pears flower and fruit from stems on stubby shoots called "spurs," which form on wood that's at least two years old. To encourage more spurs to develop, prune long sideshoots back to four buds, and the shoots at the tip of each branch by up to a third of their new growth.

CHERRY TREES

Vigorous sweet cherries are best fan-trained against a wall, while sour types can be grown as trees. Sour cherries fruit on last summer's growth—to encourage new shoots, cut back some older stems to healthy shoots in early fall. To prune trained sweet cherries, cut the sideshoots to six leaves in late summer, then to three in early fall.

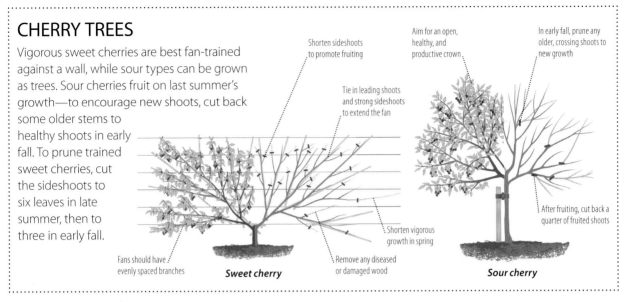

Shorten sideshoots to promote fruiting

Tie in leading shoots and strong sideshoots to extend the fan

Aim for an open, healthy, and productive crown

In early fall, prune any older, crossing shoots to new growth

Fans should have evenly spaced branches

Shorten vigorous growth in spring

Remove any diseased or damaged wood

After fruiting, cut back a quarter of fruited shoots

Sweet cherry

Sour cherry

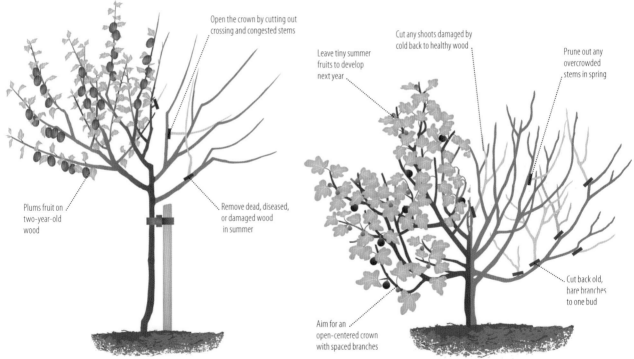

Open the crown by cutting out crossing and congested stems

Cut any shoots damaged by cold back to healthy wood

Prune out any overcrowded stems in spring

Leave tiny summer fruits to develop next year

Plums fruit on two-year-old wood

Remove dead, diseased, or damaged wood in summer

Cut back old, bare branches to one bud

Aim for an open-centered crown with spaced branches

PLUM TREES

Established plum trees need little pruning, which is done in summer to prevent silver leaf disease, see p.186. Cut out diseased or damaged branches, and remove crossing or crowded growth to let light and air into the crown.

FIG TREES

Remove shoots damaged by cold in spring, along with any that are badly placed or overcrowded. Promote new growth by cutting older branches back to one bud. Pick off any unripe fruit that are larger than peas in the fall.

Soft fruit anatomy

Undemanding to grow and a delicious summer treat, most soft fruit are produced year after year on woody plants that either take the form of clumps of tall stems, or attractive, medium-sized bushes. The leafy, low-growing, perennial plants that bear strawberries will only crop well for a few seasons

CANE FRUIT

Given good, moist soil and shelter from wind, raspberries, blackberries, and related hybrids will flourish. Their long, often thorny stems, known as canes, emerge as suckers each year from the base of the plant.

Fruit develops on the current or last year's canes

Flowers need to be pollinated by insects before fruit will form

Fruit should be picked when fully ripe, so check your plants regularly

Canes emerge at the base of stems or from the roots

PROVIDING SUPPORT
To stop tall canes from bowing under the weight of fruit or breaking in strong wind, regularly tie them onto supporting posts or wires as they grow.

CANE FRUIT
New fall-fruiting raspberries can crop in their first season; other cane fruit will crop well in their second year.

Raspberries

Blackberries

Hybrid berry

BUSH FRUIT

Currants, gooseberries, and blueberries all need fertile, well-drained soil, some sunshine, and enough space to allow good airflow to prevent fungal diseases. Apart from these simple requirements, they are easygoing, needing only basic pruning to keep them neat and cropping well.

STRAWBERRIES

These perennial plants will grow for a number of years, but many growers prefer to renew their strawberry bed every three years to prevent pests and diseases from building up.

Runners Stems carrying baby plants grow during summer. You can use these to create new healthy plants.

Fruit Flowers need to be pollinated to set fruit, so ensure insects have easy access to plants grown under cover.

NETTING

All soft fruit should be covered with netting before it ripens to stop birds from eating the berries before you.

Many insect pests will attack the foliage. Check for symptoms

Plant fruit bushes away from frost pockets to prevent damage to their flowers

BUSH FRUIT

Bush fruit are ideal for small gardens because they are self-pollinating, which means they don't need another nearby.

Blueberries

Red and white currants

Gooseberries

Different bush fruit crop on different-aged stems. Check before pruning

The roots may die if the soil becomes waterlogged

BLUEBERRY GROWING IN POT

Unless you have acidic soil, grow blueberries in large containers filled with lime-free, acidic potting mix.

What's wrong with my soft fruit?

Succulent and sweet, soft fruit are a favorite of birds, and without a tough outer skin, they are also prone to rot as they ripen. Respond quickly to marked, curling, and eaten leaves during the growing season, and good yields of tasty fruit can still be had.

WHY ARE THE LEAVES TURNING YELLOW THEN BROWN IN SUMMER?

Do the stems look healthy?

Has the weather been dry?

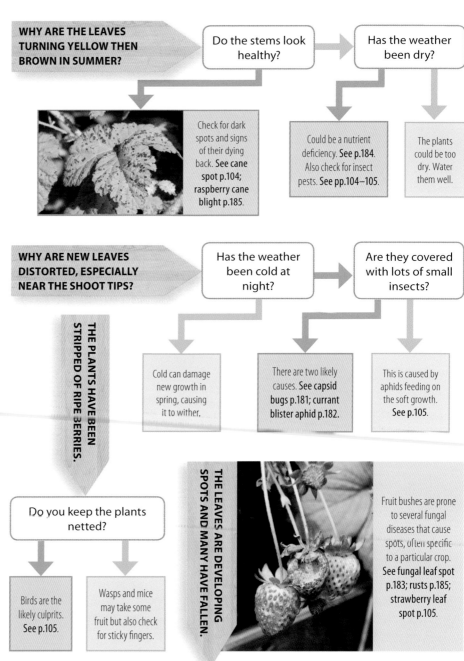

Check for dark spots and signs of their dying back. **See cane spot p.104; raspberry cane blight p.185.**

Could be a nutrient deficiency. **See p.184.** Also check for insect pests. **See pp.104–105.**

The plants could be too dry. Water them well.

WHY ARE NEW LEAVES DISTORTED, ESPECIALLY NEAR THE SHOOT TIPS?

Has the weather been cold at night?

Are they covered with lots of small insects?

Cold can damage new growth in spring, causing it to wither,

There are two likely causes. **See capsid bugs p.181; currant blister aphid p.182.**

This is caused by aphids feeding on the soft growth. **See p.105.**

THE PLANTS HAVE BEEN STRIPPED OF RIPE BERRIES.

Do you keep the plants netted?

Birds are the likely culprits. **See p.105.**

Wasps and mice may take some fruit but also check for sticky fingers.

THE LEAVES ARE DEVELOPING SPOTS AND MANY HAVE FALLEN.

Fruit bushes are prone to several fungal diseases that cause spots, often specific to a particular crop. **See fungal leaf spot p.183; rusts p.185; strawberry leaf spot p.105.**

WHY DOESN'T THE PLANT CROP WELL, IF AT ALL?

Have you planted it recently?

It will need time to establish. Check that you planted it correctly. **See How to plant fruit crops p.86.**

Have you kept it well watered and fed?

Keep it well watered while in flower. Flowers and fruitlets drop if too dry.

Are you sure it's growing in the right location?

Check the plant's preferred growing conditions. **See Choosing the right site p.85.**

Are you sure you pruned it correctly?

Check the plant for signs of pests and diseases. **See Soft fruit clinic pp.104–105.**

Correct pruning is often essential for strong flowering and fruiting. **See Pruning fruit bushes pp.106–107.**

Do you water and feed regularly?

Feeding and watering promotes healthy growth and encourages a good crop.

Is the plant getting old, in need of replacing?

Check for signs of pests and diseases. **See Soft fruit clinic pp.104–105.**

Are there plenty of bees in your garden?

THE FRUIT DON'T RIPEN FULLY, OR TAKE A LONG TIME.

Most fruit need sun in order to ripen properly, and poor weather and shady growing conditions can delay this. Ensure your plants aren't shaded and keep them well watered.

The flowers must be pollinated to set fruit. Try growing flowering plants nearby to attract more pollinating insects.

Soft fruit clinic

Soft fruit are simple to grow, but their enticing sweetness and delicate skins make them easy pickings for pests, and vulnerable to fungal diseases just as you are ready to pick the delicious harvest. Successful cultivation of these crops is all about being one step ahead by spotting problems early and keeping pests at bay.

Why is foliage marked with yellow patterns?

All soft fruit can be affected by their own types of viruses, but older strawberry plants are particularly prone. Symptoms include marks on the leaves; misshapen leaves, flowers, and fruit; weak growth; and poor yields, which gradually worsen. See Viruses p.187.

Q **What damage do capsid bugs do to fruit bushes?**

A During summer, these small green sap-sucking insects feed at the shoot tips. Leaf cells die where the bugs have fed, forming tears as the leaves grow. Young growth can also become distorted. **See p.181.**

Q **Why are the fruits covered with mold?**

A Fluffy, gray fungal growth that starts as brown patches on fruit is caused by gray mold. Spread in the air and in water droplets, this is a common disease in wet summers and if fruit touch damp surfaces. **See p.183.**

▲ **CANE SPOT SYMPTOMS**

▲ **HEALTHY RED CURRANTS**

GRAY MOLD DESTROYS FRUIT

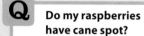

Q **Do my raspberries have cane spot?**

A Raspberry cane spot is a fungal disease that also affects blackberries, causing pale-centred purple blotches on canes from early summer. Similar spots can then spread onto leaves and fruits, the bark may split where large spots have developed, and canes may die. Simply prune out infected stems.

Q **What's eating the gooseberry's leaves?**

A Where the leaves of gooseberries, red currants and white currants have rapidly been stripped back to the stems, the pale gray, black-spotted larvae of gooseberry sawfly can be found. Repeated attacks occur from mid-spring to midsummer, weakening the plants, although they usually recover. **See p.186.**

Diagnostic chart

Symptoms	Diagnosis
 **Clusters of green, gray-green, or black insects** on young growth in spring and summer. Shoot tips are curled and smaller than normal; older leaves are covered in honeydew.	**Aphids** attack all soft fruit, damaging plant tissues while feeding. They cause distortion, reduced growth, and can also spread viral infections. **See Aphids, p.180; Viruses, p.187.**
 **In spring and early summer,** currants, particularly red currants, develop blistered leaves at their tips, with a distinctive yellow and red coloration. Insects are below the leaf.	**Currant blister aphids** overwinter on plants as eggs and hatch in spring to suck the sap of new leaves, weakening the plant. Their pale yellow coloring makes them easy to see. **See p.182.**

 Q What are the maggots in my raspberries?

A Dry patches at the top of ripe berries are a sign that there may be a cream-colored raspberry beetle larva feeding inside. They also feed on blackberries and other cane fruit. **See p.185.**

DISEASED FRUIT

PERFECT STRAWBERRIES

Is it birds taking all the fruit, even those that aren't ripe?

Birds will attack all types of soft fruit as they ripen, and will either pluck off the fruit whole or peck small beakfuls from unprotected plants. They often target fruit before fully ripe. See p.180.

Q Why are gooseberries coated in white dust?

A Gooseberry mildew, a fungal disease, coats infected foliage, stems, and fruit in a layer of powder that resembles talcum powder. Young growth can become misshapen and die back if badly affected, and although edible, infected fruit turns an unappetizing brown. See p.183.

Q What's wrong with my strawberries?

A Deep red, pale-centered patches on the leaves are a sign of strawberry leaf spot, a fungal infection that usually occurs during summer or, occasionally, spring. It does little harm. Puckered and distorted fruit are caused by poor pollination, often due to bad weather or few insects during flowering. **See Fungal leaf spot, p.183.**

Strawberry leaf spot   *Poor pollination*

Pruning fruit bushes

Easy to master and quick to do, pruning your fruit bushes correctly helps form them into an attractive shape and keep them a manageable size. A few well-placed cuts also promote good health by removing any dead and diseased shoots, and can increase harvests by encouraging plenty of strong, fruit-bearing wood.

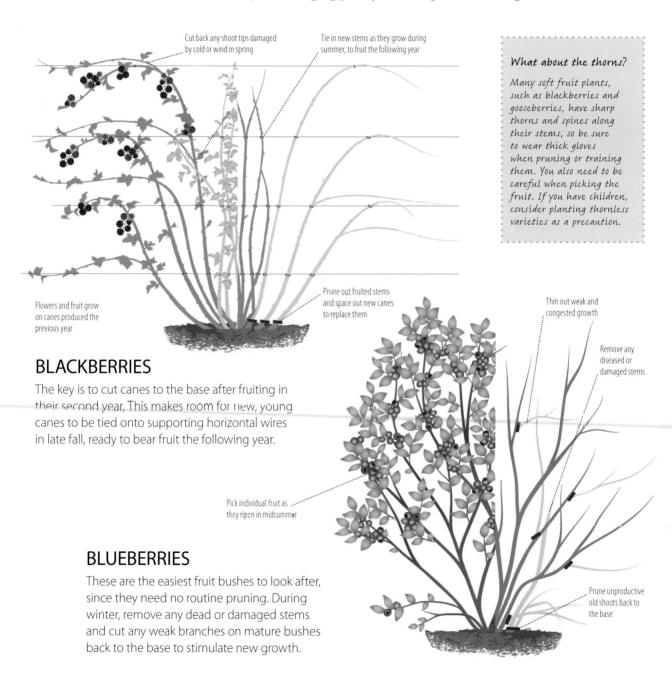

Cut back any shoot tips damaged by cold or wind in spring

Tie in new stems as they grow during summer, to fruit the following year

Flowers and fruit grow on canes produced the previous year

Prune out fruited stems and space out new canes to replace them

What about the thorns?

Many soft fruit plants, such as blackberries and gooseberries, have sharp thorns and spines along their stems, so be sure to wear thick gloves when pruning or training them. You also need to be careful when picking the fruit. If you have children, consider planting thornless varieties as a precaution.

BLACKBERRIES

The key is to cut canes to the base after fruiting in their second year. This makes room for new, young canes to be tied onto supporting horizontal wires in late fall, ready to bear fruit the following year.

Pick individual fruit as they ripen in midsummer

Thin out weak and congested growth

Remove any diseased or damaged stems

Prune unproductive old shoots back to the base

BLUEBERRIES

These are the easiest fruit bushes to look after, since they need no routine pruning. During winter, remove any dead or damaged stems and cut any weak branches on mature bushes back to the base to stimulate new growth.

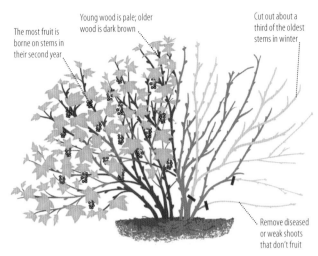

The most fruit is borne on stems in their second year

Young wood is pale; older wood is dark brown

Cut out about a third of the oldest stems in winter

Remove diseased or weak shoots that don't fruit

BLACK CURRANTS

Black currants fruit best on the previous year's wood and should be pruned once during their winter dormancy, cutting a third of the oldest stems back to a healthy young shoot near the base, to encourage new growth.

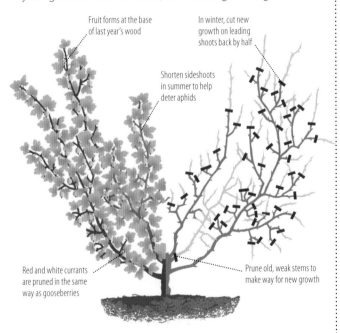

Fruit forms at the base of last year's wood

In winter, cut new growth on leading shoots back by half

Shorten sideshoots in summer to help deter aphids

Red and white currants are pruned in the same way as gooseberries

Prune old, weak stems to make way for new growth

GOOSEBERRIES & OTHER CURRANTS

These bushes are all pruned twice a year to create an open framework of branches. In midsummer, prune only the sideshoots back to five leaves, then in winter cut the lead stems back by half and sideshoots to two buds only.

RASPBERRY CANES

Summer- and fall-fruiting raspberries are easy to prune. Summer types produce berries on canes in their second year, which should be cut out at the base after fruiting, to be replaced with the new canes that have grown during summer. Fall types flower and fruit on the current season's canes, which are cut down in late winter, making space for new growth.

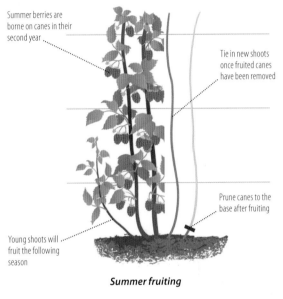

Summer berries are borne on canes in their second year

Tie in new shoots once fruited canes have been removed

Young shoots will fruit the following season

Prune canes to the base after fruiting

Summer fruiting

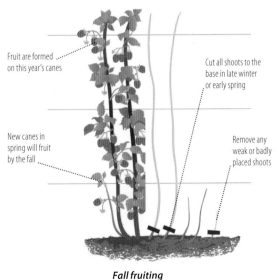

Fruit are formed on this year's canes

Cut all shoots to the base in late winter or early spring

New canes in spring will fruit by the fall

Remove any weak or badly placed shoots

Fall fruiting

The **ornamental** garden

The diversity of plants in the ornamental garden adds rich layers of color and texture, giving year-round appeal. From long-lived trees and shrubs to annual bedding plants, from all-season lawns to ephemeral bulbs, the huge range means there is something for every corner of every yard. It also means that there are a lot of plants, with different needs and ailments to get a grip on, too. This section is packed with information to give ornamental plants a healthy start, and provides advice on keeping them trouble-free. Divided according to plant type, anatomy guides explain how a plant's structure influences growth, maintenance, and problems. Charts and question-and-answer pages aid quick diagnosis and point to the best ways to solve issues.

How to grow ornamentals

The incredible diversity of ornamental plants available, which ranges from bulbs to climbers, and annuals to trees, makes it really important to understand the needs of every plant you choose, right from the start. That way you can give it the best conditions possible, enabling it to grow strongly and shrug off attacks by pests and diseases.

Right plant right place

As obvious as this gardening mantra sounds, almost every gardener must be guilty of ignoring it at some point and planting a shade-lover in full sun, or a delicate specimen in the full force of the wind. While these poor plants often survive, they never perform well, at best having their flowers or new leaves spoiled by the weather, or at worst succumbing to the many pests and diseases that prey on weakened plants.

This disappointing fate is easily avoided by taking a look at your garden and working out the range of growing conditions it has to offer. Some, such as light and wind levels, are fairly easy to gauge, while soil moisture may need to be checked throughout the year. It is also advisable to measure the pH of your soil, using one of the simple testing kits available from garden centers, and finding out which plants it suits.

Also watch for what are known as "frost pockets" during cold spells, where icy air gathers and frost takes a long time to lift. These usually occur in dips or at the bottom of slopes, and are somewhere that only the hardiest plants should be grown.

Plants exist that can cope with all conditions, from large trees to grass mixes for lawns, so it is best to do some research. Plant what suits your yard, rather than trying to change the conditions to suit the plants. Make the most of what gives your site its character, for example where drainage is poor, create a lush bog garden, or if the soil is acidic, plant beautiful rhododendrons and camellias that other others will envy.

If you're not sure where to start, look at what grows well in nearby gardens and plant the same in yours. Buy plants at a local nursery where they are raised in similar weather conditions to those in your yard, and staff can also provide reliable advice. To test conditions, just buy and try a single plant. If it fails, you've not lost much, and if it does well, you can go back and buy more of the same, along with related plants that have the same requirements.

Choosing healthy plants

A quick check and some common sense are enough to ensure that plants are in a good condition before

AVOIDING PROBLEMS

Disease resistance Even if conditions are perfect, replanting any plant related to one that has been removed due to disease is unlikely to succeed. Many diseases live in the soil for years, waiting to infect a new host plant, so grow something else instead. Many modern cultivars have been bred to be resistant to certain common diseases. Seek them out and take advantage of these naturally healthy plants, where they are available.

(above) **Textural planting** Underplanting trees makes best use of the space and allows you to create contrasting effects, such as bare trunks with foamy flowers.

(left) **Perfect partners** Combine plants that enjoy the same growing conditions. Choose a mixture of plant types for the longest, most varied show of color.

buying them. This is worthwhile, not only because healthy plants will grow better, but also because it's best to avoid bringing pests and diseases into your garden. For this reason it's always best to tactfully examine any gifts from friends' gardens too.

Look for plants that are a full, attractive shape, with bright green leaves and no roots pushing out of the base or at the top of the pot. Be wary of very weedy pots, especially with trees and shrubs, since this can indicate a pot-bound plant that has been in its container for too long. Watch out for pest damage on leaves, since whatever caused it could still be on the plant or in the medium. Also look for any signs of rot or mold.

Deciduous trees and shrubs, along with herbaceous perennials and climbers, can be bought when they are dormant and leafless. If this is the case, look for a good shape, undamaged bark and stems on woody plants, and evidence of plenty of healthy buds on all. Bulbs are also usually bought when dormant and should feel firm, with no signs of mold, and their outer skin intact.

Bare-root or container-grown?

Everyone is familiar with the pot-grown plants found in garden centers, but trees, shrubs, and sometimes herbaceous perennials are also available bare-root. All this means is that they have been grown in a nursery field and lifted for sale, so do not come in a pot. Pot-grown plants offer the convenience of being available and plantable all year round, but a wider range of plants is usually available bare-root from specialty nurseries, often via mail order and at lower prices. Since they can only be lifted when dormant, bare-root trees and shrubs are only available from late fall to early spring—slightly longer for perennials. They can therefore only be planted at this time of year, and should always be put into the ground as soon as possible.

Before planting ornamentals

Every plant has its own individual soil requirements, so it is advisable to check the label or a good book first. However, it is always good practice to remove all weeds from the planting area, particularly deep-rooted perennials, which will be difficult to extract once the new plant is growing and can resprout if even the tiniest section of root remains. The addition of a good quantity of well-rotted manure or garden compost also helps to improve the soil structure and fertility. Lime-free potting mix can be worked into soil to improve its structure where acid-loving plants are to be planted, although this will not make the soil itself acidic.

Good drainage is essential for most plants. Where it is poor, dig down to check for any compacted layers, which should be thoroughly broken up. Drainage can also be improved by incorporating plenty of grit and potting mix into heavy, clay soils. Bulbs are particularly prone to rotting in damp conditions, and will benefit from a layer of grit at the bottom of their planting holes.

Plan before planting To avoid disturbing your plants later, decide on their final positions in the bed before starting to plant them out.

The best time to plant

Try to be kind to your plants and avoid extremes when introducing them to their new environment. Of course, different plants have their own needs, but common sense suggests that it is never a good idea to plunge roots (or a spade) into winter soil that is frozen or sopping wet. Equally, few plants will enjoy being thrust into dry summer soil, when they're in full leaf and have no established roots to draw in the moisture needed during hot weather.

As a rule, the warm soil, mild weather, and gentle rains of fall and spring provide the best planting conditions and, because many plants are either losing their leaves or coming into growth, their roots have chance to establish before heavy demands are made of them.

Deciduous trees and shrubs can be a major investment in the garden. To give them the greatest chance of success, plant them without leaves between late fall and early spring. The warmth retained in fall soils makes this the ideal time for most. Evergreens are far better planted in spring, as they come into growth. Spring and fall are also the best times

to plant climbers and perennials. Those that are less hardy do better when started in spring, so they are well established before any cold weather.

The optimal time to plant bulbs depends on when they flower. Those that bloom in spring should be planted in fall. Summer-flowering types can also be planted in fall or early spring, while fall-flowering bulbs should be placed in position by late summer. Bulbs that perform well planted when in leaf, such as snowdrops, should be carefully moved after flowering.

Displays of patio plants are often created twice a year. Those that flower during winter and spring are ideally put into position during the early fall, while half-hardy summer bedding is usually planted out after the risk of frost has passed in late spring or early summer. They can also be started off under cover.

AVOIDING PROBLEMS

Planting clematis Always plant clematis 2in (5cm) deeper than they were in their pots. This encourages buds to develop below soil level, which will shoot away if the plant is struck by clematis wilt, see p.181.

How to plant

Probably the single best way to get your plants off to a healthy start is to plant them correctly. One common mistake is to plant at the wrong depth, which can lead to plants drying out or toppling over if planted too shallowly, or to the risk of fungal diseases if planted too deeply. As a general rule, trees, shrubs, climbers, perennials, and patio plants should all be planted at the same level as they were in their pot. Use the soil mark on the stems of bare-root trees and shrubs as a guide when replanting. Planting depths for bulbs vary, but most types are usually planted to a depth that is about three times their height.

Allowing plants enough space to grow is also an important consideration when planting. This is particularly true for trees and shrubs that have the potential to become large and need room to develop their attractive forms. Check plant labels and books, which usually give the size after ten years of growth, and plant accordingly. Fill any resulting large gaps with herbaceous perennials or patio plants that can easily be removed. Climbers are commonly grown singly, but don't crowd them with other plants while they establish. Herbaceous perennials and patio plants are normally spaced so the leaves of neighboring plants will just touch when fully grown. Ideally, most bulbs should be placed two or three times their width apart.

Water all plants, except bulbs, well before planting. Dig a hole comfortably large enough for the roots, and work in potting mix or grit as required. Spread out the roots of bare-root plants or tease out the

Better planting Taking time to plant correctly will be rewarded by a better display that lasts longer. The plants will also be less prone to problems.

AVOIDING MISTAKES WHEN PLANTING

If planted correctly, new plants will establish more quickly and have a good display sooner. The basic techniques involved are simple enough, although it is easy to make simple mistakes that can affect how well the plants will perform. Most of these can be avoided by taking your time when planting and not rushing—it will be time well spent.

Right way up When planting bulbs and bare-root perennials, make sure you know which way they should be planted. Bulbs can rot if planted facing down, while perennials may be slower to establish.

Firm in properly Air pockets can easily be left beneath new plants unless they are firmed in well. These voids can cause roots to dry out and die, or can fill with water, causing the roots to rot.

Avoid rain shadows Soil next to walls and fences can be very dry because it is sheltered from the rain. When planting in these areas, position plants at least 12in (30cm) into the border, and water them well.

outer roots of those in pots, and position the plant in the hole. Ensure it is at the right depth, fill soil back around the roots, firm gently with your hands, and water well. Bulbs can be planted singly in small holes, or in groups in larger holes. Check that the bulb is the right way up at the base of the hole, and cover with soil.

Providing support for plants

Many ornamental plants need additional supports, which can be either permanent or temporary. A stake, driven into the soil before planting, helps steady trees in windy conditions while their roots establish. After three or four years the roots should anchor the tree sufficiently, and the stake can be removed.

The requirements of climbing plants vary depending on their method of attaching to surfaces. Some need a substantial support system put in place before planting, but even those like ivy that can cling vertically to walls benefit from stakes or netting until established.

Perennials and bulbs with tall flowers can be damaged during bad weather. Wire mesh or twiggy supports, put in place as growth begins in spring, allow plants to grow through and cover them, giving a natural appearance, while the plants are well supported. Flowering stems can also be staked individually.

Growing in containers

All types of ornamental plants can be successfully grown in containers, and many glorious gardens are populated entirely with plants in pots. Although plants in containers require a lot more attention than those in the soil, planting in pots is popular because it offers many opportunities to utilize extra space and manipulate growing conditions. Don't be afraid to mix plants from different groups to create exciting displays and provide a long season of interest.

Choosing containers Once you have selected plants, the priority is to find a suitable container for them. As always, good drainage holes in the base are essential. Large, long-lived plants, such as trees and shrubs, need a pot that will comfortably accommodate their roots, but don't like too much spare space, so only allow up to 4in (10cm) extra width. Climbers require deep pots that are sturdy and stable enough to hold their supports if necessary. Bulbs need containers with excellent drainage that allow them to be planted at the right depth. Fast-growing perennials and patio plants are best given large pots.

AVOIDING PROBLEMS

Preventing damage Mulches and fertilizers are beneficial to plants when applied correctly, but unless you are using a liquid foliar feed, they must only touch the soil and not the plant itself. Solid fertilizers can scorch any stems, leaves, or flowers they come into contact with, while mulches laid right up to the stems and crowns of plants can allow fungal diseases to develop.

Which potting mix Use a soil-based potting mix for long-term specimens, such as trees, shrubs, climbers, and some perennials. A lighter, multi-purpose mix usually suits patio plants, particularly those in hanging baskets, and is often adequate for bulbs, although specially formulated, free-draining bulb medium will give the best results. Use lime-free potting mix for acid-loving plants, such as rhododendrons and camellias.

Plant in containers as you would in the ground, adding a layer of broken pots or coarse gravel to the bottom of pots with few drainage holes. Firm mix carefully around plants, especially where there are several in the pot, and water well.

The right site The greatest advantage of pots is that they can be moved into the plant's ideal growing conditions whenever required.

Clear view Providing support not only protects plants from damage, it also improves their display in the yard by holding the flowers and stems well.

Colorful containers Well-maintained containers can add color to all parts of the garden. The more containers you have, however, the more time you will need to spend watering and fertilizing them. Don't plant more than you can look after.

Ornamentals prone to problems

All ornamental plants can be affected by pests and diseases, but some are particularly susceptible to problems. Some gardeners choose to avoid such plants altogether, but it is worth looking for species and cultivars with resistance to common diseases, checking new plants for signs of pests and diseases before planting them in your garden, and watching out for the early signs of ailments.

Ornamental cherry trees can be damaged by aphids (p.180), bacterial canker (p.180), blossom wilt (p.181), shothole (p.186), and silver leaf (p.186). Roses are troubled by aphids (p.180), rose black spot (p.185), rust (p.185), powdery mildew (p.185), and gray mold (p.183). Some viburnums fall prey to aphids (p.180), scale insects (p.186), viburnum beetles (p.187), and whiteflies (p.187).

Clematis often suffer from clematis wilt (p.181), aphids (p.180), slug and snail damage (p.186), and powdery mildew (p.185). Hostas are a real favorite of slugs and snails (p.186), as are delphiniums, which also suffer from numerous fungal diseases.

Lilies are troubled by lily beetles (p.183) and vine weevils (p.187), and narcissi bulbs can be infected by viruses (p.187), fungal diseases, eelworm (p.182), and bulb flies (p.184).

Many plants will flourish in a sheltered spot in full sun, but some prefer shade, while others cope admirably on exposed balconies and roof terraces. Tender plants can also be moved indoors for winter, then back outside in spring.

Watering and feeding The main drawback of container gardening is that the plants rely on you to provide their water and nutrients. All pots should be checked regularly and watered if necessary, which could be twice daily during hot summer spells. To help reduce maintenance and the risk of plants becoming stressed because of drought, incorporate water-absorbing polymers into the potting mix when planting, or even install an automatic irrigation system.

Fertilizing during the growing season is best carried out regularly— even weekly for hungry patio plants—using an appropriate liquid fertilizer or by mixing granules of slow-release fertilizer into the potting mix during planting.

Plants grown in pots for more than one season should be repotted annually into larger pots until they reach the desired size. After that, replace the top 2in (5cm) of potting mix from the pot each spring, or apply a mulch of garden compost.

AVOIDING PROBLEMS

Watch out Several pests and diseases are particularly common among pot-grown plants. The cream, c-shaped grubs of vine weevil (p.187) feast on roots, while aphids (p.180) suck sap from soft leaves. Gray mold (p.183) and rots are quick to set in where drainage and air circulation are poor. Powdery mildew (p.185) spoils foliage when the potting medium is kept too dry.

ROUTINE CARE

The range of ornamental plants is huge and their problems are varied. Many different plants are prone to the same problems, which can often be prevented with basic routine care.

Watering

Soil improved with organic matter holds moisture well, reducing the need for watering. However, many newly planted specimens will still need regular watering in their first season. Plants need less watering once fully established, unless they are planted in the dry soil at the base of walls and fences.

Never water in the full heat of midday and always direct the water at the soil, not on the plants. Soak the soil well so water penetrates deeply.

Mulching

Mulching in spring adds organic matter to the soil, helps retain moisture and warmth, and controls

Routine care Regular watering and feeding will encourge strong, healthy growth and a better show of color.

Keep tidy Clearing away plant and garden debris is an effective and simple way to help avoid many pests and diseases.

weed growth. A generous layer of composted bark, garden compost, or well-rotted manure are all highly beneficial to the soil.

Fertilizing

If the soil has been improved, newly planted ornamentals shouldn't need feeding. However, fertilizer will help established plants, particularly if their leaves show signs of nutrient deficiency. Spring is the best time to apply fertilizers, giving plants a boost as they begin growing.

Well-rotted manure or organic fertilizers, such as bone meal, release nutrients slowly. Liquid fertilizers and inorganic products are ideal for a quick pick-me-up. Use specially formulated fertilizers that are suitable for acid-lovers, when needed.

Garden hygiene

Weeds, fallen leaves, and other plant debris helps spread pests and diseases. Always keep the soil around your plants clear to maintain a garden that looks tidy and is healthy.

Correct pruning

Always be sure to prune trees and shrubs at the right time of year. Badly timed pruning can leave plants prone to disease, cause stems to bleed sap heavily, and prevent flowering. Also make sure that cuts are made correctly, since poorly pruned wood can die back and become infected.

Check ties

As trees, shrubs, and woody climbers grow, tight ties can cut into their expanding stems, causing significant damage that can provide an entry point for disease. Check ties on trees at least every spring, and those on other plants more often. Loosen, replace, or remove them as required.

Leave bulbs to grow

The leaves of bulbous plants help fatten the bulbs for next year's flowers, and should be left to die down naturally, without being tied up or trimmed off. Where bulbs grow in grass, leave the surrounding area unmown until the leaves have faded.

AVOIDING PROBLEMS

Prevent overcrowding Congested clumps of bulbs and herbaceous perennials often look tired and don't flower well. Lifting and dividing them, usually while they are dormant, allows you to replant vigorous, healthy plant material that will flower prolifically. See p.155.

GARDEN LAWNS

Lawns may appear the same but there are actually many different mixes of grasses available to suit a variety of growing conditions and the purpose the lawn serves. Choosing the right mix for your yard will make maintaining healthy green grass much simpler.

Lawns can be established by sowing seed, which is cost effective, or laying turf, for quick results. Spring and fall are the best seasons for both methods. Whichever way you choose, good soil preparation is essential. Clear the area of weeds, expecially perennials, and improve sandy soil with potting mix. On heavy soil improve drainage by digging in sharp sand or installing a drainage system if water pools often.

Dig or rototill the soil, remove any large stones, and rake the site level. To prevent hollows from appearing in the lawn as the soil settles, firm the soil by treading it evenly with your feet. Level any dips that form during treading, and rake the surface to a fine tilth, taking care to remove stones if sowing grass seed.

Ideally sow seed in warm, moist conditions, at the rate recommended. To make this easier, mark the ground

Main feature The lawn is usually one of the largest, most conspicuous features in a garden, and often the most heavily used. An unkempt lawn can spoil an otherwise beautiful yard, although nearly all can be revived with time and effort—and maybe sod.

into regular sections, using stakes, and measure the correct amount of seed per section into a cup. This can then be sown evenly over the soil— repeat until the whole area is sown. Rake lightly, water using a sprinkler if there is no rain, and protect the seed from birds with netting.

Sod should be laid onto moist soil very soon after purchase. Start at the edge of the lawn and lay the sod in straight lines, standing on planks on the sod already laid, rather than on

the prepared soil. Cut the edges to the desired shape once all sod is laid. Tamp down sod with the back of a rake, and water during dry weather until the grass has rooted through.

Avoid heavy use of new grass until established, which could be up to three months for sod, or one year for seed. Cut new grass lightly when it reaches about 2in (5cm) tall.

Caring for lawns

The key to easy lawn care is to mow little and often. Cutting one-third of the leaf length each week in summer is less stressful for grass than letting it grow longer and cutting less often. Trim edges regularly and recut them annually to keep grass from spreading.

Established lawns benefit from scarifying with a rake in the fall to remove dead foliage and moss. Lawns can also be aerated to help loosen compacted soil by spiking the area all over with a garden fork.

AVOIDING PROBLEMS

Feed well for strong growth Healthy, well-fed lawns look more attractive, withstand wear and tear, and are less likely to become overrun with weeds. Apply a spring/summer fertilizer in early summer, and a specially formulated lower nitrogen feed at the start of fall. Always apply lawn fertilizers at the rate recommended on the packet. Overfeeding can scorch and damage new growth.

RESCUE

Trees, shrubs, and climbers

Since they are frequently used as specimen plants, prominently positioned in the garden, it is particularly important to keep trees, shrubs, and climbers healthy and looking at their best. A basic understanding of their needs, found in the anatomy guides that follow, will make this easier. Diagnostic charts and question-and-answer pages also help pinpoint the cause of symptoms. Take heed of the pruning and training advice given, which can spell the difference between flower-covered glory and a tangled mess.

Garden tree anatomy

Avoid problems with trees by selecting specimens that suit the space, soil type, and climate in your yard. Many trees only reach a modest size and have several seasons of interest, making them ideal for smaller yards. Taking care to prepare soil well will be rewarded with many years of healthy growth.

EVERGREEN TREES

The backbone of any garden, evergreen trees remain in leaf all year and come in the form of needle-bearing conifers, or sometimes broadleaved trees. Spring is the best time to plant evergreens, which will all naturally drop some old needles or leaves while in growth during late spring and summer.

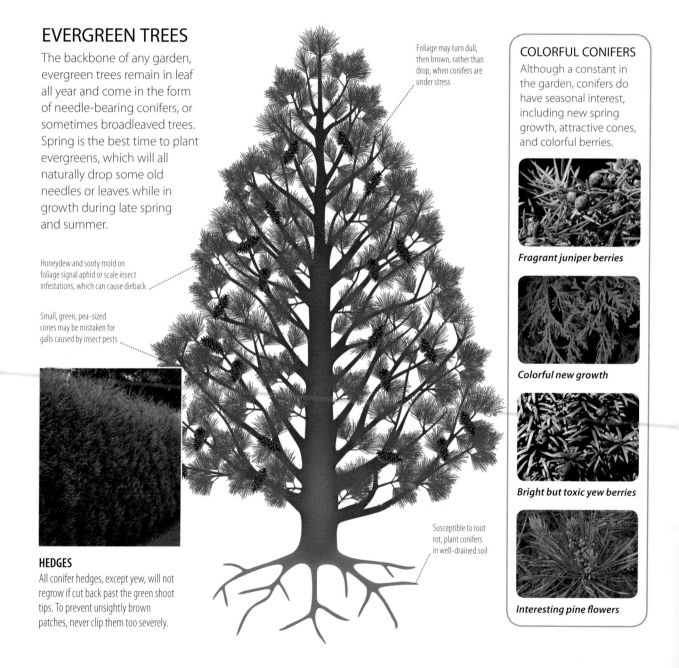

Foliage may turn dull, then brown, rather than drop, when conifers are under stress

Honeydew and sooty mold on foliage signal aphid or scale insect infestations, which can cause dieback

Small, green, pea-sized cones may be mistaken for galls caused by insect pests

Susceptible to root rot, plant conifers in well-drained soil

HEDGES
All conifer hedges, except yew, will not regrow if cut back past the green shoot tips. To prevent unsightly brown patches, never clip them too severely.

COLORFUL CONIFERS
Although a constant in the garden, conifers do have seasonal interest, including new spring growth, attractive cones, and colorful berries.

Fragrant juniper berries

Colorful new growth

Bright but toxic yew berries

Interesting pine flowers

DECIDUOUS TREES

Losing leaves in the fall has many advantages for deciduous trees. Bare branches are less prone to wind damage, and pests and diseases fall away with the foliage. Their annual leaf fall, often in a vivid range of fall tints, can also expose attractive bark and branch patterns.

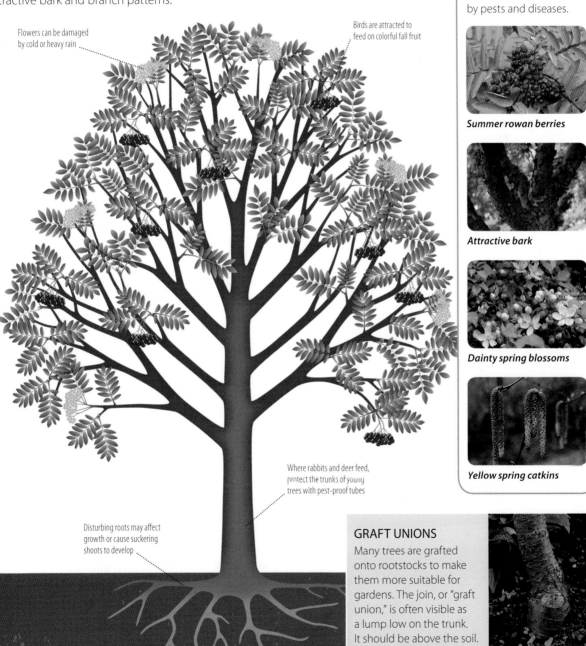

Flowers can be damaged by cold or heavy rain

Birds are attracted to feed on colorful fall fruit

Where rabbits and deer feed, protect the trunks of young trees with pest-proof tubes

Disturbing roots may affect growth or cause suckering shoots to develop

SEASONAL INTEREST

Deciduous trees can have year-long appeal, bearing flowers, fruit, berries, and bark. Most are unaffected by pests and diseases.

Summer rowan berries

Attractive bark

Dainty spring blossoms

Yellow spring catkins

GRAFT UNIONS

Many trees are grafted onto rootstocks to make them more suitable for gardens. The join, or "graft union," is often visible as a lump low on the trunk. It should be above the soil.

What's wrong with my garden tree?

Trees benefit from year-round scrutiny to keep them in good health. In winter check bark for injury, and bare branches for signs of disease and dead wood. When in leaf, look closely for symptoms visible on the leaves and step back to assess the overall condition of the tree.

WHY IS MY CONIFER TURNING YELLOW AND BROWN, AND DYING BACK?

Is the tree changing color all over?

Patchy discoloration can be caused by a number of pests and diseases. **See Garden tree clinic pp.124–127**

Conifers are sensitive to drought, **see p.126**, and also waterlogging, which causes the roots to die, **see p.125**.

WHY ARE THE LEAVES TURNING YELLOW THEN BROWN IN SUMMER?

A MATURE TREE HAS WILTED AND APPEARS TO BE DYING.

Did the symptoms develop quickly?

This is possibly just old age— trees do naturally die. Also see honey fungus p.126.

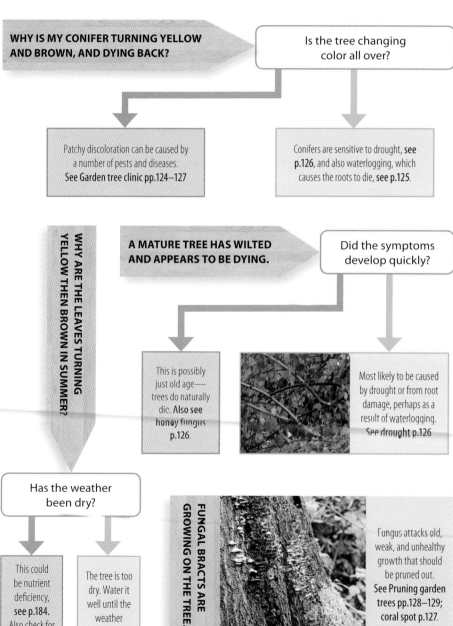

Most likely to be caused by drought or from root damage, perhaps as a result of waterlogging. See drought p.126

Has the weather been dry?

This could be nutrient deficiency, see p.184. Also check for insect pests.

The tree is too dry. Water it well until the weather changes.

FUNGAL BRACTS ARE GROWING ON THE TREE.

Fungus attacks old, weak, and unhealthy growth that should be pruned out. **See Pruning garden trees pp.128–129; coral spot p.127.**

MY TREE DOESN'T FLOWER OR FRUIT WELL, AND LOOKS SICKLY. WHY?

Have you planted it recently?

If it hasn't established well, check to ensure that you planted it correctly. **See How to plant p.113.**

Have you kept it well watered and fertilized?

Watering and fertilizing are essential to help new trees establish and grow.

Is it growing in the right spot?

Check the plant's preferred growing conditions. **See Right plant right place p.110.**

Do you prune it regularly?

Pruning encourages flowers, fruit, and healthy growth. **See Pruning garden trees pp.128–129.**

Check for pests and diseases. **See Garden tree clinic pp.124–127.**

A LARGE BRANCH HAS STARTED TO DIE BACK. WHAT HAS CAUSED THIS?

Are there signs of physical damage to the stem or bark?

Damaged branches often die but other stems are unaffected. It may caused by wind, or damage by squirrels or deer.

Are there large cracks or open sores in the bark?

THE YOUNG LEAVES AND STEMS ARE INFESTED WITH INSECTS.

Many insect pests infest trees, but only young or weak trees need treatment. **See aphids p.180; scale insects p.186.**

This could be caused by the disease bacterial canker. **See p.180.**

Some serious fungal diseases cause branches to die. **See honey fungus p.126; phytophthora root rot p.185; verticillium wilt p.186; fireblight p.182.**

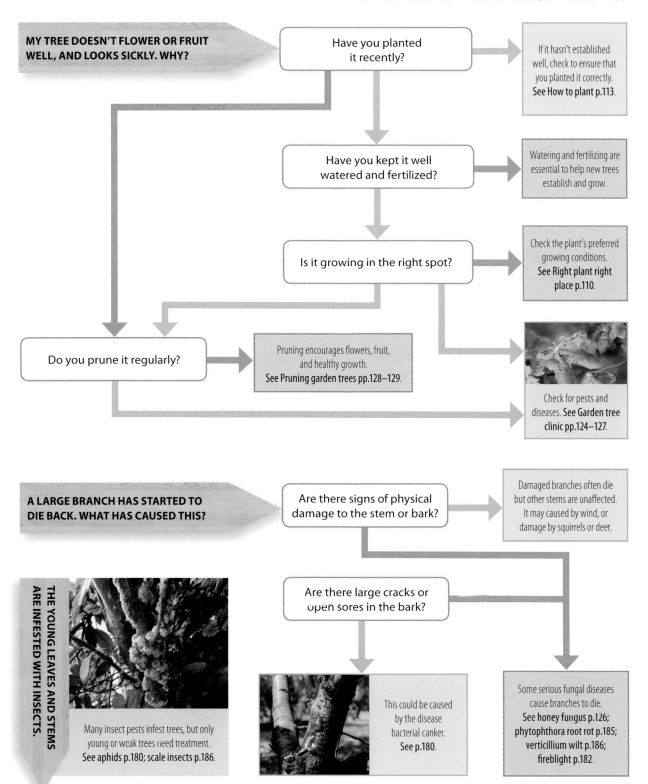

Garden tree clinic

Often large enough to allow minor problems to go unnoticed, it pays to keep an eye on trees—both up close and from a distance—to prevent something serious from developing. Check leaves and bark for signs of insect and disease damage, and step back to look for signs of environmental stress, such as wind damage.

Why are young leaves pale and crisp?

Where leaves appear bleached and become papery, sometimes turning brown, scorch may be the problem. Caused by intense or hot sunlight, it can affect soft, young leaves near the tips, and is likely to be worse where raindrops on the foliage magnify the sun's rays.

Q Why are the flowers dying off and turning brown on the tree?

A Blossom wilt is a fungal disease that causes spring flowers of ornamental crabapples and cherry trees to turn brown, die, and remain in place. It is worse in damp weather and may affect nearby leaves. **See p.181.**

Q What is eating lots of holes in the leaves?

A Yellow-green colored winter moth caterpillars feed on the leaves of many deciduous trees as they unfurl in spring. They also make nests by pulling leaves together with silk. Damage can be severe. **See p.187.**

SIGNS OF DECAY **SYMPTOMS ON LEAVES** **WINTER MOTH DAMAGE**

Q What is growing out from the trunk?

A Semi-circular growths of bracket fungus appear on the roots, trunk, or branches of trees, usually after humid summer and fall weather. The fungus gradually weakens the tree by feeding on its tissues, increasing the chance of limbs falling. **See Pruning garden trees, pp.128–129.**

Q Is this bacterial canker on a cherry blossom?

A In damp springs and falls, bacterial canker produces areas of sunken bark on ornamental cherry trees. These patches may exude a syrupy, amber substance. Growth is affected, with small, yellow leaves, or stem tips dying back. In spring, the leaves may develop brown spots and tiny holes. **See p.180.**

How can I tell if my trees are affected by a soil nutrient deficiency?

 Magnesium deficiency causes yellowing around leaf edges and between veins, particularly in older leaves, often because heavy rain has washed magnesium from the soil. Acid-loving trees are prone to iron deficiency and lime-induced chlorosis on alkaline soil, which also causes yellowing and brown patches between leaf veins. Trees can show symptoms for several years before gradually declining and dying back. **See Nutrient deficiencies, p.184**.

Magnesium deficiency

Lime-induced chlorosis

Q **What are these red pimples on my maple leaves?**

A Acer gall mites feed on the leaves of sycamores and maples, triggering the formation of distinctive, upright, red growths on the leaves. Although dramatic looking, it is harmless to the tree.

HEALTHY FOLIAGE

POOR PRUNING

GROWTHS ON FIELD MAPLE

Q **What are the symptoms of waterlogged soil?**

A The signs of waterlogging closely resemble those of drought, as leaves often yellow and fall early. This is because poor drainage can cause the roots to rot, meaning that they can't supply the rest of the plant with water. Dark roots that break easily are a sure sign that rot has set in. Try to improve soil drainage.

Q **Why is it important to prune correctly?**

A Pruning trees in the right way helps them to heal quickly and prevents disease from entering through the wounds. Good cuts leave the branch collar, which promotes quick healing. Cutting flush with the trunk removes the collar and leaves a large wound—long stumps encourage disease. **See Pruning garden trees, pp.128–129**.

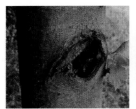

Cutting flush to the trunk

Decaying pruning stump

A healthy branch collar

Q **Why is my conifer tree dying back?**

A Several pests and diseases affect conifers, which can be slow to show symptoms. Pestalotiopsis is a fungal disease that causes individual shoots to appear scorched and brown. Where spruce needles turn yellow or brown and drop in late winter and spring, green spruce aphid may be feeding on the sap. Adelgids are sap-sucking insects covered in a white, waxy coating that cause growth to turn yellow. See Pestalotiopsis p.185; Aphids (green spruce) p.180; Adelgids p.180.

Pestalotiopsis

Green spruce aphid

Adelgids

Q **What is tunneling through the leaves?**

A Numerous trees, including beech, holly, and laburnum, can be attacked by leaf miners, usually during spring and summer. The larvae of various insects eat through the internal tissues of leaves, creating cream, yellow, or brown trails, where they can sometimes be seen. Severe infestations can be unsightly, especially on evergreen trees, but mined leaves rarely affect overall tree health.

HEALTHY CONIFER GROWTH

HONEY FUNGUS ON ROOTS

HOLLY LEAF MINER DAMAGE

Q **What are the tree symptoms of drought?**

A Drought can cause leaves to turn yellow and fall early, poor growth, the dropping of flowers, and poor fruit formation. Whole branches may die back, and in severe droughts, established mature trees may die completely. Recently planted trees are most at risk. See Watering p.116.

Q **Does my tree have honey fungus?**

A Infected trees may die gradually or in a single season. Groups of tan-colored toadstools grow around the trunk or roots in late summer or fall, and creamy fungal growth develops beneath the bark at the base of the trunk. Black, shoelacelike fungal strands spread out into the surrounding soil. See p.183.

Diagnostic chart

Symptoms	Diagnosis
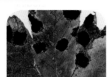 **Unmistakable large,** slightly raised, shiny, black spots appear on the leaves of sycamores and other maples in spring and summer. The leaves may fall from the tree early.	**Acer tar spot** is a common fungal disease that infects the foliage. Although it looks dramatic, the disease causes little damage to the tree and doesn't require treatment. Rake up any fallen leaves.
 **A white, powdery coating** covers first the upper and sometimes later the lower surface of leaves, usually during summer. This can cause leaves to yellow and become distorted.	**Powdery mildew** is a fungal disease that often commonly infects plants under stress due to dry conditions, or where the air surrounding the leaves is stagnant and humid. **See p.185.**

Q **Are the orange bumps on branches due to coral spot?**

A Bright orange lumps on bark are a sure sign that the branch is dead and infected by coral spot. This infection can spread into healthy tissue and may cause significant dieback. **See p.182.**

WIND-DAMAGED BRANCH **WEAKENED TREE TRUNK**

What are the vigorous shoots growing up from the base of the tree?

These shoots are "suckers" and can occur naturally or if shallow roots are damaged. They should be removed as close to the source as possible by tearing rather than cutting them.

Q **Why is wood torn or broken?**

A Trees can suffer physical damage in many ways. Passing vehicles, wind, heavy snow, and vandals can all break tree limbs, leaving an open wound that increases the risk of infection. Cut broken branches back with sharp tools to help prevent disease. **See Pruning garden trees, pp.128–129.**

Q **Why is bark damaged around the stake?**

A Trees will grow around tight ties and stakes left in place, which also allows disease in and may weaken the main trunk. It is vital to inspect tree ties and stakes regularly to check that they are not rubbing against the tree when it moves, wearing away the bark and leaving it vulnerable to disease.

Pruning garden trees

Trees with enough room to grow need little pruning once they are mature. Keep them looking good by removing any dead or diseased wood, and retaining the tree's natural form. Problems arise when trees outgrow their space. Lifting the canopy by removing lower branches helps allow in more light, and pollarding may provide a solution for certain trees.

How do I prune correctly?

Accurate pruning cuts made with clean, sharp tools allow trees to heal quickly and minimize the risk of disease. Cut stems back just above a healthy bud. Branches should be removed just beyond their "branch collar"—the area where they join the trunk. See **Why is it important to prune correctly?** *p.125.*

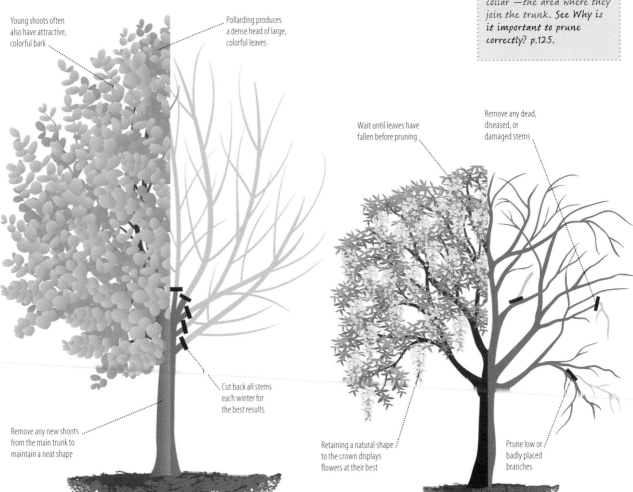

Young shoots often also have attractive, colorful bark

Pollarding produces a dense head of large, colorful leaves

Cut back all stems each winter for the best results

Remove any new shoots from the main trunk to maintain a neat shape

Wait until leaves have fallen before pruning

Remove any dead, diseased, or damaged stems

Retaining a natural shape to the crown displays flowers at their best

Prune low or badly placed branches

TREES FOR LEAVES

Pollarding—cutting branches back to the trunk—is used to promote attractive new leaves on trees, such as willow and eucalyptus. The branches are cut back in this way every year or two during winter, and then resprout.

TREES FOR FLOWERS

Keep pruning to a minimum where trees are grown for flowers to retain a natural shape, and to avoid removing shoots that will produce blossoms. Excessive pruning also promotes leafy growth at the expense of the flowers.

CONIFERS

Conifers generally have beautiful natural outlines and are usually best left unpruned unless they are damaged or attacked by disease. It is particularly important not to remove the top leading shoot if you want to retain the natural shape, and to cut out any other vertical shoots that compete with it as soon as they appear.

New growth can be bright, golden-yellow

Clipping limits growth and enhances form

Carefully cut out any dead foliage

A tall, columnar shape is a feature of cypresses

Remove any untidy, horizontal stems

Cypress

Take care not to damage the leading shoot

Trimming encourages dense growth

Prune out any shoots spoiling the natural outline

Pine

Retaining a natural shape looks good year-round

Remove any crossing stems

Prune weak or diseased growth in winter

Ornamental bark makes a lovely winter feature

Removing the lower branches helps expose more of the bark

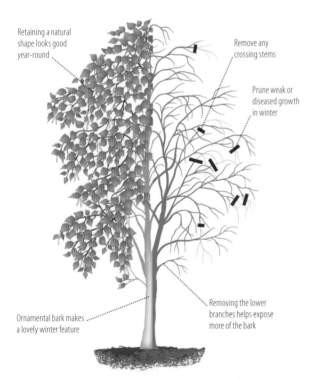

Spring flowers can be reduced by excessive pruning

Keep an open center to the canopy to let in light and air

A well-balanced spread of branches gives trees an attractive outline

Remove any diseased or damaged wood

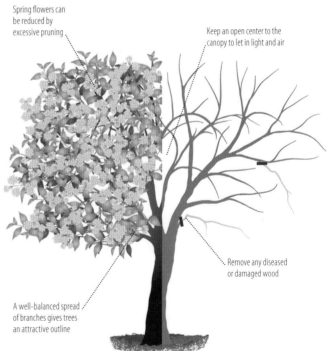

TREES FOR BARK

These trees need to look attractive with bare branches, so good pruning is essential. Maintain the tree's natural form, thin lower branches and any overcrowded growth to help showcase the bark in winter light.

TREES FOR FLOWERS AND FRUIT

Careful pruning is needed to retain these trees' year-round appeal. Only prune to remove dead or damaged wood, or where growth blocks access or views. Prune during winter; flowering cherries are pruned in summer.

Garden shrub anatomy

Although incredibly varied, shrubs commonly have a framework of woody stems, rather than a single trunk. Often—although not always—long-lived, they need the right growing conditions, plenty of space, regular care, and attention to flourish. Stress caused by lack of water, nutrients, or poor pruning can leave them prone to problems.

EVERGREENS

The structure of many gardens, evergreen shrubs retain their leaves or needles year round, although older leaves dropping in summer is no cause for concern. Even hardy evergreens are prone to damage by frost and cold winds, and prefer a sheltered site.

PRUNING
Evergreens usually only require light pruning to remove spent flowers, and dead or diseased wood. This is usually done in spring or after flowering.

TYPES OF EVERGREENS
Whether they are grown for their attractive flowers, compact shapes, or glossy foliage, evergreens have many uses in the garden, and are ideal for screens.

Scented flowers

Compact shape

Attractive year-round leaves

Permanent groundcover

Water spring-flowering shrubs in summer when new buds are forming

Shoot tips can be damaged by frost, wind, intense sunlight, and pests

Drought and waterlogging are common problems for shrubs

Insect pests easily hide in evergreens. Check leaves for damage or symptoms

DECIDUOUS SHRUBS

Losing their leaves in fall has advantages for deciduous shrubs and their owners. A fiery fall display often precedes leaf drop, and many shrubs have attractive bark in winter. They also drop any pests and diseases harbored in the foliage each fall.

UNUSUAL APPEARANCES

Certain shrubs grown for their novel appearance can be surprising when first seen, such as the twisted hazel, (*Corylus avellana* 'Contorta'), with its contorted stems. Vividly variegated shrubs can also seem alarming, and although unusual, this growth is normal and perfectly healthy.

Sudden changes in leaf color and shape often indicate a problem

Flowers can be lost if shrubs are incorrectly pruned

Some shrubs can be pruned to produce colorful, young stems

Winter is the easiest time to check bark for damage, pests, and diseases

Some shrubs produce new shoots from the base, and may spread

Regular watering and annual mulching helps keep shrubs healthy

PRUNING

As a rule, deciduous shrubs are pruned after flowering, or in early spring if new growth bears flowers or colorful bark.

DECIDUOUS SHRUBS

In good health, deciduous shrubs deliver everything from bold winter color and spring foliage to scented summer flowers.

Colorful winter stems

Scented winter flowers

Bold foliage and flowers

Attractive summer flowers

What's wrong with my garden shrub?

Although the foliage and flowers on shrubs can be spoiled by pests, diseases, and unfavorable weather, the problems are rarely serious. Leaves often show the first signs of trouble, but don't overlook yellowing foliage caused by nutrient deficiency when checking for bugs and mold.

WHY HAS A LARGE BRANCH STARTED TO DIE BACK?

Are there signs of physical damage to the stem or bark?

Damaged branches often die but other stems are unaffected. Branches can be damaged by wind, squirrels, or rabbits.

Various serious fungal diseases cause branches to die back. **See honey fungus p.183; phytophthora root rot p.185; verticillium wilt p.186.**

WHAT IS EATING MY SHRUB?

Is it mainly the leaves and soft growth?

Are the stems and bark chewed?

Many pests feed on shrub leaves. **See capsid bug p.181; caterpillars p.181; viburnum beetle p.137; vine weevils p.137; winter moth p.187.**

Most likely caused by larger pests. **See deer, squirrels, and rabbits p.182.**

THE LEAVES ARE CHANGING COLOR—THEY LOOK SICK.

Do they have a mottled or streaked appearance?

It could be a nutrient deficiency. **See p.184.**

Most probably caused by spider mites, **see p.186,** or a virus, see **p.187.**

THE NEW SHOOTS AND FLOWERS HAVE DIED BACK.

Probably just cold damage. The damage won't spread.

Has the weather been cold at night?

This could be dieback **p.182;** fireblight **p.182;** scorch **p.135.**

MY SHRUB DOESN'T FLOWER OR FRUIT. IT LOOKS SICK.

Have you planted it recently?

If it hasn't established well, check that you planted it correctly. **See How to plant p.113.**

Have you kept it well watered and fertilized?

Watering and fertilizing are essential to help new shrubs establish well.

Are you sure it's growing in the right spot?

Check the plant's preferred growing conditions. **See Right plant right place p.110.**

Do you prune it regularly?

Pruning encourages flowers, fruit, and healthy growth. **See Pruning garden shrubs pp.138–139.**

Check the shrub for signs of pests and diseases. **See Garden shrub clinic pp.134–137.**

WHY ARE THE LEAVES DISTORTED AND UNSIGHTLY?

Can you see any insects on the affected growth?

This could be caused by gall insects, which are harmless or virus. **See p.187.**

THE LEAVES ARE COVERED WITH SOMETHING POWDERY.

A white coating will be powdery mildew, **see p.185.** If it's black or brown, it's sooty mold, **see p.136.**

THE BRANCHES HAVE ORANGE BUMPS ON THEM.

This is coral spot, a fungus that attacks old, weak, or unhealthy growth. **See Pruning garden shrubs pp.138–139.**

Many insects affect leaves. **See aphids p.137; scale insects p.137; bay sucker p.137; leaf miners p.137; thrips p.186.**

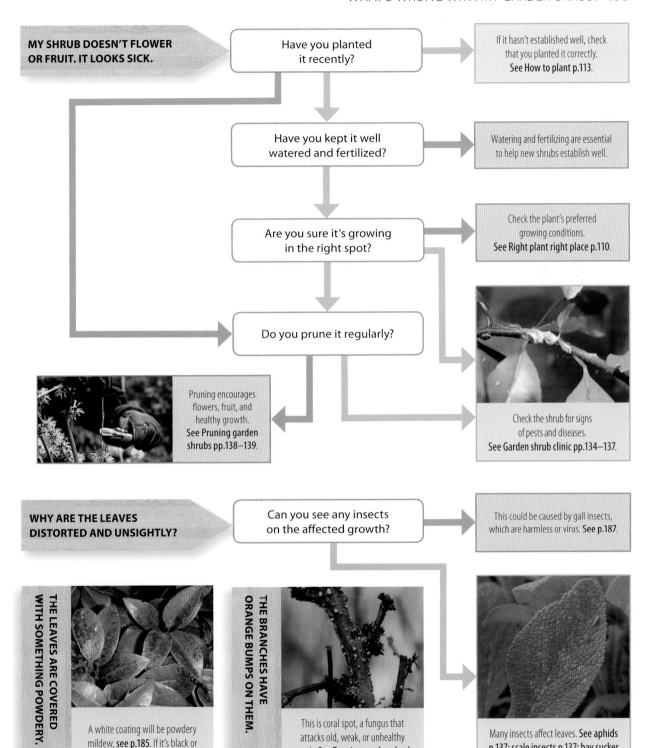

Garden shrub clinic

Most garden shrubs are robust plants that, given good growing conditions, can easily tolerate a little damage from common pests and diseases. To prevent these issues from becoming serious and spoiling the plant's appearance, it's always wise to site shrubs correctly, and be vigilant in order to catch problems early.

Why don't my shrubs produce any berries?

Only female flowers set berries, and only when pollinated. Many shrubs that fruit have both male and female flowers, but others produce them on separate plants that need to be planted closely for pollination to occur. Badly timed pruning can also prevent a crop of berries.

Q What causes the brown patches on camellia leaves?

A Camellia leaf blight is a fungal disease that infects these shrubs in wet or humid conditions. Leaves develop brown speckled patches and drop off. Infection may spread, causing stems to die. **See p.181.**

Q Why are the flowers turning brown and unsightly?

A Heavy rain can damage delicate petals, causing them to look bruised, turn brown, and sometimes to fall. Petals that remain often fade and turn moldy, particularly in double blooms—remove damaged flowers.

▲ **SPRING LEAVES**   ▲ **REVERTED GREEN GROWTH**   **RAIN-DAMAGED FLOWERS**

Q Has my shrub been damaged by cold?

A Cold can damage a wide range of shrubs but most commonly kills the soft young leaves of slightly tender plants in spring. Leaves and stems, as well as buds and flowers, turn brown or black, and die back, while the rest of the plant appears healthy. Cut back the damaged growth when conditions improve.

Q Why is my variegated shrub turning green?

A Variegated shrubs are usually first propagated from a parent plant with plain green leaves that produced a variegated sport. Sometimes their growth will revert to the plain green of the parent, and, since these shoots are usually more vigorous, they should be cut out as soon as they are seen.

What's eating my lavender plant?

 Metallic green-and-purple striped insects are rosemary beetles, which feed on rosemary and lavender, as do their gray larvae, from summer to spring. Damage is minor.

 What's wrong with my shrubs growing in containers?

 Shrubs in pots rely on regular watering and fertilizing to stay healthy. Dull, wilting leaves are the first sign of underwatering, but they will soon yellow and begin to drop if plants remain dry. Underwatering during summer can also result in spring-flowering shrubs, such as rhododendrons, producing few flowers the following season. Plants in old soil mix that are not fertilized are a sickly yellow, look sparse, and do not grow. **See Growing in containers p.114**.

Poorly watered shrub   *Malnourished shrub*

PROBLEM-FREE PLANT   **HEALTHY LEAVES**

Why are the leaves on my rose plant curled up into tubes?

Rose leaf rolling sawflies roll up leaves in spring and summer to shelter their eggs. Their caterpillars eat the tubes but cause little harm. Rolled leaves should be picked off.

  What causes brown spots on leaves?

 Circular brown spots that sometimes enlarge and join together, and develop tiny black spots on their surface, are fungal leaf spots. These are caused by a range of fungi and are usually more prevalent in damp conditions, particularly when plants are stressed or weakened by other factors. **See p.183**.

How do I recognize scorch on my shrub?

Bright sunlight can scorch shrubs, with delicate young leaves and petals being particularly prone in sunny conditions. Affected areas often become pale and papery, sometimes turning brown. Water droplets can increase the problem by intensifying sunlight. Pick off the leaves that look worst.

What's wrong with my roses?

 Many pests and diseases are associated with roses. Rose black spot is a fungus that produces rough-edged, black spots on leaves during spring and summer, causing them to yellow and fall early. Badly infected plants can lose all their leaves but usually recover later. Rose rust is also a fungal disease, resulting in bright orange spots on the leaves from late spring into summer, which may also drop if badly affected. **See Rose black spot p.185; Rusts (rose) p.185.**

Black spot   *Rust*

Why are my mahonia leaves changing color?

 Foliage of mahonias that turns shades of bright yellow, orange, and red, with bright orange specks on the upper leaf surface, has been infected with mahonia rust, and often falls early. This fungal disease overwinters on fallen leaves and proliferates in humid conditions, but rarely causes lasting damage. Many other shrubs also suffer with their own forms of rust but the damage is usually superficial, not serious. **See Rusts, p.185.**

DISEASE-FREE ROSES

HEALTHY CAMELLIA LEAVES

DISEASED MAHONIA LEAVES

Why did shrubs die during winter?

 Shrubs vary enormously in their tolerance to cold, making it vital to choose appropriate plants for your local climate, taking into account exposure to wind and rain too. A particularly hard frost or cold spell can kill established shrubs, and poor drainage will also finish off sun-lovers, such as lavender and cistus.

How do I recognize sooty mold?

 Sooty mold forms dark powdery fungal growth on leaves already coated with honeydew, the sticky excretion from sap-sucking insects. It suggests the presence of aphids or scale insects, which need to be treated. Wipe the leaves clean. **See Sooty mold p.186; Aphids p.180; Scale insects p.186.**

Q Why have the branches broken, and does it matter?

A Shrub stems can be damaged by wind, snowfall, or accidental slips during pruning. Foliage will quickly die on broken branches, which should be pruned back cleanly to prevent diseases.

 AN AFFECTED BOXWOOD STEM

Q Why is the growth on my boxwood shrub stunted?

A Where new shoots on boxwood bushes show slow growth in spring, and new leaves are close together with a puckered look, boxwood sucker is likely to be the culprit. The tiny, pale green nymphs of this insect suck the sap from new growth, leaving white, waxy excrement in the curled leaves. Mature shrubs are rarely harmed, but new plants should be treated. **See p.181.**

Diagnostic chart

Symptoms	Diagnosis
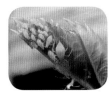 **Leaves, particularly on new growth**, become deformed and often sticky with honeydew during spring and summer. Clusters of insects can be seen on leaves and stems.	**Aphids** are small sap-sucking insects that may be green, yellow, black, pink, or brown and will feed on almost any shrub. They multiply rapidly and can badly damage young leaves. **See p.180.**
 **In late spring and early summer** the foliage of viburnums is rapidly eaten, sometimes right down to the veins, by yellow larvae with black spots. Plants can be heavily defoliated.	**Viburnum beetles** overwinter on the bark as eggs and hatch in spring into grubs that eat the leaves. The dull brown adult beetles also eat the foliage but are less damaging. **See p.187.**
 **Notches are eaten into the leaf edges** of many shrubs from spring to fall—rhododendrons and hydrangeas are often badly affected. Plants may also grow slowly.	**Adult vine weevils** are small, matte-black insects, that feed on leaves at night. Their brown-headed, cream, c-shaped grubs eat bark from the roots of shrubs, resulting in poor growth. **See p.187.**
 **Small, brown or pale gray, waxy bumps** can be found underneath leaves and on the stems of shrubs. There may also be sticky honeydew and sooty mold on upper leaf surfaces.	**Scale insects** feed on the sap of shrubs from the safety of their domed shells, and there are many species. They can be found on plants year-round and lay eggs during summer. **See p.186.**
 **The edges of bay leaves thicken**, turn yellow, and curl inward during summer, then later turn brown and dry. Often only one side of the leaf shows any symptoms.	**Bay sucker insects** feed inside the protection of the deformed leaves, then emerge as adults covered in a white, fluffy wax. Damage to the plant is not usually serious enough to treat.
 **The leaves of many shrubs** may be riddled with winding trails made up of damaged tissue that is usually pale cream or brown. Plant growth is not usually affected.	**Leaf miners** feed within the leaf tissues during spring and summer as larvae, creating tunnels where they are sometimes visible if held up to the light. Damage is minor —treatment is not required.

Pruning garden shrubs

Shrub pruning can be confusing because its purpose
is often to encourage flowers, which no gardener wants to
inadvertently cut off. It is easy, however, to work out when
and how to prune each shrub correctly, making the garden more colorful.

*What is the best way to
prune evergreen shrubs?*

*Most evergreens require
little pruning, except to
remove shoots that have
died due to disease or cold
damage. As a rule, the best
time to prune to shape or
limit their size is right
after flowering, when shoots
should be cut back to a
healthy bud. Also remove
weak and wayward stems.*

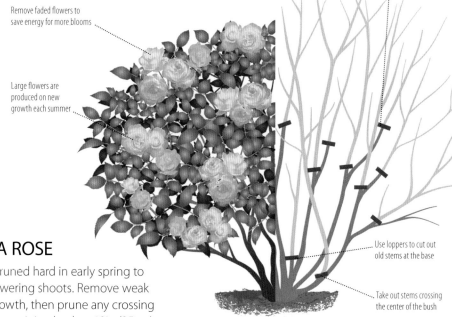

Remove faded flowers to
save energy for more blooms

Large flowers are
produced on new
growth each summer

Prune the stems to
outward-facing
buds

Use loppers to cut out
old stems at the base

Take out stems crossing
the center of the bush

HYBRID TEA ROSE

These roses are pruned hard in early spring to
stimulate new flowering shoots. Remove weak
and unhealthy growth, then prune any crossing
stems. Cut those remaining back to 10in (25cm).

Small flowers cover the
whole plant in summer

Cut out any weak, twiggy
growth in early spring

Clipping over with shears
helps retain a compact shape

PATIO ROSES

If their flowering and shape
are good, these roses need
minimal pruning to remove
dead or crowded stems, and to
retain a compact form. If untidy,
prune in spring, cutting any
vigorous shoots back by half.

SUMMER PRUNING

Many shrubs that flower in spring or early summer, such as forsythia and *Deutzia*, should be pruned in summer after flowering. Cut back the shoots that flowered, take out weak and dead growth, and remove up to a fifth of the oldest stems each year to encourage strong, new growth.

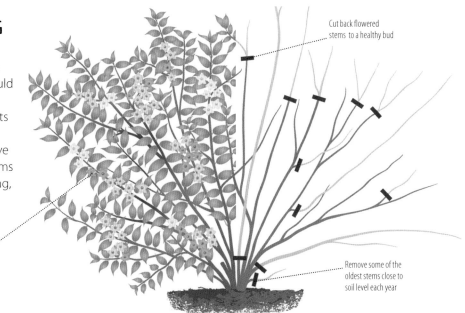

Cut back flowered stems to a healthy bud

Flowers are produced on last year's wood; encourage new growth

Remove some of the oldest stems close to soil level each year

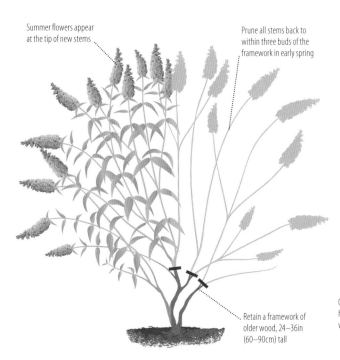

Summer flowers appear at the tip of new stems

Prune all stems back to within three buds of the framework in early spring

Retain a framework of older wood, 24–36in (60–90cm) tall

SPRING PRUNING

Summer-flowering shrubs that bloom on the new year's growth are best pruned in spring. The butterfly bush, (*Buddleja*), is a good example, and can be pruned hard. In early spring, cut all shoots back close to the old wood.

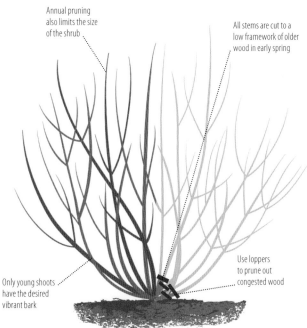

Annual pruning also limits the size of the shrub

All stems are cut to a low framework of older wood in early spring

Only young shoots have the desired vibrant bark

Use loppers to prune out congested wood

SHRUBS FOR STEMS

Some shrubs are grown for their colorful winter stems. Only the bark on young dogwood (*Cornus*) and willow (*Salix*) has these dramatic tones. For a vibrant display, cut back to a low framework annually in early spring.

Climbing plant anatomy

This diverse group of plants ranges from tender climbers, grown as annuals from seed each year, to large, woody perennials that can cover entire buildings. Grown for their attractive foliage, flowers, or berries, many climbers only run into difficulties when growing conditions are poor, or supports and pruning are inappropriate.

SELF-CLINGING CLIMBERS

Tiny roots, sent out from the fast-growing stems of these plants, grip firmly onto their supporting surface, allowing them to climb unaided. Their vigor means it is more often the plants themselves that need to be kept in check, rather than pests and diseases.

Flowers attract many beneficial pollinating insects to the garden

Dense glossy leaves shelter insect pests and fungal diseases, but plants usually shake them off

Cut back soft shoot tips where climbers are growing out of bounds

CLINGING CLIMBERS
These plants can flourish on shady walls, providing year-round interest, such as evergreen foliage, and fall color.

Attractive summer flowers

Evergreen foliage

Dazzling fall tints

WALL DAMAGE
Sound walls can cope with clinging roots, but climbers work into gaps in damaged masonry, enlarging them. Keep eaves and gutters free of climbers.

Sturdy, woody stems need no extra supports, but are hard to remove when unwanted

Add plenty of compost to soil to help keep roots moist

TENDRIL CLIMBERS

Many climbing plants produce twisting tendrils at the shoot tips, which seek out supports to grasp and help the plant grow vertically. Tying them into a suitable supporting framework as they establish gives them a strong start. Their long, soft stems are easily damaged by bad weather and pests.

THE ONLY WAY IS UP

Tendrils are not the only method used to pull plants skyward. Twining leaf stalks are used in a similar way by clematis to grip, while morning glory (*Ipomeae*) twists its main stems around supports as they grow.

Solid supports help plants climb and protect fragile stems from weather damage

Leafless tendrils reach out and coil around whatever they find

TENDRIL TYPES

Many tendril climbers perform best in a sunny spot. A number are not hardy, but thrive grown under cover or as annuals.

Hardy exotic climber

Hardy annuals

Tender annuals

Tender perennial climber

SUITABLE SUPPORTS

Short tendrils need a lot of opportunities to coil around thin supports, like wire, netting, or twiggy branches. Trellis is ideal for tying in many other climbers.

Remember when planting on fences and pillars that flowers always face the light

Improve soil and water regularly for healthy plants and a good display

What's wrong with my climber?

Vigorous and vibrant when healthy, climbing plants can suffer problems when planted in poor conditions or not given appropriate supports. Check in spring and summer that new growth is healthy, pruned, and tied in as required, and that pests are not hiding in the lush foliage.

WHY ARE THE LEAVES ON MY CLIMBER BECOMING DISCOLORED?

Are they covered with brown spots or a white powder?

Spider mites cause mottled, pale leaves. **See p.186.**

Brown spots mean it's fungal leaf spot, **p.183.** White powder is powdery mildew, **p.145.**

WHY HAS MY CLEMATIS SUDDENLY WILTED?

Are there any broken stems or ones that appear chewed?

Could be clematis wilt. **See p.145.** Also check for aphids **p.144** and scale insects **p.186.**

Stems can be broken by strong wind, but snails are often the cause of chewed stems. **See p.144.**

WHY DO THE LEAVES ON MY CLIMBER LOOK BATTERED AND UNSIGHTLY?

Is it in a bright, open site?

Sounds like scorch caused by strong, dry winds. Strong sun can also scorch the leaves. **See p.145.**

Does the soil dry out?

Improve the soil with lots of well-rotted organic matter to retain moisture.

Check for other symptoms. **See Climbing plant clinic pp.144–145.**

WHY DOES IT LOOK SICKLY AND NOT GROW WELL?

THE FLOWERS ARE AT THE TOP OF THE PLANT WHERE I CAN'T SEE THEM.

THE NEW STEMS ARE GROWING AWAY FROM THEIR SUPPORT.

IT'S SWALLOWING MY GARDEN WHOLE.

Your plant needs pruning and training.
See Pruning climbing plants pp.146–147.

Have you planted it recently?

Are you sure it's growing in the right spot?

Check the plant's growing requirements.
See Right plant right place p.110.

Have you kept it well watered?

Regular watering and feeding are essential for new climbers to establish well.

Check for other symptoms. **See Climbing plant clinic pp.144–145.**

Is it planted against a wall or fence?

The soil at the base of walls and fences can be very dry, due to rain shadow. Water your plant well.

ESTABLISHED ROSES, CLEMATIS, AND WISTERIA FLOWER POORLY.

Do you prune them each year?

Do you fertilize the plant each spring?

Pruning encourages flowers and strong growth.
See Pruning climbing plants pp.146–147.

Be sure you are pruning at the right time of year—it makes a difference.
See Pruning climbing plants pp.146–147.

Try feeding the plant regularly.
See Routine care p.116.

Check for signs of pests and diseases.
See Climbing plant clinic pp.144–145.

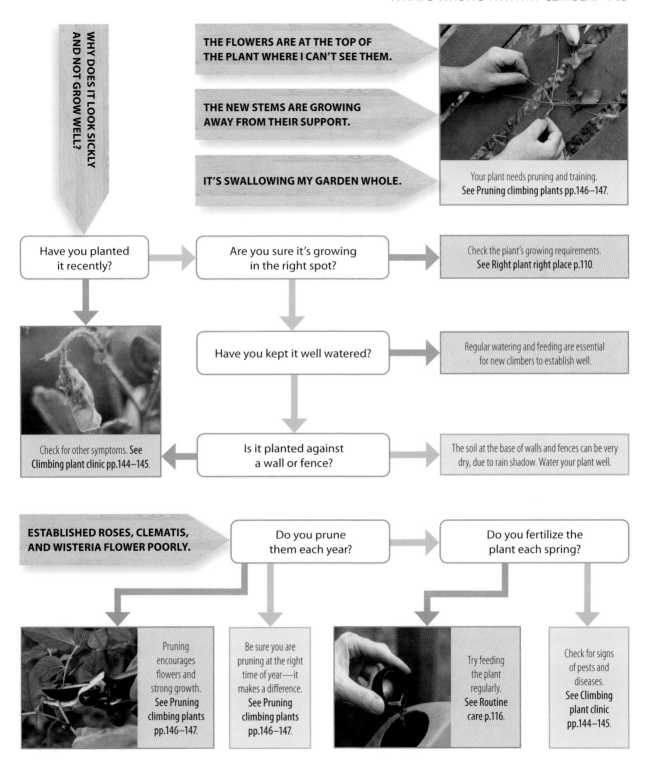

Climbing plant clinic

Often grown in poor soil at the base of walls, where the sheltered conditions favor pests and diseases, it is no surprise that a few common complaints affect many climbers. Given good care however, along with the right supports and regular pruning, these plants overcome problems to create a glorious display.

Should I be concerned about scale insects?

Scale insects thrive on climbing plants grown on sheltered walls, and are easy to spot on stems and undersides of leaves. They suck sap, affecting growth, and encourage sooty mold, which stops light and air from reaching leaves. See Scale insects p.186; Sooty mold p.186.

Q Why doesn't my climbing plant climb properly?

A All climbing plants, even self-clinging types like ivy, need tying to their supports to get them growing in the right direction. Select supports that suit the way your plant grows to help it take off quickly.

Q How do I recognize aphids on my climbing plant?

A Young growth is a magnet for aphids, which are usually green, often with a yellow or brown tinge. They quickly multiply, causing young leaves to curl and can reduce overall growth and display. **See p.180**.

SNAIL-DAMAGED CLIMBER **FLOWERING WISTERIA** **GREEN APHIDS ON SWEET PEAS**

Q What is eating my climbing plants?

A Snails often hide on walls, trellises, and fences during the day, only to come out at night to chew irregular holes in the leaves and flowers. Their rasping teeth are also capable of eating through stems, which can lead to large portions of the plant dying back if damage is near the base. **See p.186**.

Q Why doesn't my wisteria flower?

A Wisterias can be shy to flower, so help encourage plenty of cascading spring blooms by cutting back the long, vigorous, leafy shoots in late summer. This helps focus the plant's energy on flower-bud production. Training the main stems horizontally, rather than vertically, also promotes flowering.

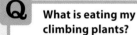

Diagnostic chart

Symptoms	Diagnosis
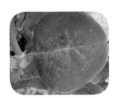 **Circular brown or gray-brown** patches appear on the leaves of ivy plants, sometimes marked with rings of tiny, raised black spots. Infected leaves may have numerous spots.	**Ivy leaf spot** is a common fungal disease, which may be found throughout the year. Although infected leaves look unsightly, the plant's overall health is not affected and no treatment is required.
 **Upper leaf surfaces develop a powdery**, white covering, which can spread to flowers and stems, and cause leaves to fall early. It occurs from midsummer into early fall.	**Powdery mildew** is a fungal disease found frequently in climbers grown against walls, where the soil easily dries out and the dense foliage is surrounded by humid air. **See p.185.**

 Will my plant recover from clematis wilt?

A This is a fungal disease that causes clematis to wilt suddenly. Although it looks dramatic, most plants usually reshoot from the base. All dead growth should be pruned out. See p.181.

NIBBLED LEAVES

CONTROLLED CLIMBER

Why are leaves turning brown and crispy on the sides and tips?

Exposed to the full force of the wind on walls and fences, leaves and flowers on climbing plants are easily damaged. Prune dead stems, water well, and provide shelter to help them recover.

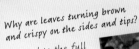

 Q What is eating notches in the leaf edges?

A Adult vine weevils are usually responsible for this pattern of foliage damage at any time between spring and fall. The dull, matte-black beetles are easiest to see when they emerge to feed at night. They eat only leaf edges, so most climbers can withstand the damage. However, this pest can severely harm other plants growing nearby and should be controlled. **See p.187.**

 Q How can I prevent climbers from becoming overgrown?

A Some climbers grow incredibly quickly during summer and can swamp neighboring plants. They may even find their way onto roofs and gutters, where they can cause damage. The only way to prevent this is to prune them at least once a year in spring or after flowering. If a climber still proves too rampant, replace it with something slower growing. **See Pruning climbing plants pp.146–147.**

Pruning climbing plants

The prospect of dealing with the vigorous growth of many climbing plants can seem daunting, but when tamed by annual pruning and training, they become easily manageable, flower more profusely, and never get anywhere near gutters or roofs. Having good supports in place, knowing how to prune each climber correctly, and getting the timing right are the recipe for success.

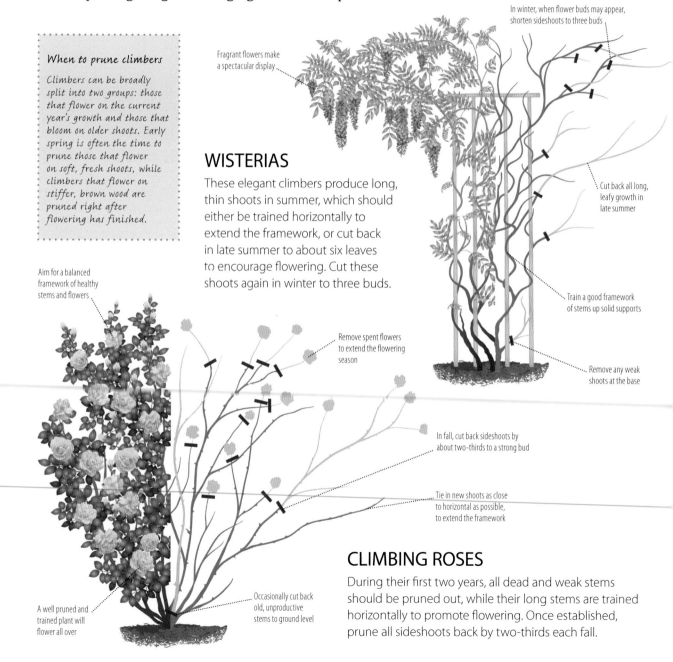

When to prune climbers

Climbers can be broadly split into two groups: those that flower on the current year's growth and those that bloom on older shoots. Early spring is often the time to prune those that flower on soft, fresh shoots, while climbers that flower on stiffer, brown wood are pruned right after flowering has finished.

In winter, when flower buds may appear, shorten sideshoots to three buds

Fragrant flowers make a spectacular display

WISTERIAS

These elegant climbers produce long, thin shoots in summer, which should either be trained horizontally to extend the framework, or cut back in late summer to about six leaves to encourage flowering. Cut these shoots again in winter to three buds.

Cut back all long, leafy growth in late summer

Train a good framework of stems up solid supports

Remove any weak shoots at the base

Aim for a balanced framework of healthy stems and flowers

Remove spent flowers to extend the flowering season

In fall, cut back sideshoots by about two-thirds to a strong bud

Tie in new shoots as close to horizontal as possible, to extend the framework

CLIMBING ROSES

During their first two years, all dead and weak stems should be pruned out, while their long stems are trained horizontally to promote flowering. Once established, prune all sideshoots back by two-thirds each fall.

A well pruned and trained plant will flower all over

Occasionally cut back old, unproductive stems to ground level

CLEMATIS

Pruning clematis is complicated by the fact there are three groups that need pruning in different ways. Group 1 plants, such as *C. montana*, don't need annual pruning, although can be cut back after flowering in spring if overgrown. Large, early-summer flowering Group 2 plants, such as *C.* 'Nelly Moser', bloom on last season's growth, so cut back lightly to healthy buds in early spring. Late-flowering Group 3 clematis, such as *C. tangutica*, flower on new growth; prune to their lowest buds in early spring.

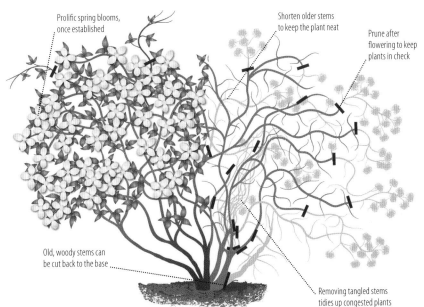

Prolific spring blooms, once established

Shorten older stems to keep the plant neat

Prune after flowering to keep plants in check

Old, woody stems can be cut back to the base

Removing tangled stems tidies up congested plants

Group 1: Early flowering clematis

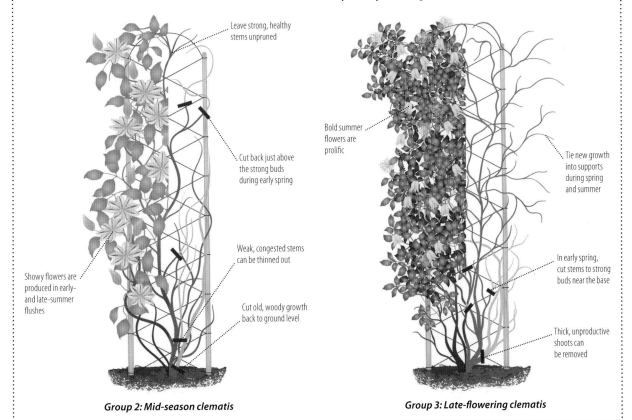

Leave strong, healthy stems unpruned

Cut back just above the strong buds during early spring

Weak, congested stems can be thinned out

Cut old, woody growth back to ground level

Showy flowers are produced in early- and late-summer flushes

Group 2: Mid-season clematis

Bold summer flowers are prolific

Tie new growth into supports during spring and summer

In early spring, cut stems to strong buds near the base

Thick, unproductive shoots can be removed

Group 3: Late-flowering clematis

RESCUE

Perennials, bulbs and bedding

Used to create seamless swathes of color in our gardens, perennials, bulbs, and bedding plants are incredibly diverse, with plants suitable for almost every situation. The anatomy guides for each plant group in this section illustrate some of this variety and give advice on planting and routine care. Common pests, diseases, and cultural problems are also easily diagnosed using the flowcharts and question-and-answer pages, with solutions to help maintain a vibrant display.

Perennial plant anatomy

These tough, often long-lived plants, have soft growth that dies down each fall and overwinters as roots and buds in the soil, ready to shoot up again the following spring. As the plant dies down every year, pests and diseases are eliminated, meaning these versatile plants are often trouble-free and easy to grow.

SPREADING PERENNIALS

Rapid growth marks out this group of perennials, which cover ground quickly by sending up shoots from shallow roots or underground stems, or rooting stems above ground. They are easy to grow, encounter few problems, and often thrive in difficult conditions.

Many perennials start dying back after flowering

Dense mats of foliage can be prone to powdery mildew in dry soils

CARPET OF GROWTH
Spreading perennials make excellent groundcover plants, because their quick growth and dense carpets of foliage make it difficult for weed seedlings to establish.

Fleshy underground stems and roots spread quickly, but can become invasive

Lift rooted sections and transplant for easy propagation

SPREADING PLANTS
Robust and frequently evergreen, spreading perennials are ideal for filling spaces and growing beneath larger shrubs.

Winter and spring color

Leafy bamboo grasses

Evergreen foliage

Summer flowers

CLUMP-FORMING PERENNIALS

Many of the best-known colorful perennials form clumps with a fibrous root system that produces new shoots each year. Others regrow annually from deep taproots, which make the plants more difficult to move and divide. Both are a quick and easy route to a vibrant garden.

CLUMPING BAMBOO

Bamboos are large evergreen grasses with segmented woody stems and delicate divided leaves that grow in dense clumps. Many varieties are vigorous and, once established, they can spread over a large area.

Deadheading regularly will prolong the display of flowers

Large leaves can wilt quickly in hot weather, but recover with an evening watering

Tender new shoots are prone to cold or slug and snail damage

Damage to roots by vine weevil grubs or rot cause wilting foliage

PERENNIALS THAT FORM CLUMPS

A huge range of vibrant clump-forming perennials exists, so there is almost guaranteed to be something to suit every garden. Choose perennials to suit your conditions for strong growth that resists attack.

Drought-tolerant plants

Sun-loving perennials

Late summer color

Attractive seed heads

Moisture-loving perennials

Early-flowering plants

What's wrong with my perennials?

Protection from pests is key for perennials as their tender new growth heads skyward in spring. Once in full leaf, plants usually cope well with any attacks, but keep an eye on vulnerable shoot tips and flower buds, which can be spoiled by insects and fungal infection.

THE STEMS FLOP OVER AND LOOK UNHEALTHY. WHAT CAN I DO?

Is it growing at the back of a border or in a shady spot?

Some perennials have weaker stems and need additional support. Insert stakes and tie the stems to them. **See p.154.**

Shade and competition can encourage weak, leggy growth that is prone to flop over. Consider moving the plant elsewhere.

WHY DOES THE PLANT KEEP WILTING DURING THE DAY?

Has the weather been warm and dry lately?

Don't worry. Many perennials often wilt when it's hot out. Water them well in the morning or evening.

Is your soil light and free draining?

Plants dry out quickly in lighter soils, even during brief dry spells. Water them regularly.

Are there insect pests or signs of damage on the stems?

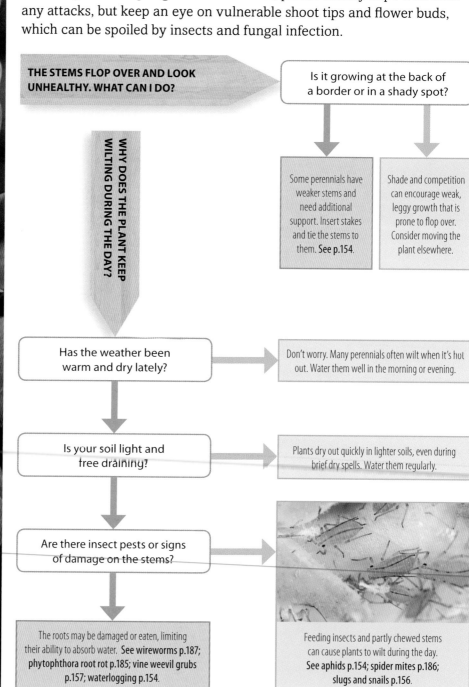

The roots may be damaged or eaten, limiting their ability to absorb water. See wireworms p.187; phytophthora root rot p.185; vine weevil grubs p.157; waterlogging p.154.

Feeding insects and partly chewed stems can cause plants to wilt during the day. See aphids p.154; spider mites p.186; slugs and snails p.156.

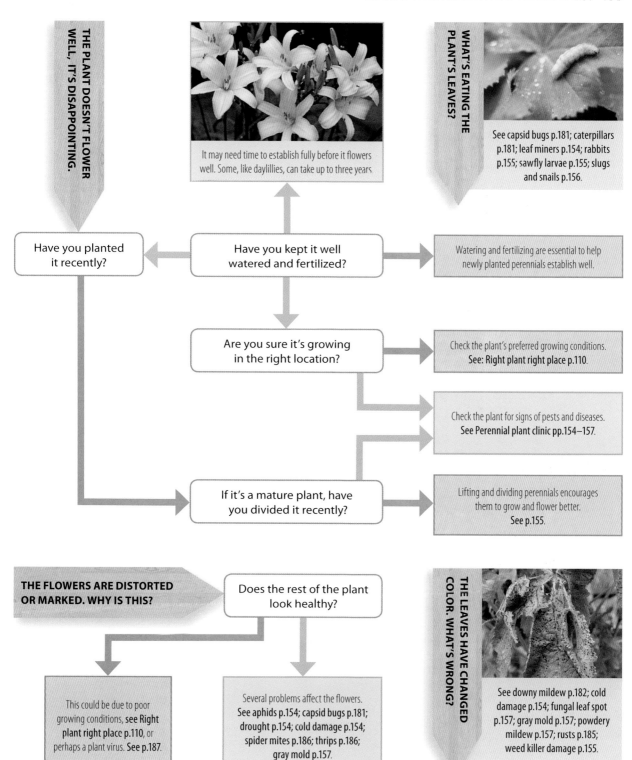

THE PLANT DOESN'T FLOWER WELL. IT'S DISAPPOINTING.

It may need time to establish fully before it flowers well. Some, like daylillies, can take up to three years.

WHAT'S EATING THE PLANT'S LEAVES?

See capsid bugs p.181; caterpillars p.181; leaf miners p.154; rabbits p.155; sawfly larvae p.155; slugs and snails p.156.

Have you planted it recently?

Have you kept it well watered and fertilized?

Watering and fertilizing are essential to help newly planted perennials establish well.

Are you sure it's growing in the right location?

Check the plant's preferred growing conditions. **See: Right plant right place p.110.**

Check the plant for signs of pests and diseases. **See Perennial plant clinic pp.154–157.**

If it's a mature plant, have you divided it recently?

Lifting and dividing perennials encourages them to grow and flower better. See p.155.

THE FLOWERS ARE DISTORTED OR MARKED. WHY IS THIS?

Does the rest of the plant look healthy?

This could be due to poor growing conditions, see Right plant right place p.110, or perhaps a plant virus. **See p.187.**

Several problems affect the flowers. **See aphids p.154; capsid bugs p.181; drought p.154; cold damage p.154; spider mites p.186; thrips p.186; gray mold p.157.**

THE LEAVES HAVE CHANGED COLOR. WHAT'S WRONG?

See downy mildew p.182; cold damage p.154; fungal leaf spot p.157; gray mold p.157; powdery mildew p.157; rusts p.185; weed killer damage p.155.

Perennial plant clinic

Perennials usually stay healthy thanks to the fact that their growth dies back in fall and can be removed along with any lingering pests and diseases. Specific ailments target some, and tender new growth may be attacked by common pests and fungal diseases, but if well cared for, these plants grow and thrive.

Can aphids cause much damage to plants?

Aphids form large groups and suck the sap from perennials, and are often found on soft, new stems. Heavy infestations can reduce plant growth, and the damage done to young leaves causes them to curl. Aphids also spread viral diseases. See Aphids, p.180; Viruses, p.187.

Q My perennials are wilting, are they too dry or too wet?

A A lack of water reaching the leaves results in wilting, either because the soil is very dry, or because it is waterlogged and causing the roots to die. Check the soil then either water the plant or improve drainage.

Q What can I do to prevent cold from damaging my plants?

A Brown leaves in spring, which wilt and die, may be caused by cold. During mild spring weather, plants start into growth but are then hit by cold spells. Protect them with fabric or move them to a sheltered spot.

UNSUPPORTED PLANTS

LEAF MINER DAMAGE

LEAVES DAMAGED BY COLD

Q Why have my healthy plants collapsed?

A With large flowers and no woody stems to support them, many perennials struggle to stay upright in wet or breezy weather. Keep them standing by installing supporting twiggy sticks, poles and twine, or commercially produced stakes in spring, which plants will grow through and conceal.

Q Should I worry about leaf miners?

A Many perennials develop pale, tunneled areas in their leaves—the larvae of various insects feed inside them. Although this looks unattractive, the damage caused is rarely severe enough to affect a healthy, established plant. Simply pick off any mined leaves to limit the spread of the pests.

How do I know if it's rabbits eating my plant?

 When established plants are rapidly destroyed or badly damaged, especially in rural areas, rabbits are likely to be the culprits. Keep them out of the garden if you can.

Why has my established perennial stopped flowering well?

 Many perennials spread quickly, forming congested clumps that are bare in the middle, and less free-flowering than before. This is easily remedied by lifting the clump in late fall or early spring, and dividing it into several sections containing healthy young shoots and roots that can be replanted. Most plants can be teased apart once lifted, and the woody central portion discarded. Take the opportunity to remove weeds from the clump and improve the soil before replanting.

Dig up the plant

Split into sections

Replant healthy pieces

HEALTHY SOLOMON'S SEAL

UNAFFECTED FOLIAGE

What's caused the leaves and buds to become twisted and deformed?

If affected plants are near an area recently sprayed with weed killer, they may possibly have been hit by airborne droplets. Established plants often recover; water and fertilize well.

Are sawflies a big problem on plants?

Small caterpillarlike sawfly larvae can rapidly defoliate *Aquilegia*, Solomon's seal, and *Aruncus* in late spring and summer. Plants can tolerate some damage but will be weakened after several seasons, especially when attacks occur in late spring. Remove the larvae as soon as possible; check plants often. **See p.186.**

Why have the leaf tips turned dry and brown?

The foliage of perennials can be damaged or scorched by the weather. The most common symptoms are crisp, brown patches at the leaf edges and shoot tips, and the browning of flowers. Dry wind and bright sunlight are usually to blame. Provide shelter and keep plants well watered.

Q **How can I keep spreading perennials under control?**

A Many spreading perennials create dense mats of foliage and flowers, making them great groundcover plants. However, this rapid growth can result in them becoming invasive. Luckily most are simple to control because they spread via stems just below the soil surface. To tame the plant, every piece of these fleshy stems must be unearthed with a fork, leaving a clump the desired size. Overly vigorous plants are best removed to prevent the problem from recurring.

Euphorbia cyparissias

Persicaria bistorta

Q **Should I worry about slugs and snails?**

A Since they have no woody growth and grow close to soil level, many perennials are particularly vulnerable to damage by slugs and snails. New shoots, which can be chewed off overnight during wet spring weather, need to be protected. Mature plants cope well with holes in their leaves during the growing season, but as summer progresses, hostas and other leafy plants can be spoiled without protection. See p.186.

RAMPANT SPREAD

HEALTHY PEONIES

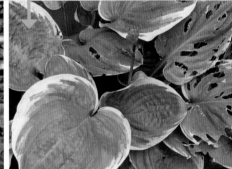

SLUG-EATEN HOSTAS

Q **Why are stems rotting off at the base?**

A If parts of the plant are collapsing due to decay at soil level, where the stems and roots meet, this is crown rot. Caused by bacteria or fungi, it is common where plants have been planted too deeply, or mulch has been spread too close to the stems. Clear away soil or mulch to expose the base.

Q **What's causing peony buds to turn brown?**

A Peony wilt is a fungal disease that causes the buds on infected plants to wither and turn brown, sometimes along with stem bases, which causes whole shoots to die. In wet weather, wilted areas can develop fluffy, white fungal growth. Remove affected shoots to prevent its spread. See p.184.

Q Why aren't my daylilies opening?

A Flower buds that don't open and turn brown are a symptom of hemerocallis gall midge. The fly maggots feed on the flower bud, causing thickened and crimped petals. **See p.183**.

GALL MIDGE DAMAGE

Q Should I be worried about vine weevils on my plants?

A Adult vine weevils are matte-black beetles, about ½in (1cm) long, that eat notches in the leaf edges of many perennials from spring to fall. Although leaves look bad from their nibbling, it is actually their cream, c-shaped grubs that cause real damage, feeding on plants with fleshy roots between fall and spring, causing slow growth, wilting, and eventually death. **See p.187**.

Diagnostic chart

Symptoms	Diagnosis

Gray-brown patches appear on the leaves of hellebores, merging to create large areas of dead tissue. Flower stems may also be infected, turning brown and collapsing.

Hellebore leaf blotch is a fungal disease that is particularly prevalent in wet weather. Infected leaves should be removed promptly to prevent the infection from spreading. **See p.183**.

The upper leaf surface looks dull and becomes covered in a fine, white, fungal growth that looks like talcum powder. The infection may also spread to the flowers and stems.

Powdery mildew is a fungal infection, common in mid- to late summer on many perennials, such as *Acanthus* and *Aster*. It it is encouraged by dry soil and humid air around leaves. **See p.185**.

Leaves develop bright orange spots above, with corresponding puffy orange growths below, which can merge, killing parts of the leaf and giving it a ragged appearance.

Hollyhock rust is a common fungal condition that usually appears during spring and summer, but is worse in wet seasons. Remove all fallen leaves to help prevent infection. **See Rusts p.185**.

Perennials develop round, gray-brown patches on their leaves, which may join to form large dead patches, or kill the leaf. Overall growth is not usually affected.

Fungal leaf spots are caused by a range of different fungi, all of which thrive in moist conditions. The spores linger among fallen leaves, unless cleared, to reinfect plants the following year. **See p.183**.

Plant growth is distorted and stunted, and leaves may develop vivid yellow streaked, mottled, or mosaiclike markings. Flowers may also fail or open with pale streaks.

Viruses can infect perennial plants, some of which cause clear symptoms, while others are less obvious. They can be spread by insects, soil-living nematodes, and by tending infected plants. **See p.187**.

Leaves and stems develop areas of fuzzy, gray fungal growth, usually after insect or physical damage has occurred. Growth above the infection often yellows and dies.

Gray mold is an extremely widespread fungus, easily spread in the air and water droplets. It usually infects plants through an existing injury, so cut back damaged growth cleanly. **See p.183**.

Patio and bedding plant anatomy

Highly popular for a quick burst of color or to fill gaps, these bold plants perform spectacularly when well cared for. To produce strong, free-flowering plants with more resistance to ailments, protect half-hardy summer bedding from cold, ensure plants in pots have good drainage, and keep them well fed and watered all summer.

TENDER PERENNIALS

These patio stalwarts cannot tolerate cold, so do not plant out until early summer. Despite often being discarded, they can be kept somewhere bright and frost-free in winter, or easily propagated by cuttings to flower the following year.

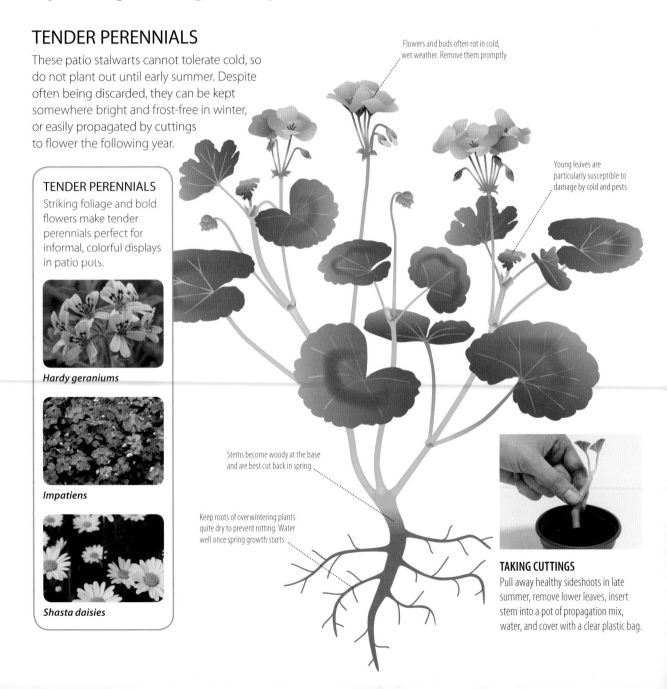

Flowers and buds often rot in cold, wet weather. Remove them promptly

Young leaves are particularly susceptible to damage by cold and pests

Stems become woody at the base and are best cut back in spring

Keep roots of overwintering plants quite dry to prevent rotting. Water well once spring growth starts

TENDER PERENNIALS

Striking foliage and bold flowers make tender perennials perfect for informal, colorful displays in patio pots.

Hardy geraniums

Impatiens

Shasta daisies

TAKING CUTTINGS

Pull away healthy sideshoots in late summer, remove lower leaves, insert stem into a pot of propagation mix, water, and cover with a clear plastic bag.

ANNUALS AND BIENNIALS

Quick and colorful, annuals flower from seed in a single year. Some are hardy enough to survive the winter outdoors, while others cannot tolerate cold and should only be planted out once nights are mild. Biennials are sown in early summer one year and planted into borders in early fall, ready to flower the next year. Many gardeners buy both annuals and biennials as young plants.

Flowers can be spoiled by insect pests, fungal diseases, and wet and cold weather

DEADHEADING

Regularly removing faded flowers keeps seeds from forming, forcing plants to put their energy into producing more flowers. It can also help reduce problems with fungal diseases.

Feed and water plants regularly for a lush, long-lasting display

Watch leaves for wilting, yellowing, and damage, which signal problems

Plant at the same depth as before; too deep, it will rot, too shallow and plants dry out

VINE WEEVILS

The succulent roots of many annuals and biennials are a favorite food source for vine weevil larvae, which can be particularly damaging in pots.

SHORT-LIVED COLOR

Sow hardy annuals directly into warm spring soil. Plant out half-hardy annuals in early summer, having sown them indoors in early spring.

Sunflowers (annual)

Lobelia (annual)

Wallflowers (biennial)

Marigolds (annual)

Alyssum (annual)

What's wrong with my patio plant?

Often planted out while young and still tender, many of these colorful plants frequently fall victim to late spring frost. Their soft growth is also vulnerable to fungal diseases, particularly when plants are grown closely together, and their pots are poorly drained or kept too dry.

WHY IS MY PLANT WILTING?

Are the roots growing out the base of the pot?

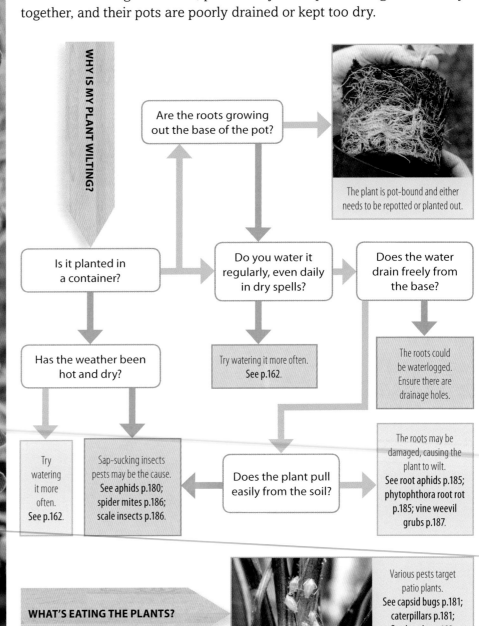

The plant is pot-bound and either needs to be repotted or planted out.

Is it planted in a container?

Do you water it regularly, even daily in dry spells?

Does the water drain freely from the base?

Has the weather been hot and dry?

Try watering it more often. See p.162.

The roots could be waterlogged. Ensure there are drainage holes.

Try watering it more often. See p.162.

Sap-sucking insects pests may be the cause. See aphids p.180; spider mites p.186; scale insects p.186.

Does the plant pull easily from the soil?

The roots may be damaged, causing the plant to wilt. See root aphids p.185; phytophthora root rot p.185; vine weevil grubs p.187.

WHAT'S EATING THE PLANTS?

Various pests target patio plants. See capsid bugs p.181; caterpillars p.181; flea beetles p.183; rabbits p.182; slugs and snails p.186.

THE PLANT DOESN'T FLOWER VERY WELL. IT'S DISAPPOINTING.

Is it planted in a sunny location?

Most patio plants need a warm, bright spot to flower well. Consider moving your plant.

Has the weather been cold, dull, and wet?

Poor weather commonly causes a poor display. Hope for better weather.

Have you kept it well watered and fed?

Regular watering and feeding are essential in summer for patio plants to have a good display.

Do you regularly remove the spent flowers?

Check for pests and diseases. **See Patio and bedding clinic pp.162–163.**

Removing faded flowers encourages the plant to produce more.

THE PLANTS SEEM WEAK AND DON'T GROW WELL.

Look closely at the plants. Can you see small insects on them?

A virus, **p.187**, can cause weak growth, as can poor growing conditions. **See Right plant right place p.110.**

See aphids p.180; capsid bugs p.181; spider mites p.186; whiteflies p.187.

THE FLOWERS ARE DISTORTED OR MARKED. WHY IS THIS?

Does the rest of the plant look healthy?

This could be due to poor growing conditions, **See Right plant right place p.110**, or perhaps a virus. **See p.187.**

This could be caused by one of several problems. See aphids p.180; capsid bugs p.181; drought p.162; spider mites p.186; thrips p.186; gray mold p.183.

THE LEAVES LOOK SICK. WHAT COULD BE WRONG?

Several things can cause this. See drought p.162; cold damage p.162; fungal leaf spot p.183; gray mold p.183; powdery mildew p.185; spider mites p.186; rusts p.185.

Patio and bedding plant clinic

Unequaled for a burst of seasonal color, patio and bedding plants grow strongly when given the right conditions. Poor drainage, along with inadequate fertilizing and watering however, are the root of many problems for pot-grown plants. Insect pests and fungal diseases also thrive on their soft growth and can spoil the show.

How can I recognize the signs of root rot?

Many bedding plants have soft stems that are prone to fungal foot and root rots. These cause mature plants and seedlings alike to wilt, often showing soft, dark tissue around the base of the stem. Affected plants yellow and die, and their roots often rot. See *Phytophthora* root rot p.185

Q **What has damaged the shoot and leaf tips overnight?**

A Summer bedding plants cannot tolerate cold and may be damaged by spring weather. Affected growth becomes limp, turns brown, and dies back. Cut back to healthy buds and protect plants with fabric.

Q **What damage do vine weevils do to bedding plants?**

A The cream, c-shaped grubs feed on the roots of bedding plants, especially primulas, cyclamen, and begonias. A real problem in pots from early fall to spring, they sever roots, killing plants. **See p.187**.

WILTING PETUNIAS   **SIGNS OF COLD DAMAGE**   **DISEASED LEAVES**

Q **What's causing plants to look dull and limp?**

A Densely packed into pots and grown in full sun during summer, it's no wonder that bedding plants often wilt due to a lack of water. During warm spells, containers may need watering thoroughly twice a day. Never rely on rainfall or allow potting mix to dry out—it can be hard to rewet.

Q **Should I worry about fungal leaf spot?**

A Fungal leaf spot causes pale brown or gray circular patches on leaves. These can spread and may join together, killing the whole leaf, while the rest of the plant remains healthy. Although not usually a serious problem, the disease occurs most often when growing conditions are poor. **See p.183**.

Q Why is the display so short-lived?

A Flowering profusely is hard work for plants, and they need help to sustain a good display for a long period. Plants flower to produce seed, and will channel their energy into seed heads at the expense of forming new flower buds. This makes it vital to remove fading flowers from plants regularly, so that they never set seed and keep producing more blooms. Regular fertilizing, especially with tomato fertilizer, enables plants to flower and look their best.

Remove spent flowers

Feed plants regularly

Q Why are plants crawling with ants and aphids?

A Aphids suck sap from bedding plants, weakening their display. Ants feed on the aphids' sticky excretions and protect them from predators, but are harmless to plants. **See Aphids p.180**.

RUNNING TO SEED

APHIDS ON A FLOWER

Why are my plants turning moldy and collapsing?

This is gray mold, which infects plant tissue, causing it to turn brown and develop gray fungal growth. It is worse in wet conditions, where drainage is poor, or plants are crowded. See p.183.

Q How can I identify powdery mildew?

A Powdery mildew is a fungal disease that forms a fine, dusty white coating on the leaves of many bedding plants, especially pansies and begonias. Growth may be poor, and affected leaves can yellow and distort. Dry roots and damp air leave plants at risk of attack—keep them well watered. See p.185.

Q What damage do thrips do to plants?

A Thrips are insects that feed on the flowers and leaves of bedding plants, causing silvery flecking on leaves, but more noticeable white splotches on petals. Large numbers of thrips can ruin flowers and prevent buds from opening. Mainly a summer pest, they can infest plants brought inside for winter. See p.186.

Garden bulb anatomy

All bulbous plants have a modified part of their anatomy that swells to store the food made by their leaves, enabling them to survive a dormant period underground. Despite being hidden, this fat storage organ is tempting to animal and insect pests, and also prone to fungal diseases, especially in wet conditions.

BULBS AND CORMS

Like onions, true bulbs are formed from layers of fleshy leaves or leaf bases, known as scales. Corms, on the other hand, are more solid and made up of the swollen bases of stems. Both have flat bases and tapering tops, which mean there is no excuse for planting them upside-down.

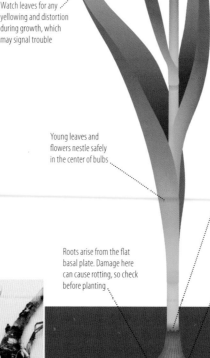

Watch leaves for any yellowing and distortion during growth, which may signal trouble

Young leaves and flowers nestle safely in the center of bulbs

The papery outer skin protects bulbs and corms, and prevents them from drying out

Roots arise from the flat basal plate. Damage here can cause rotting, so check before planting

Fleshy scales or a corm store food to fuel growth, so the bigger the better

LEAVES FEED THE BULBS
Food produced in the foliage is stored in the bulb for next season's growth. Allow leaves to die down naturally before removing for bigger bulbs and better flowers.

BABY BULBS
New bulbs, called offsets, are produced at the base of the bulb. As they grow, the bulbs become overcrowded and flower less, so should be lifted and divided.

BULBS TO GROW
Bold and bright, many bulbs and corms perform excellently when planted in well-drained borders or naturalized in grass.

Tulips (bulb)

Daffodils (bulb)

Crocus (corm)

Lilies (bulb)

TUBERS AND RHIZOMES

Tubers are swollen, usually irregular or knobby, stems or roots, while rhizomes are fat stems that grow horizontally at, or just below, the soil surface. Rhizomes often spread rapidly and a single plant can produce numerous tubers, making it easy to expand your stock.

DRYING OUT

With no protective skin, some tubers dry out when lifted and then won't grow well. Buy cyclamen and *Erythronium* tubers packed in moist potting medium or growing in pots.

Stake tall, showy flowers, such as dahlias and lilies, to keep them from blowing over

FLESHY ROOTS

Leave hardy tubers, such as cyclamen, undisturbed, but tender plants, like dahlias, can be stored in a frost-free place for winter.

Many tubers and rhizomes produce striking foliage, unlike most other bulbous plants

Tubers and rhizomes are solid, like a potato, with no protective skin

Shoots appear from buds or eyes. Ensure they are present and planted pointing upward

Roots emerge directly from tubers and rhizomes, which can make planting them the right way up difficult

FLOWERS

Varieties of dahlia with large flowers may need supporting with stakes to prevent them from falling over.

Dahlias (tuber)

Iris sibirica (rhizome)

Cyclamen (tuber)

What's wrong with my garden bulbs?

Bulb health is easiest to gauge when plants come into leaf and flower, when poor growth, marked leaves, and a lack of flowers can indicate pests and diseases, or poor growing conditions. Stored and newly bought bulbs should always be firm and mold-free before planting.

MY STORED BULBS HAVE ROTTED.

Did you keep them dry, frost-free, and well ventilated?

Bulbs need these conditions to store well. Try again next year.

The bulbs may have been harboring disease when you lifted them. Buy fresh bulbs and try again.

MY BULBS HAVE COME UP, BUT WHY ARE THERE ARE NO FLOWERS?

Did you plant them recently?

Established bulbs should be lifted and divided every few years to encourage flowering.

Are you sure you planted them at the correct depth?

Bulbs planted too shallowly often don't flower. **See How to plant p.113**.

WHAT'S EATING THE LEAVES AND FLOWERS?

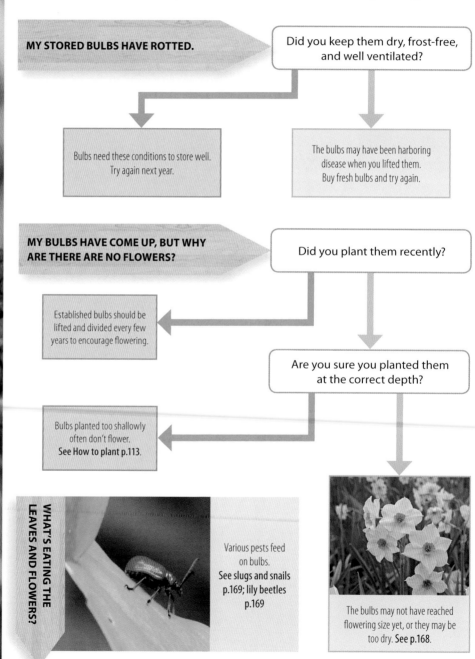

Various pests feed on bulbs. **See slugs and snails p.169; lily beetles p.169**

The bulbs may not have reached flowering size yet, or they may be too dry. **See p.168**.

MY NEW BULBS HAVEN'T COME UP.

Did you plant them at the correct time of year?

> Bulbs planted later than normal often come up and flower later as a result. Wait a little longer.

Are you sure the bulbs were fully hardy?

> Some bulbs, such as begonias and freesias, are tender and can be killed by low temperatures.

Is your soil heavy clay or poorly drained?

> Most bulbs like good drainage and may rot in heavy, wet soils.

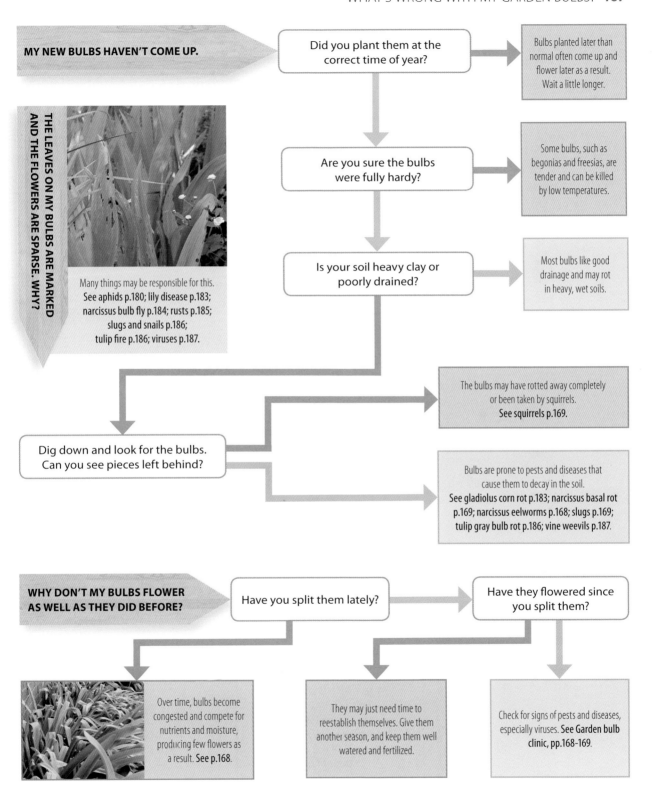

THE LEAVES ON MY BULBS ARE MARKED AND THE FLOWERS ARE SPARSE. WHY?

Many things may be responsible for this. See aphids p.180; lily disease p.183; narcissus bulb fly p.184; rusts p.185; slugs and snails p.186; tulip fire p.186; viruses p.187.

Dig down and look for the bulbs. Can you see pieces left behind?

> The bulbs may have rotted away completely or been taken by squirrels. **See squirrels p.169.**

> Bulbs are prone to pests and diseases that cause them to decay in the soil. **See gladiolus corn rot p.183; narcissus basal rot p.169; narcissus eelworms p.168; slugs p.169; tulip gray bulb rot p.186; vine weevils p.187.**

WHY DON'T MY BULBS FLOWER AS WELL AS THEY DID BEFORE?

Have you split them lately?

Have they flowered since you split them?

> Over time, bulbs become congested and compete for nutrients and moisture, producing few flowers as a result. **See p.168**.

> They may just need time to reestablish themselves. Give them another season, and keep them well watered and fertilized.

> Check for signs of pests and diseases, especially viruses. **See Garden bulb clinic, pp.168-169.**

Garden bulb clinic

Bulbs planted in the perfect spot will often flower profusely without any problems for years, but many can be affected by viruses, a range of fungal diseases, and a few pests. Knowing common symptoms will help you spot problems quickly during the bulbs' rapid growth spell and prevent the issues from spreading.

Do my daffodils have a virus or eelworms?

Distorted and stunted leaves and flowers can be caused by either problem, and all affected bulbs should be destroyed promptly. To identify the cause, slice a bulb in half crosswise. If brown rings are visible in the flesh, the bulb was infested with eelworms.

Q How do I recognize tulip gray bulb rot?

A This fungal disease affects many bulbs, including alliums, crocuses, daffodils, snowdrops, and tulips. Infected bulbs rot and develop thick, gray mold, or form weak, distorted leaves that quickly die. See p.186.

Q Why are canna lilies growing poorly? Do they have a virus?

A Canna lilies are prone to several viruses that cause the leaves of infected plants to develop pale or yellow stripes, weak or distorted growth, and poor flowers. There is no cure—destroy infected plants.

HEALTHY DAFFODILS   **WELL-SPACED BULBS**

DISEASED CANNA LEAVES

Q Why haven't my new bulbs flowered?

A Bulbs that fail to flower are said to be blind. Newly planted bulbs may be too small to flower and should be left to grow. A lack of care during the growing season also impairs flower-bud formation. Water your bulbs well, give them some high-potassium fertilizer, and remove their leaves once faded.

Q Does overcrowding harm bulbs?

A Congested bulbs steadily produce fewer flowers, and may become weak because of the intense competition for water and nutrients. Pests and diseases also spread easily where bulbs are grown densely packed together. Lift and divide crowded bulbs in fall—discard any that are unhealthy.

Diagnostic chart

Symptoms	Diagnosis
 **Brown rot spreads from the root end** of the bulb, sometimes accompanied by thick fungal growth where the roots originate. Stored bulbs dry out and those in the ground rot.	**Narcissus basal rot** is a fungal disease, which is at its worst during hot summer weather. It is found in the soil, where bulbs harboring mild infections can easily go unnoticed. **See p.184.**
 **Bulbs lifted for storage or grown in pots** develop molds or rots, which either damage an area of the bulb's surface or cause the whole bulb to rot, often leaving just the outer skin.	**Fungal diseases** attack bulbs damaged during lifting, stored in damp conditions, or kept too moist while dormant in pots. Only store healthy, undamaged bulbs, and use paper, not plastic, bags.

Q **Would squirrels dig up and eat garden bulbs?**

A Gray squirrels are partial to crocus and tulip bulbs, which are easy for them to unearth from the soil or pots after planting in the fall. Use chicken wire to protect new bulb plantings.

SLUG-DAMAGED LEAVES

PEST-FREE LILIES

Why are the flower buds on healthy plants brown and shriveled?

Bulbs are sensitive to their growing conditions during the formation of flower buds, and a lack of water at this critical stage can later cause buds to abort and fail to open.

Q **Are slugs and snails attacking my bulbs?**

A The lush foliage and tender flowers of many bulbs are a prime target for slugs and snails. Early spring bulbs often escape damage since they come into leaf and flower before the pests become active, but late spring-, summer-, and fall-flowering bulbs can all suffer, especially in wet seasons. **See p.186.**

Q **How do I recognize lily beetles?**

A Foliage, flowers, and seed pods of lilies and fritillaries are eaten by adults and grubs, often badly damaging plants. The pudgy, orange-red grubs can be found during midsummer, covered in their black excrement. The easy-to-see adult beetles are bright scarlet with a black head, and feed from spring into fall. **See p.183.**

Lily beetle grubs   *Adult beetle*   *Typical damage*

RESCUE

Lawns

A healthy, well kept lawn provides the perfect offset for beds and borders, while patchy, weed-riddled grass can make even a neat garden look scruffy. The key to a lush, green lawn is to first understand the way grasses grow, and to keep them strong and able to outcompete weeds with regular mowing and feeding. Quick diagnosis and treatment makes all common problems much easier to deal with, and keeps grass handsome and hard-wearing.

Garden lawn anatomy

Everyone knows that lawns are made of grass, but few realize that a mix of different grass species goes into making good turf. This mix, plus the growing conditions, determine how fine or hard-wearing a lawn will be. Regular maintenance is key, with mowing, weeding, raking, and aeration essential to keep grass growing well.

LAWN STRUCTURE

Dense, green grass is made up of an enormous number of individual grass plants that spread and knit together. Grasses produce long, narrow leaves from growing points, or "crowns," that set close to soil level. When mown, leaves regrow from the crown, allowing the lawn to be trimmed repeatedly without any ill effects. The way many grasses spread also makes them ideal for producing a thick, green carpet. Popular turf grasses often form dense clumps by sending out new shoots, called "tillers" from the base of the parent plant. More vigorous grasses, used for hard-wearing lawns, send out long stems that produce new plants along their length, and can easily spread into surrounding borders.

REMOVING THATCH

As new grass blades appear, older ones naturally die off. This creates a tangled layer of tan-colored dead matter, known as thatch, which should be raked from a lawn each year, either by hand or using a scarifyier. This will help to keep the grass thick, allow rain to reach the roots, deter moss, and keep fungal diseases from developing.

GRADES OF SOD

Choose the right sod for the appearance and durability you require. High-quality sod consists of fine grasses that create an even color and texture, and can be mown closely. Utility grass is harder wearing with a coarser texture. It contains ryegrass and will tolerate heavy use

Trim lawn edges regularly and recut them every spring to stop grass from spreading

Weeds commonly grow in between the grass plants

Pests may feed on the dense fibrous roots, causing patches of grass to yellow

Shallow roots quickly absorb surface water, but can't reach deeper reserves

LAWN WEED KILLERS

Selective lawn weed killers are available, which are capable of killing broadleaf lawn weeds, while leaving grass blades unharmed. This is a useful way to rid large lawns of weeds, where grubbing them out by hand would be impractical. Do not use weed killers on new lawns that are less than six months old. When using liquid weed killers, take care that the spray or droplets don't drift onto garden plants, especially those in surrounding borders.

APPLYING WEED KILLERS

Weed killers are available as concentrated liquids that should be diluted before use, and are applied using a watering can or hand sprayer. Dry or granular weed killers can be spread by hand or by using a lawn spreader. Never exceed the recommended dose rate given on the packet—doing so may damage or even kill the lawn.

Watch the lawn for areas of discoloration, which can indicate pests or disease on the foliage

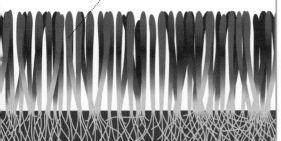

COMMON LAWN WEEDS

A surprising number of creeping and rosette-forming perennial weeds can flourish in lawns, despite regular mowing. Good lawn care promotes vigorous grass growth, which will help prevent weeds from establishing. Remove all weeds that appear promptly to prevent them from spreading.

Plantain

Buttercup

Dandelion

White clover

Slender speedwell

Sheep's sorrel

Yarrow

Oxalis

Dock

Mind-your-own-business

What's wrong with my lawn?

It is wise to keep a check on your lawn's well-being year-round, not only to watch for signs of disease, pests, and weeds, but also to look at the growing conditions. Improving drainage, well-timed watering, and mowing at the right height all help keep grass healthy.

WHY IS MY LAWN SO THREADBARE AND PATCHY?

WHAT CAUSES THE YELLOW PATCHES IN THE GRASS?

If the patches appear at random, the likely cause is animal urine. **See p.179.** If the patches develop in the same spot, there may be buried debris under the grass. Dig down a little and check.

Is your lawn shaded or regularly damp or dry?	Lawns struggle in these conditions, leading to weak growth. Improve the soil and try to reduce the shade cast by nearby shrubs.
Do you cut it at regular intervals?	Leaving the grass to grow too long before mowing encourages bald patches to develop, as does mowing too short. **See Caring for lawns p.117.**
Is your lawn used heavily?	Wear and tear can lead to patchy grass. Look after it and give it chance to grow back. **See p.177.**
Do you feed your lawn regularly?	

Look for signs of leather jackets, which eat the roots during summer, causing areas of grass to die. **See p.177.**

Regular fertilizing promotes growth, and if mown regularly, a thick, healthy lawn. Don't exceed the dose when fertilizing because this may scorch the lawn, causing bald patches. **See p.177.**

WHY IS MY LAWN ALWAYS FULL OF MOSS? IT ALWAYS GROWS BACK.

Is your lawn shaded for periods of the day?

Shade weakens grass but encourages moss to grow. **See p.176**.

Does your lawn often feel damp under foot, even in summer?

Poor drainage also encourages moss to grow at the expense of grass. **See p.176**.

Do you rake your lawn periodically?

Lawns develop a buildup of plant debris that reduces airflow and holds moisture, encouraging moss. Rake your lawn two or three times during summer.

WHY DO PILES OF SOIL APPEAR ON THE LAWN—DO THEY MATTER?

Is each pile about the size of a quarter?

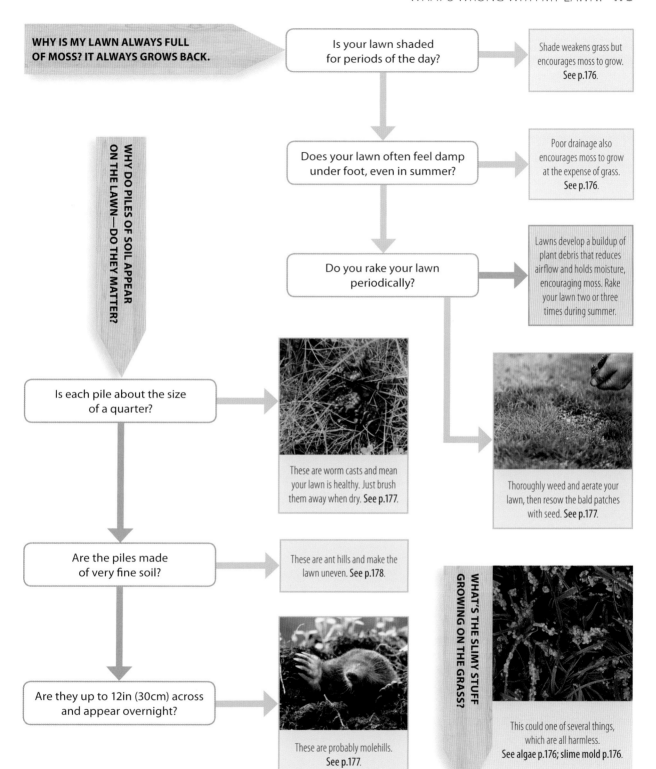

These are worm casts and mean your lawn is healthy. Just brush them away when dry. **See p.177**.

Thoroughly weed and aerate your lawn, then resow the bald patches with seed. **See p.177**.

Are the piles made of very fine soil?

These are ant hills and make the lawn uneven. **See p.178**.

Are they up to 12in (30cm) across and appear overnight?

These are probably molehills. **See p.177**.

WHAT'S THE SLIMY STUFF GROWING ON THE GRASS?

This could one of several things, which are all harmless. See algae p.176; slime mold p.176.

Garden lawn clinic

A healthy lawn is a matter of pride for many gardeners, but even if you don't covet pristine turf, regular maintenance will keep growing conditions favorable and make a green landscape easier to achieve. Ailments often indicate an underlying problem, which it is best dealt with, as well as treating the pest or disease.

Are the slimy patches caused by algae?

In patches where grass growth is poor, algae will often develop on the soil, forming green or black-tinged slimy patches. Unlike grass, algae thrives in moist, shady areas and places where the soil is compacted and poorly drained. See Caring for lawns p.117.

Q What are the pale red patches developing on the lawn?

A Patches of small, jellylike fungal threads in shades of pink and pale red are a sign of red thread. This disease is most common after heavy rain—infected areas are often killed and appear bleached. **See p.185.**

Q My lawn has slime mold. Should I be concerned?

A Slime molds produce gray, yellow, or orange bumpy growths along blades of grass in summer and fall. They are not parasitic and are thought harmless. Use a hose to wash them off or wait for heavy rain.

LAWN MOSS

POOR DRAINAGE

SLIME MOLD ON GRASS

Q How can I control the moss in my lawn?

A Moss flourishes in shade and poorly drained soil, so improve conditions and aerate the lawn by spiking annually with a fork, and increase light levels by cutting back overhanging branches. Kill moss using lawn sand and remove it when dark brown, using a wire rake or a powered lawn scarifier.

Q Why is my lawn always damp underfoot?

A Bad drainage results in water pooling at the soil surface, which will kill grass and encourage the growth of moss and algae. Aerating the lawn in early fall by pushing a garden fork into the soil at regular intervals reduces compaction and improves drainage. Very wet lawns may need drains installed.

Q What can I do about worm casts?

A Worm casts are made by active earthworms during spring and fall, which help aerate the soil. If they spoil the look of the lawn, let the casts dry out and brush them into the borders.

Q How can I fix bare patches?

A Most well-used lawns have areas that become worn and bare. If it's possible not to walk on them for a while, reseed bald patches in spring or fall by raking the soil loose, adding a little potting soil, and scattering and raking in grass seed. Alternatively, to prevent worn areas from developing, install slabs or stepping stones in heavily used areas. Place them level with the lawn surface so they don't come into contact with the lawn mower blades.

Sowing seed on bald spots   *Preventing worn patches*

When is the best time of year to fertilize a lawn?

As grass clippings are removed, soil nutrients can run low. Apply lawn fertilizer in late spring and a low nitrogen fertilizer in fall at the recommended rate, then water it in.

TOADSTOOLS IN GRASS   **BALD PATCH IN LAWN**

Q Why are there toadstools in the lawn?

A Various toadstools appear in grass, from honey fungus growing on roots to fairy rings that grow from circles of yellowing grass. Since toadstools are the fruiting bodies of fungal growth beneath the soil, little can be done to control them except to remove them before they release their spores to minimize spread.

Q What can I do about molehills on the lawn?

A The damage caused by a few molehills can easily be repaired and reseeded, but where many occur, deterrents may be needed.

Q Is my lawn suffering from leatherjackets?

A Small, yellow-brown spots in the grass may indicate the presence of leatherjackets. These are the large, soil-dwelling larvae of crane flies, which sever the roots of grass, causing it to die back. Once damage is done, it is too late to act, but encouraging starlings into the yard can help control their numbers.

Why do patches of grass die in winter?

A Fusarium patch is a disease that causes areas of grass to yellow and die during late fall and winter, often after a covering of snow. The patches may merge together, forming larger areas of dead grass. In damp conditions, tufts of grass develop white fungal growth and stick together. It is most common on lawns fed with a high-nitrogen feed during fall, which should be avoided.

There are small ant hills on the lawn. Are they harmful?

A Ants frequently tunnel under lawns during summer to make nests, creating small hills with the soil they remove during digging. The soil rarely damages grass and can be brushed away.

Will my lawn survive during a drought?

A Drought can result in patches of grass, or even the entire lawn, turning yellow or brown. It may look alarming, but grass recovers its green color quickly after rain or a thorough evening watering.

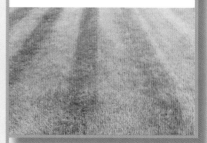

 SCORCHED GRASS

RAKE LEAVES IN FALL

SIGNS OF DROUGHT

Can lawn fertilizer harm grass?

A Applying too much lawn fertilizer can scorch grass and may kill it, creating bare patches. Unevenly applied fertilizer will also cause the lawn to grow at different rates in different places, making it uneven. For the best results, use a calibrated lawn spreader or evenly apply measured amounts by hand.

Should I rake up fallen leaves?

A One of the most important lawn maintenance tasks is to rake up any leaves that drop onto grass in fall. This is because leaves create a dense covering, particularly when wet, which excludes light from grass, turning it pale yellow and weak. The decaying mat can also encourage fungal diseases.

Does dog urine damage the lawn?

 Dog urine, especially from female dogs, is very high in nitrogen and will quickly damage grass, leading to ugly bare patches. Wash it away using plenty of water.

Q **How can I get rid of the cracks in new sod?**

A New sod may shrink slightly once laid, leaving ugly gaps. These can be filled using good, fine garden soil, then lightly sprinkled with grass seed, and watered well.

Q **Can I use creeping herbs instead of grass for a lawn?**

A Creeping herbs will form an attractive, fragrant lawn, but will not withstand much wear and tear. Herb lawns can also be short-lived, lasting just a few years, and high maintenance.

 EFFECTS OF SHADING

 NEGLECTED LAWN

ATTRACTIVE HERB LAWN

Q **Why does grass thin close to buildings and trees?**

A Large buildings, trees, and shrubs all cast shade, which does not suit most turf grasses. The shelter created also prevents rain from reaching the lawn, and the roots of trees and shrubs will compete for the little moisture available. Reduce shade by cutting back plants, water well during dry spells, and use a grass mix designed for shady lawns.

Q **How can I restore a lawn that has been neglected?**

A If the lawn is riddled with weeds, it may be easier to remove it and start again. If not, dig out all large weeds, then mow, weed, and fertilize regularly. Grass is resilient, so you should be able to restore a lawn within a single season.

Give the lawn a good mow

Starting from scratch

A–Z of common pests and diseases

Once your plant's problem is diagnosed, a quick response is important to control it and, if possible, prevent it from recurring the following year or spreading to other plants growing nearby. These pages suggest both chemical and non-chemical techniques for treating pests and diseases where available, to allow you to select the best course of action for your garden.

ADELGIDS
Symptoms In spring or early summer sap-sucking insects can be seen on shoot tips, often covered in a white, waxy secretion. Foliage yellows and galls may form, but growth usually unaffected.
Plants affected Conifers, particularly pines and silver firs (*Abies*).
Prevention None available.
Treatment Often unnecessary—a suitable insecticide can be used in late winter to prevent egg laying.

APHIDS
Symptoms Distorted leaves, especially at shoot tips, reduced growth, and sticky honeydew on leaf surfaces that can develop black sooty mold (p.186). Severe infestations can kill younger plants.
Related types Black bean, green spruce, mealy aphids.
Plants affected Almost all garden plants.
Prevention Minimize or pinch back soft young growth where possible.
Treatment Squash between fingers, encourage predatory insects, or use a suitable insecticide.

APPLE BITTER PIT
Symptoms Apples develop small, brown, sunken spots on skin, pale brown flecks in flesh, and may have a nasty, bitter taste. This can happen on the tree or in storage.
Plants affected Apples
Prevention Caused by calcium deficiency in fruit, usually because of dry conditions. Keep plants well watered and mulched.
Treatment Affected apples are often spoiled. Water well next year and apply a mulch in spring to retain soil moisture.

APPLE AND PEAR CANKER
Symptoms Starting with patches of sunken, cracked, flaky bark on branches, the affected area will often swell and can cause the branch to die back.
Plants affected Apples, pears, hawthorns, poplars, and willows.
Prevention Ensure good drainage, add lime to acidic soils. Avoid susceptible apple varieties.
Treatment Remove infected spurs and branches by cutting back to healthy wood with clean, sharp tools. Treat with a suitable fungicide right after harvest, and again when some leaves have fallen.

APPLE AND PEAR SCAB
Symptoms Brown, scabby marks appear on fruit and leaves. The skins of badly affected fruits can crack, and may rot.
Plants affected Apples, pears, crabapples, ash, *Cotoneaster*, *Pyracantha*.
Prevention Rake up and remove fallen leaves to help stop the spread of infection.
Treatment Grow resistant cultivars and remove infected stems. Treat smaller trees with a suitable fungicide.

ASPARAGUS BEETLE
Symptoms In summer adult beetles and larvae eat foliage and bark. Stems die back above damage.
Plants affected Asparagus
Prevention Burn old stems in late fall to kill beetles.
Treatment Pick off beetles and larvae by hand or spray with a suitable pesticide.

BACTERIAL CANKER
Symptoms Areas of bark sink and die, sometimes oozing sticky resin. Affected stems can die back and leaves are peppered with shothole (p.186).
Plants affected Plums, cherries, peaches, apricots, and ornamental *Prunus*.
Prevention Prune these trees in mid- to late summer.
Treatment Cut back to healthy wood and paint cuts with wound paint. Use suitable fungicides in late summer and fall.

BACTERIAL LEAF SPOT
Symptoms Dark, dead patches, often with a surrounding yellow halo, on leaves.
Plants affected Many plants.
Prevention Avoid overhead watering.
Treatment Remove affected leaves quickly. It can indicate a more serious ailment.

BEAN SEED FLY
Symptoms Seedlings grow slowly and have damaged stems and ragged leaves, or fail to germinate at all.
Plants affected Green and runner beans.
Prevention Protect outdoor sowings with fabric or sow seeds under cover in pots.
Treatment Nothing can be done by the time damage is visible.

BIRDS
Symptoms Holes pecked in apples, plums, and other large fruit, while currants and berries are eaten entirely. Tree blossoms may also be damaged and spring bedding plants may lose their flowers. Pigeons strip the leaves of garden greens.
Plants affected Tree fruit, soft fruit, and garden greens.
Prevention Cover crops with netting before fruit ripens or seeds germinate.

Treatment Netting quickly after first damage is seen will allow garden greens to recover or save remaining fruit.

BLOSSOM WILT

Symptoms Spring blossoms turn brown in spring and nearby shoots die back from early summer. Dead blossoms and shoots lingers on the tree and develop cream-colored spots in wet weather.
Plants affected Fruit trees, ornamental cherries, and crabapples.
Prevention Remove rotten fruit and grow resistant cultivars where possible.
Treatment Cut out and burn infected shoots. Use a suitable fungicide.

BOXWOOD SUCKER

Symptoms In spring, leaves on new growth remain bunched together and become wrinkled.
Plants affected Boxwood
Prevention None available.
Treatment Clipping mature plants removes damage. Treat young plants using a suitable pesticide in spring.

BROWN ROT

Symptoms Fruits soften and turn brown around wounds where infection has occurred. Cream-colored spots form on the skins; infected fruit may remain on tree.
Plants affected Fruit trees, ornamental cherries, and crabapples.
Prevention Remove all rotten fruit from tree and ground. Net trees if possible to prevent bird damage.
Treatment Use a suitable fungicide while the tree is flowering.

CABBAGE ROOT FLIES

Symptoms Seedlings and recently transplanted garden greens grow slowly, wilt, and die. White maggots can be found eating their roots.
Plants affected The cabbage family, including rutabagas and turnips.
Prevention Practice crop rotation and prevent flies from laying eggs by placing collars around transplants or protecting with row cover.

Treatment Apply an appropriate biological control. No chemical controls are available.

CAMELLIA GALL

Symptoms Large, off-white growths appear in place of leaves from early summer. The rest of the plant is unaffected.
Plants affected Camellias
Prevention Remove galls when first seen.
Treatment None available.

CAMELLIA LEAF BLIGHT

Symptoms Brown patches form on leaves, which then develop tiny black spots. Leaves may fall and affected stems can die back.
Plants affected Camellias
Prevention Dispose of all fallen leaves.
Treatment Remove infected growth. No chemical controls are available.

CANE SPOT

Symptoms From early summer, purple spots with silvery centers appear on stems, and sometimes leaves. Canes may be killed if the spots spread, splitting the bark.
Plants affected Blackberries, raspberries, and hybrid cane fruits.
Prevention Avoid susceptible cultivars.
Treatment Prune out infected canes. Use a suitable fungicide.

CAPSID BUGS

Symptoms Shoot tips become tattered and full of holes, and flower buds may be deformed or fail to develop from late spring to fall. Damage to young apples results in tan-colored bumps on skins of mature fruit.
Related types Apple capsid
Plants affected Many vegetables, herbaceous plants, shrubs, and apple trees.
Prevention None available.
Treatment Plants often cope well with damage, but appropriate insecticides can be used.

CARNATION TORTRIX MOTH

Symptoms Leaves joined together with silky threads turn brown and dry, after the caterpillar living inside has fed on them.
Plants affected A range of herbaceous plants and shrubs.

Prevention None available.
Treatment Squash any caterpillars found between the leaves or use an appropriate insecticide.

CARROT RUST FLIES

Symptoms Roots are eaten by small white larvae, causing brown tunnels. This can kill seedlings, stunt growth, and spoil crops.
Plants affected Carrots, parsnips, parsley, celery, celeriac, and Florence fennel.
Prevention Practice crop rotation. Protect crops with 2ft (60cm) high barriers or a covering of fabric. Minimize thinning—it attracts adult flies. Grow resistant cultivars.
Treatment Use a suitable nematode biological control to reduce numbers of larvae, or a suitable pesticide for adult flies.

CATERPILLARS

Symptoms A lacelike pattern of damage that appears rapidly on leaves is often caused by butterfly and moth caterpillars, which come in variety of sizes and colors.
Related types Cabbage white, winter moth.
Plants affected Many plants.
Prevention Use of fine netting prevents butterflies from laying eggs on leafy vegetables.
Treatment Remove eggs and caterpillars by hand, treat with a suitable biological pest control or pesticide.

CHOCOLATE SPOT

Symptoms Small, circular brown spots on leaves can enlarge and spread to stems, pods, and flowers, reducing yields and, in serious cases, killing plants.
Plants affected Broad beans
Prevention Grow on well-drained soil and leave plenty of space between plants for good air circulation. Remove all infected plant material and rotate crops.
Treatment Suitable fungicides may provide protection if applied before infection, but none is effective once symptoms are established.

CLEMATIS WILT

Symptoms Leaves wilt, leaf stalks turn black, and whole stems quickly wilt and die.

Whole plants may sometimes be killed.
Plants affected Clematis, especially large-flowered hybrids.
Prevention Provide good moist soil, water and feed regularly, and mulch annually. Plant resistant types.
Treatment Cut out wilted shoots to the base. No chemical controls available.

CLUBROOT
Symptoms Drastically swollen roots lead to weak growth, purple-tinged leaves, wilting, and sometimes, plant death.
Plants affected Garden greens, including related root crops, such as rutabagas, and related ornamental plants (e.g., wallflowers).
Prevention Add lime to acidic soils, improve drainage, keep soil weed-free, and grow resistant cultivars.
Treatment There is no treatment for infected plants.

CODLING MOTH
Symptoms A hole appears in the skin of ripe fruit, and flesh is spoiled by the tunnels and excrement of small caterpillars.
Plants affected Apples and pears.
Prevention Pheromone traps hung in trees in late spring show if the moths are present to help time pesticide application correctly.
Treatment The nematode *Steinernema carpocapsae* kills overwintering caterpillars when applied in fall. Use a suitable pesticide from early to midsummer.

COMMON POTATO SCAB
Symptoms Rough, bumpy, brown patches appear on the surface of tubers and roots, but are usually superficial.
Plants affected Mainly potatoes, but also beets, radishes, rutabagas, and turnips.
Prevention Add organic matter and water to keep soil moist while tubers develop. Do not lime soil before potato crop. Grow resistant cultivars.
Treatment None available.

CORAL SPOT
Symptoms Small, salmon-pink pustules appear on dead wood and can cause further dieback.

Plants affected Many trees and shrubs.
Prevention Prune correctly, during dry weather, without leaving long stubs that are prone to infection.
Treatment Cut out infected areas back to healthy wood. No fungicides are available.

CURRANT BLISTER APHID
Symptoms In spring and early summer, leaves at shoot tips develop red or yellow raised areas, with pale yellow insects underneath. Growth and fruiting are rarely affected.
Plants affected Red, white, and black currants.
Prevention Encourage beneficial insects.
Treatment Not worthwhile once symptoms appear. Overwintering eggs can be killed with a suitable insecticidal wash midwinter, or apply an appropriate insecticide in early spring.

DAMPING OFF
Symptoms Seedlings don't come through the soil or quickly collapse and die.
Plants affected Seedlings
Prevention Use fresh potting mix, clean pots, and tap water when sowing seeds to prevent infection. Sow thinly and provide good ventilation. A suitable fungicide, watered onto seedlings, is effective.
Treatment None available.

DEER, RABBITS, AND SQUIRRELS
Symptoms Leaves, flowers, stems, and bark may be nibbled or destroyed. Stems can be partially chewed, which then die back. Bulbs can be unearthed and eaten. Even large plants can be killed or damaged.
Plants affected Most plants.
Prevention Fence the garden to keep deer and rabbits out. Shield young trees with protective tubes, and cover vulnerable plants and bulbs with chicken wire.
Treatment Cut back damage to healthy growth where possible, and protect the plant from further attack.

DIEBACK
Symptoms Stems fade and die, with wilting leaves and sometimes dark patches

on bark. Symptoms may begin at the base, shoot tip, or from a wound, spreading into healthy tissue.
Plants affected Many plants.
Prevention Avoid waterlogging and drought. Prune correctly to minimize chances of fungal infection.
Treatment Cut out all affected stems.

DOWNY MILDEW
Symptoms Patches of yellow or brown discoloration on upper leaf surface, with pale mold beneath. Badly affected leaves can die. It is worse in wet weather.
Related types Brassica, lettuce, onion, and pansy downy mildew.
Plants affected A wide range.
Prevention Avoid overhead watering, leave space between plants, and keep greenhouses well ventilated to reduce humid air around plants. Grow resistant vegetable cultivars.
Treatment Remove infected leaves. No suitable fungicides are available.

EELWORMS
Symptoms Stunted, distorted growth, and swollen stems are common signs of infection. Tiny, pale, hairlike worms can often be found living in bulbs, stems, or near roots of infected plants.
Related types Narcissus, onion, phlox, and potato cyst eelworms.
Plants affected Many types of plants.
Prevention Destroy infested plants. Practice crop rotation and don't replant related ornamentals in the same site.
Treatment None available.

FIREBLIGHT
Symptoms Blossoms wilt and die, as do adjacent shoots. Brown leaves remain on the plant. Infections seep white slime in wet weather, and sunken areas of bark may form. Infection spreads and can kill plants.
Plants affected Apples, pears, and related plants, such as cotoneaster and pyracantha.
Prevention Clean pruning tools to avoid spreading infection.
Treatment Cut out and burn any infected wood immediately.

FLEA BEETLE
Symptoms Small, round holes in leaves that may not go all the way through. Seedlings are particularly susceptible. Beetles jump off leaves when disturbed.
Plants affected The cabbage family, including arugula, mizuna, and ornamentals, such as wallflowers.
Prevention Cover germinating vegetables with fabric to keep beetles out.
Treatment Use a suitable insecticide.

FUNGAL LEAF SPOT
Symptoms Gray or brown spots on leaves, which may remain circular or join together and kill whole leaves. Circles of tiny black dots are sometimes visible.
Related types Celery, currant and gooseberry, ivy, and strawberry leaf spot.
Plants affected A wide range.
Prevention Remove or rake up infected leaves. Ensure good growing conditions.
Treatment Not always necessary. Suitable fungicides can be used for some plants.

GLADIOLUS CORM ROT
Symptoms Foliage has yellow spattering at tips, gradually developing downward into stripes. Leaves eventually die. Corms form raised, brown markings and dry out during storage.
Plants affected Gladioli, crocuses, and bulb-forming irises.
Prevention Check corms before planting and only plant healthy corms in a new, disease-free site each year.
Treatment Destroy infected plants.

GOOSEBERRY MILDEW
Symptoms A powdery, pale gray coating develops on leaves, stems, and fruit. Fruit skins turn brown and shoots can die back.
Plants affected Gooseberries and black currants.
Prevention Grow resistant cultivars and avoid high-nitrogen fertilizers that encourage vulnerable soft growth.
Treatment Cut out affected growth and prune to create an open bush that allows air in. Use a suitable fungicide.

GRAY MOLD
Symptoms Leaves, flowers, and fruit show a burst of fluffy gray fungal growth, which spreads rapidly in wet conditions. Affected areas can die and fruit rots.
Plants affected Fruit, vegetables, and many ornamentals.
Prevention Clear away all dead plant material, and ensure good ventilation in greenhouses.
Treatment Remove any affected parts of the plant immediately. No suitable fungicides are available.

HALO BLIGHT
Symptoms Wet-looking spots form on leaves, which turn dark with a yellow halo surrounding them. Leaves then yellow and may die, reducing yields.
Plants affected Green and runner beans.
Prevention Only buy fresh seed from a reputable supplier.
Treatment Destroy infected plants.

HELLEBORE LEAF BLOTCH
Symptoms Dark brown, dead areas appear on leaves. Stems may also be affected, causing them to collapse.
Plants affected Hellebores, particularly *Helleborus niger*.
Prevention Remove infected leaves. Cut back old leaves as new shoots emerge.
Treatment None available.

HEMEROCALLIS GALL MIDGE
Symptoms Flower buds look swollen and don't open. They are infested with small white maggots.
Plants affected Daylilies (*Hemerocallis*)
Prevention Grow late-flowering cultivars, which may escape damage.
Treatment Destroy affected buds quickly.

HONEY FUNGUS
Symptoms Plants die back over several seasons, or quite suddenly. Leaves may be small and take on fall colors early. Bark near ground level sometimes splits, with white fungal growth between the bark and wood. Honey-colored toadstools may emerge in fall.

Plants affected Many woody plants and herbaceous perennials.
Prevention Choose plants more resistant to infection, such as bamboo, bay, and yew.
Treatment Dig out and burn infected plants, including the stump and roots. Remove black fungal threads from the soil.

LEEK MOTH
Symptoms Pale patches on stems, where brown-headed caterpillars can sometimes be seen feeding inside. Damage to stems can halt growth and cause rot to set in, killing plants.
Plants affected Leeks, onions, shallots, and garlic.
Prevention Cover crops with row cover.
Treatment Pick silky cocoons from leaves. No suitable pesticides are available.

LILY BEETLE
Symptoms Bright red beetles and their larvae eat lily leaves and sometimes flowers.
Plants affected Lilies and fritillaries.
Prevention None
Treatment Pick off beetles and larvae when seen. Treat with a suitable pesticide in spring and summer.

LILY DISEASE
Symptoms Brown oval spots spread over leaves, which wilt and die. Flower buds can be distorted, and infected stems collapse.
Plants affected Lilies
Prevention Remove all spent plant material in fall.
Treatment Destroy infected leaves. No suitable fungicide available.

MICE
Symptoms Seeds and bulbs are dug up and eaten, sometimes leaving young shoots lying on the soil. Mature fruit and vegetables can also be nibbled on the plant or in storage.
Plants affected Bulbs, beans, peas, sweet corn, and other vegetables and fruit.
Prevention Sow crops in pots out of reach. Firm soil well around newly planted bulbs.
Treatment Set mouse traps, taking care to conceal them from birds, pets, and children.

NARCISSUS BASAL ROT

Symptoms Pale pink fungus is visible on stored bulbs, which rot from the root end. Leaves turn yellow and plants don't flower.
Plants affected Daffodils (*Narcissus*).
Prevention Do not plant or store bulbs showing symptoms. Lift bulbs and plant in a new site each year.
Treatment Destroy infected plants and bulbs. No suitable fungicide available.

NARCISSUS BULB FLIES

Symptoms Large maggots feed on the center of bulbs from midsummer, resulting in spindly leaves and no flowers in spring.
Plants affected Daffodils (*Narcissus*) and snowdrops.
Prevention Plant only firm bulbs from reliable suppliers. Adult flies lay eggs in late spring and early summer, when plantings can be protected with row cover.
Treatment Destroy infected bulbs. No suitable insecticide available.

NUTRIENT DEFICIENCIES

Symptoms Foliage takes on yellow and red coloring, and growth and flowering are poor. Plants may start to die back but there are no signs of pests or diseases present.
Related types Iron – leaves of acid-loving plants most commonly turn yellow between veins and brown at edges. Magnesium – yellowing between leaf veins, sometimes tinged red.
Nitrogen – yellow leaves and weak growth. Potassium – plants flower and fruit poorly, with yellow and purple patches, and brown edges on the foliage.
Plants affected All plants, particularly fruit and vegetables; plants in containers; and those grown on sandy, acidic, or alkaline soils. Acid-lovers are especially at risk of iron deficiency if planted in alkaline soil.
Prevention Improve soil annually with well-rotted organic matter, such as garden compost. Repot or replenish potting mix of container-grown plants regularly. Fertilize and water plants routinely. Only grow plants suitable for your soil type.
Treatment Apply suitable fertilizers containing the nutrients in short supply.

ONION FLIES

Symptoms In early summer foliage wilts and young plants can die as their roots are eaten by maggots. In late summer maggots tunnel into bulbs, encouraging rotting.
Plants affected Onions, shallots, leeks, and garlic.
Prevention Plants grown from sets are less susceptible. Cover beds with fabric to prevent egg laying.
Treatment Lift and destroy affected plants. Use a suitable biological control.

ONION THRIPS

Symptoms White flecks develop on foliage during summer, and pale yellow or black insects can be seen on leaves.
Plants affected Onions, shallots, and leeks.
Prevention Cover with fabric in spring.
Treatment Often none required. Use a suitable pesticide if necessary, or biological control during warm weather.

ONION WHITE ROT

Symptoms Foliage yellows and wilts. Roots rot, and white fungal growth can be seen at the base of bulbs. Black fungal bodies remain viable in soil for at least seven years.
Plants affected Onions, shallots, leeks, and garlic.
Prevention Avoid introducing infected plants or soil into the garden. Practice crop rotation.
Treatment Destroy infected plants and remove the surrounding soil. No suitable fungicide available.

PARSNIP CANKER

Symptoms Orange-brown, roughened areas are found around the top of roots.
Plants affected Parsnips
Prevention Sow resistant cultivars and improve soil drainage. Protect from carrot rust flies with row cover since damage allows infection.
Treatment None available.

PEA AND BEAN WEEVILS

Symptoms Notches are eaten from leaf edges by gray-brown beetles. It is not usually harmful.

Plants affected Peas and broad beans.
Prevention None available.
Treatment Often unnecessary, but heavy infestations can be treated with a suitable insecticide.

PEA MOTH

Symptoms Small, white caterpillars are found feeding inside pea pods in summer.
Plants affected Peas
Prevention Early spring and late summer sowings of fast-maturing peas should miss the egg-laying period. Cover crops with row cover or insect mesh.
Treatment Spray with a suitable insecticide as the flowers fade.

PEACH LEAF CURL

Symptoms Leaves become distorted, with thickened patches that often turn bright red and fall prematurely. Plant vigor and crop is reduced as a result of leaf drop.
Plants affected Peaches, nectarines, apricots, and almonds.
Prevention Grow cultivars with resistance. Keeping shoots dry prevents infection, so sheltering wall-trained trees with clear plastic from early winter until late spring is worthwhile. Move pot-grown trees inside.
Treatment Spray with a suitable fungicide just before leaves fall and in late winter.

PEAR MIDGE

Symptoms Fruitlets blacken from the flower end and drop off in early summer. Small maggots can be found inside.
Plants affected Pears
Prevention Pick up infected fruitlets to keep larvae from going into soil to pupate.
Treatment Use a suitable pesticide just before blossoms open.

PEONY WILT

Symptoms Foliage develops brown patches, buds wilt and fail to open, and whole stems can collapse in early summer.
Plants affected Peonies
Prevention Clear away all plant debris.
Treatment Remove infected stems quickly and burn or compost. No suitable fungicide is available.

PESTALOTIOPSIS
Symptoms Leaves yellow and brown from the shoot tip, and stems can die back. Can result in brown patches in conifer hedges.
Plants affected Many conifers.
Prevention Healthy plants are more resistant, so keep well watered and prune at the correct time of year.
Treatment Prune out infected growth.

PHYTOPHTHORA ROOT ROT
Symptoms Wilting and yellowing foliage, leading to branch dieback and eventually death, as a result of the roots rotting.
Plants affected Many trees and shrubs.
Prevention Ensure good soil drainage.
Treatment Remove and destroy infected plants and replace the soil near their roots.

PLUM MOTH
Symptoms Pale pink caterpillars and their dark excrement are found inside ripe fruit.
Plants affected Plums
Prevention Use a pheromone plum moth trap from late spring to midsummer to catch male moths.
Treatment Treat the tree with a suitable insecticide when moths are found in trap.

POTATO BLACKLEG
Symptoms From early summer, foliage appears weak and yellow, and stems turn black and rot at the base. Tubers often rot.
Plants affected Potatoes
Prevention Rotate potato crops, grow resistant cultivars, and buy seed potatoes from a reputable source.
Treatment Dispose of infected plants quickly. No suitable fungicides available.

POTATO AND TOMATO BLIGHT
Symptoms Brown, watery patches spread from the tips and edges of leaves, which quickly die. Similar spots on stems cause them to collapse. Infected tubers rot, often in storage. Tomato foliage shows similar symptoms, and fruit turns brown and rots. Plants may die back as a result.
Plants affected Potatoes and tomatoes, especially tomatoes grown outdoors.
Prevention Rotate crops, grow early-fruiting and resistant cultivars, and hill up potatoes to protect the tubers.
Treatment Cut down and destroy plants at the first sign of infection.

POWDERY MILDEW
Symptoms Leaves, stems, flowers, and sometimes fruit are covered with white, powdery fungal growth. Infected areas may discolor and distort.
Related types Apple, pansy, pea, and rose powdery mildew.
Plants affected Many plants.
Prevention Keep plants well watered. Rake up fallen leaves. Grow resistant cultivars.
Treatment Cut out affected growth. Use a suitable fungicide.

RASPBERRY BEETLE
Symptoms Fruits have dark, dried up patches and may contain maggots.
Plants affected Raspberries, blackberries, and hybrid cane fruits.
Prevention None available.
Treatment Use a suitable pesticide as fruit begins to ripen.

RASPBERRY CANE BLIGHT
Symptoms Leaves wilt and canes develop dark brown patches at the base and die. They snap easily where the bark has split.
Plants affected Raspberries
Prevention Do not replant raspberries on infected sites. Improve soil, and give plants space to grow well. Avoid damaging canes, which may allow infection in.
Treatment Cut out infected canes to the base and disinfect pruners.

RED THREAD
Symptoms Brown patches on lawns with slender red fungal growth, often during late summer and fall.
Plants affected Lawn grasses.
Prevention Scarify lawn to improve aeration, and fork to improve drainage. Remove clippings and apply nitrogen feed in spring and summer.
Treatment Apply nitrogen-rich fertilizer to the area by the end of late summer, or treat with a suitable fungicide.

ROOT APHIDS
Symptoms Plants grow slowly and often wilt in hot weather. Cream or blue-green insects can be found clustered around the stem base or roots.
Related types Lettuce and rose root aphids.
Plants affected Many ornamental and crop plants.
Prevention Covering vegetables with fabric during summer may limit attacks. Practice crop rotation.
Treatment Young lettuce can be unearthed, the aphids washed off, and the lettuce replanted. Pesticide treatment has limited effect below ground.

ROSE BLACK SPOT
Symptoms Black blotches form on leaves, which then yellow and drop prematurely.
Plants affected Roses
Prevention Rake up and destroy fallen leaves in fall.
Treatment Use a suitable fungicide as soon as symptoms appear.

ROSE REPLANT DISEASE
Symptoms New plants, positioned on the site of an old rose, put on little growth and sometimes die. Roots may be rotten.
Plants affected Roses
Prevention Replace the soil in an area larger than the established roots. Try applying high-nitrogen fertilizer and a mycorrhizal soil improver when planting. Choose a different site.
Treatment None available. Transplant to a new location and the rose may recover.

RUSTS
Symptoms Spots on the upper leaf surface develop, with raised pustules beneath. Usually orange, spots can also form on stems too. Leaves fall early; plants lack vigor and can even be killed.
Related types Bean, hollyhock, leek, mint, raspberry, and rose rusts.
Plants affected Many types.
Prevention Clear away debris in fall. Avoid using high-nitrogen fertilizer, which promotes soft growth that is easily infected.

Treatment Remove infected leaves. Use a suitable fungicide.

SAWFLIES
Symptoms Caterpillarlike larvae rapidly devour leaves, tunnel into tree fruit, or roll rose leaves into cigar shapes.
Related types Apple, gooseberry, plum, rose leaf-rolling, and Solomon's seal.
Plants affected A number of perennials and fruit trees and bushes.
Prevention Control numbers as larvae overwinter in soil to pupate and lay eggs the following year.
Treatment Squash or pick off larvae in spring and summer. Treat with a suitable insecticide.

SCALE INSECTS
Symptoms Sticky honeydew and sooty mold on upper leaf surfaces is produced by insects that live under brown or waxy white, protective scales that can be found under leaves or on stems.
Plants affected Shrubs, trees, climbers, and many greenhouse plants.
Prevention None available.
Treatment Pick off scales on small plants. Use a suitable insecticide in early to midsummer. Treat greenhouse plants with the biological control, *Metaphycus helvolus*.

SHOTHOLE
Symptoms Round brown spots form on leaves. Holes are left in the leaves when the dead tissue falls away.
Plants affected Trees and shrubs.
Prevention Water and mulch, where necessary, to improve growing conditions. Prune carefully and at the right time of year.
Treatment Can be caused by range of fungal and bacterial diseases, so look for other symptoms before taking action.

SILVER LEAF
Symptoms Leaves develop a silvery appearance and branches die back. Infected wood has a dark stain at its center.
Plants affected Plums, cherries, apricots, and rhododendrons.
Prevention Prune susceptible plants in

summer, using wound paint to seal cuts.
Treatment None available.

SLUGS AND SNAILS
Symptoms Holes eaten in leaves and flowers, destroyed seedlings, damaged stems, and chewed root crops. Plants often have a slimy trail leading from them.
Plants affected Many, but especially soft growth of seedlings, bedding plants, perennials, and vegetables.
Prevention Encourage predators into the garden. Create barriers using, for example, copper tape or slug repellents around plants. Catch them by flashlight or in sunken traps filled with beer.
Treatment A nematode biological control applied from spring to fall will reduce slugs, but is less effective on snails.

SOOTY MOLD
Symptoms A black layer develops on leaves covered with honeydew excreted by sap-sucking insects.
Plants affected Many plants.
Prevention Deal with the pest responsible.
Treatment Wipe leaves clean.

SPIDER MITES
Symptoms Pale mottling on foliage, with tiny yellow-green mites hiding underneath leaves. Heavy infestations produce silk webbing and cause leaves to fall early.
Plants affected Many grown under cover and those outdoors in summer.
Prevention None available.
Treatment Use biological control *Phytoseiulus persimilis* in warm conditions, or a suitable insecticide.

TARSONEMID MITES
Symptoms New foliage and flowers are small and distorted, and growth can stop completely. Shoot tips are infested with tiny, pale brown mites.
Plants affected Many bedding plants and perennials.
Prevention Don't introduce plants with symptoms to the garden.
Treatment Destroy affected plants. No insecticides available.

THRIPS
Symptoms Small, narrow insects can be seen feeding on leaf surfaces, and cause pale mottling on foliage.
Plants affected A wide range.
Prevention None available.
Treatment Often none required. Use a suitable pesticide if necessary, or biological control in warm weather.

TOMATO MOTH
Symptoms Leaves show pale, papery patches caused by young caterpillars. Later, large holes are eaten in the leaves and fruit. The green-brown caterpillars hide during the day and are difficult to spot.
Plants affected Tomatoes
Prevention None available.
Treatment Watch for damage and pick off caterpillars when seen, or spray with a suitable insecticide.

TULIP FIRE
Symptoms Tulip leaves become twisted and covered in brown spots, which develop gray mold in wet weather.
Plants affected Tulips
Prevention Only plant healthy bulbs. Don't plant tulips in diseased soil for three years.
Treatment Remove infected plants promptly and destroy.

TULIP GRAY BULB ROT
Symptoms Leaves fail to grow, or emerge distorted and quickly die. Infected bulbs become gray and dry as they rot, and gray fungal growth can be seen on the outside and between scales.
Plants affected Many bulbs including alliums, crocuses, lilies, daffodils, and tulips.
Prevention Do not plant infected bulbs or replant tulips in diseased soil for five years.
Treatment Lift affected plants and the surrounding soil, and throw away.

VERTICILLIUM WILT
Symptoms Wilting occurs over parts, or whole plants, and foliage yellows. Branches die back on trees and shrubs. Dark tissue under the bark is visible if stems are cut.
Plants affected A wide range.

Prevention The disease can be carried on soil and by weeds, so avoid contamination and keep weed-free.
Treatment Destroy infected plants.

VIBURNUM BEETLE
Symptoms Shrubs are defoliated by larvae from late spring to early summer, and adult beetles from midsummer into fall.
Plants affected Viburnums, including *V. tinus* and *V. opulus*.
Prevention None available.
Treatment Pick off larvae by hand or use a suitable insecticide in late spring.

VINE WEEVIL
Symptoms Adult beetles eat notches in leaf edges in spring and summer, but root damage caused by grubs during fall and winter is more serious. Plants wilt and die as their roots are attacked.
Plants affected A wide range, especially those in containers.
Prevention Pick off adult beetles by hand and encourage beneficial wildlife.
Treatment Nematodes are available as biological controls and work particularly well applied to pots in late summer. Suitable pesticides can be used to treat plants in pots, but not those in open soil.

VIRUSES
Symptoms Patterned markings and distortion on leaves, stems, and flowers, along with a loss of vigor, although plants are rarely killed.
Related types Cucumber mosaic virus, daffodil virus, and potato viruses.
Plants affected Many plants.
Prevention Control weeds and aphids, since they help spread some viruses. Grow resistant cultivars where available. Don't propagate from diseased plants.
Treatment Destroy all infected plants.

WASPS
Symptoms Holes nibbled in ripe soft skinned tree fruits, such as plums, and damage caused to tougher-skinned fruit by birds is enlarged.
Plants affected Fruit trees.

Prevention Pick fruit as soon as they ripen and avoid leaving fallen fruit beneath trees.
Treatment Hang wasp traps in branches.

WHITEFLIES
Symptoms Small white insects fly up from plants when disturbed, and excrete honeydew, which can cause sooty mold to form on leaves below.
Plants affected Many greenhouse plants, garden greens, and shrubs.
Prevention None available.
Treatment Use suitable insecticides. In greenhouses, hang up sticky yellow sheets to catch the adults, or use the biological control, *Encarsia formosa*.

WINTER MOTH
Symptoms In spring, young leaves are woven together with silky threads and eaten by yellow-green caterpillars. These holes expand as the leaves grow. Blossoms and young fruit can also be damaged, affecting yields.
Plants affected Fruit trees and other deciduous trees and shrubs.
Prevention Encourage birds into the garden to eat caterpillars, and place a sticky

grease band around the trunk in late fall to prevent females from laying eggs.
Treatment Use a suitable insecticide as leaves unfurl in spring.

WIREWORMS
Symptoms Rust-colored beetle larvae live in soil. They kill seedlings by eating through the stems and tunnel into root vegetables.
Plants affected Seedlings and root vegetables.
Prevention Dig up root vegetables promptly. Although wireworms are common on newly cultivated lawns, they usually decrease each year. Prepare and work the soil well each year.
Treatment None available.

Natural allies By caring for your plants—watering and feeding them well—and by encouraging wildlife into your garden, most plant problems can be avoided.

Index

A

acer gall mites 125
acer tar spot 127
acidic soils 13, 39, 64, 85, 88, 101
adelgids 126, 180
algae 175, 176
annuals 18, 19, 159–63 *see also* climbers
ants 32, 163, 175, 178
aphids 43, 115, 180
    climbers 142, 144
    fruit 91, 92, 95, 102, 105
    fruiting crops 48, 51
    garden bulbs 167
    garden greens 65, 67, 69
    garden shrubs 133, 136, 137
    garden trees 120, 123, 126
    leafy greens 61, 62
    patio & bedding plants 160, 161, 163
    perennials 152, 153, 154
    pod crops 78, 80
    root crops 57 *see also* specific types
        (e.g., mealy aphids)
apple capsid bugs 92, 97, 181
apple leaf miners 95
apple & pear canker 92, 96, 180
apple & pear scab 92, 96
apple powdery mildew 96, 185
apple sawflies 92, 97, 186
apples 33, 87, 88, 89, 91–8
arugula 42, 45, 59–63
asparagus 71–5
asparagus beetle 73, 75, 180

B

bacterial infections 23
    bacterial canker 92, 96, 115, 123, 124, 180
    bacterial leaf spot 180
bamboos 151
barriers 26, 121
bay sucker 137
bean chocolate spot 78, 81, 181–2
bean rust 78, 81, 186
bean seed flies 42, 79, 80, 180
bean weevils, pea & 79, 81, 184
beans 38, 39, 40, 42, 45, 77–81
bedding plants 18, 19, 112, 158–63
beet leaf miners 54, 56, 61, 62
beets 44, 53–7

beneficial insects 24–5, 28–9, 31, 32
biennials 18, 19, 159–63
biological controls 27
bird pests 26, 28–9, 181
    bulb & stem crops 72
    fruit 92, 97, 101, 102, 105
    fruiting crops 49, 50
    garden greens 23, 42, 64, 66, 67, 68
    garden trees 121
    pod crops 42, 78, 81
    seedlings 41
birds, beneficial behavior 25, 26, 29
bitter pit, apple 92, 94, 180
bitterness, leafy salads 58, 61, 62, 63
black bean aphids 78, 80, 180
black currants 22, 84, 86, 87, 101–5, 107
black spot, rose 115, 136, 185
blackberries 86, 87–8, 100, 102–5
blackberry leaf spot 102
blight *see* specific types (e.g., potato blight)
blind bulbs 168
blister aphid/mite, currant 22, 105, 182
blossom end rot 49, 51
blossom wilt 92, 97, 115, 124, 181
blueberries 22, 84, 87, 88, 101–3, 106
bolting/running to seed
    bulb & stem crops 75
    garden greens 64, 67
    leafy greens 58, 61, 62, 63
    root crops 55, 56
boxwood suckers 137, 181
bracket fungus 23, 122, 124
brassica downy mildew 67, 68
brassicas *see* specific types (e.g., cabbage)
broad beans 39, 77–81
broccoli 40, 45, 65–9
brown rot 92, 95, 181
Brussels sprouts 64, 66–9
bulb flies, narcissus 115, 167, 184
bulbs
    bulb & stem crops 39, 45, 70–5
    ornamentals 17, 111, 112, 113–14, 116, 164, 166–9
bush fruit 84–9, 101–7

C

cabbage 45, 64, 66–9
cabbage collars 26, 64
cabbage root flies 64, 66, 69, 181
cabbage white caterpillars 67, 69, 181
cabbage whiteflies 67, 68
calcium deficiency 51, 94, 180
camellia gall 181

camellia leaf blight 134, 181
cane fruit 84–9, 100, 102–5, 107
cane spot 102, 104, 181
canker
    bacterial 92, 96, 115, 123, 124, 180
    parsnip 56, 184
capsid bugs 181
    fruit 92, 97, 102, 104
    ornamentals 132, 153, 160, 161
carnation tortrix moth 181
carrot rust flies 26, 41, 55, 56, 181
carrots 40, 44, 53–7
caterpillars 28, 132, 153, 160, 181 *see also* specific
    types (e.g., cabbage white)
cauliflower 65–9
celery 71–5
celery leaf spot 73, 183
celery root 71–5
centipedes 29
chard 45, 59–63
chemical-free gardening 24–7
chemical sprays 23, 28, 31, 133, 153, 155, 173
cherries 85, 87, 90, 92–7, 98, 99
chicory 58, 60–3
chiles 40, 46, 48–51
chocolate spot 78, 81, 181–2
chlorosis, lime-induced 125
clematis 112, 115, 141, 146
clematis wilt 115, 142, 145, 182
climbing plants 15, 111, 112, 113–14, 115, 116,
    140–7
clubroot 39, 64, 66, 69, 182
clump-forming perennials 16, 116, 151–7
codling moth 89, 92, 97, 182
cold damage 12
    frost pockets 12, 85, 110
    fruit 85, 90, 92, 94, 101, 102
    fruiting crops 42, 44, 51
    garden shrubs 130, 132, 134, 136
    patio & bedding plants 158, 159, 161, 162
    perennials 151, 153, 154
    pod crops 77, 78, 81
    root crops 52, 54
    seedlings 41
common potato scab 55, 57, 182
companion planting 24, 26, 27
compost
    compost heaps 25, 27
    soil improvement 13, 24–5, 112, 140, 141, 142
conifers 120, 122, 126, 129
container growing
    fertilizer granules 33

fruit 85, 88, 90, 91, 101
ornamentals 114–15, 135, 160
pot-bound plants 20, 111, 160
vegetables 39, 43, 50
container-grown plants, buying & planting 14, 15, 84, 86, 88, 111, 113–14
coral spot 95, 122, 127, 133, 182
corm rot, gladiolus 183
corms 17, 164, 166–9
crop rotation 26, 43, 44
crown rot 156
cuckoo spit 33
cucumber mosaic virus 47, 49, 51
cucumbers & cucumber family 44, 47–51
cultivars, choosing 40, 84, 110–11, 115
currant blister aphid/mite 22, 105, 182
currant & gooseberry leaf spot 102, 183
currants 22, 84, 86, 87, 101–5, 107
cutworms 60, 62, 152, 160

D E

damping off disease 41, 42, 48, 60, 66, 182
deadheading 18, 151, 159, 161, 163
deer 28, 121, 123, 132, 182
dieback 21, 63, 97, 120, 132, 182
disease-resistant plants 40, 84, 110, 115
diseases 20–3, 180–7 see also specific diseases (e.g., downy mildews)
division
garden bulbs 164, 166, 167, 168
perennials 16, 150, 153, 155
dog lichen 175
dog urine 174, 179
downy mildew 60, 63, 67, 68, 73, 75, 153, 182
drainage & waterlogging 13
containers 88, 114
fruit trees & bushes 85, 101
fruiting crops 46, 51
garden bulbs 167
garden trees & shrubs 120, 122, 125, 130
lawns 117, 175, 176
leafy greens 61
ornamentals 112
patio & bedding plants 160, 163
perennials 152, 154
pod crops 45
root crops 44, 52, 53, 54, 56
vegetables 38
drought see weather problems
earthworms 175, 177
eelworms 115, 167, 168, 182

eggplant 46, 48–51
endive 58, 60–3

F

fairy rings 177
fasciation 33
fennel, Florence 71–5
fertilizing
containers 115, 135
fruit 88, 89
lawns 117, 174, 177, 178
ornamentals 114, 116, 143, 153, 159, 161, 163
vegetables 43, 46, 48
figs 91, 99
fireblight 92, 97, 123, 132, 183
flea beetles 183
bulb & stem crops 73
garden greens 66, 67
leafy greens 59, 61, 64
patio & bedding plants 160
root crops 54, 57
seedlings 41, 42
flies see by specific plant affected (e.g., carrot rust flies)
flowers 10, 11, 20
beneficial insect attractants 24–5, 26, 31
bulb & stem crops 70, 71, 73
fruit trees 90, 94
garden greens 45, 65–9
leafy greens 58, 59, 61, 62
ornamental plants see specific types (e.g., garden shrubs)
pod crops 76, 78, 81
root crops 52, 53 see also pollination
foliage problems 20–3, 32
bulb & stem crops 73, 75
climbers 142–5
fruit trees 22, 92, 93, 94, 95, 96
fruiting crops 46, 47, 49, 50, 51
garden bulbs 164, 166, 167, 168
garden greens 66, 67, 68, 69
garden shrubs 130–7
garden trees 120, 122–7
leafy greens 60, 61, 62, 63
leaves on lawns 178
perennials 17, 150, 152–7
pod crops 78, 81
root crops 52, 54, 56, 57
soft fruit 22, 101, 102, 104
forking, root crops 39, 53, 55, 57
froghoppers 33

frogs & toads 25, 26, 29
fruit
fruit trees 27, 33, 84–9, 90–9
misshapen 21
soft fruit 84–9, 100–7
fruit cages 85
fruiting crops 38, 40, 42, 44, 46–51
fungal diseases 20, 23, 115, 169 see also specific diseases (e.g., chocolate spot)
fungal leaf spot 183
fruit 102, 105, 183
ornamentals 135, 142, 145, 153, 157, 161, 162, 183
vegetables 60, 67, 73, 183
fungicides 23, 27
fungus see specific types (e.g., bracket fungus)
fusarium patch 178

G

gall midge, hemerocallis 157, 183
gall mites, acer 125
galls 120
camellia 181
garden bulbs 17, 111, 112, 113–14, 116, 164–9
garden greens 23, 39, 40, 42, 43, 45, 64–9
garden hygiene 25, 29, 68, 89, 90, 115, 178
garden shrubs 14–15, 111, 112, 113–14, 116, 130, 132–9
garden trees 14, 111, 112, 113–14, 116, 120–9
garlic 39, 45, 70, 72–5
germination problems
bulb & stem crops 72
fruiting crops 38, 48
garden greens 66
leafy greens 60
pod crops 38, 77, 79
root crops 55
ghost spot, tomato 33
gladiolus corm rot 167, 183
gooseberries 87, 101–5, 107
gooseberry leaf spot, currant & 102, 183
gooseberry mildew 105, 180
gooseberry sawflies 104, 186
graft unions 21, 121
grass
annual meadow grass 31
lawns 19, 117, 172–9
gray bulb rot, tulip 167, 168, 186–7
gray mold 183
fruit 104
leafy greens 60, 63
ornamentals 115, 153, 157, 161, 163
grease bands 89

green beans 38, 77–81
green spruce aphids 126, 180
greening, potato tubers 52, 55, 57
ground beetles 29

H

halo blight 78, 183
hardening off 41–2, 79
hardy perennials 16, 112, 113–14, 116, 150–7
hedgehogs 25, 29
hedges 120
hellebore leaf blotch 157, 183
hemerocallis gall midge 157, 183
herbaceous perennials 11, 16, 111, 112, 113–14, 116, 150–7
herbs 59, 63, 179
hilling up 52, 57
hollyhock rust 157, 186
honey fungus 92, 122, 123, 126, 132, 177, 183
honeydew 20, 32, 120, 136, 137, 186
hoverflies 29
hybrid berries 100, 102–5

I J K

insect collars 26, 64
insecticides 23, 27
insects see specific groups (e.g.,
    beneficial insects)
    & types (e.g., pea moth)
iron deficiency 13, 66, 125, 184
ivy 114, 140, 144
ivy leaf spot 145, 183
Jerusalem artichokes 52
June drop 33, 94
kale 45, 64, 66–9
kohlrabi 71–5

L

lacewings 29
ladybugs & ladybug larvae 25, 29, 33
lawns 19, 117, 172–9
leaf miners
    apple 95
    ornamentals 126, 137, 153, 154
    vegetables 54, 56, 59, 61, 62
leaf spot
    bacterial 180
    fungal see fungal leaf spot
leafy salad crops 40, 45, 58–63
leatherjackets 174, 177
leek moth 73, 74, 183
leek rust 73, 75, 186

leeks 70, 72–5
lettuce 40, 45, 58–63
lettuce downy mildew 60, 63
lettuce gray mold 60, 63
lettuce root aphids 61, 62, 185
lichens 33, 175
lily beetles 28, 115, 166, 169, 183
lily disease 167, 183
lime-induced chlorosis 125
liming soil 39, 64
loam 13

M

maggots
    fruit crops 92, 96, 97, 105
    vegetable crops 56, 62, 66, 73
magnesium deficiency 13, 49, 50, 125, 184
mahonia rust 136
manuring 13, 25, 39, 57, 79, 112
marrows 47, 51
mealy aphids 69, 180
mice 183
    soft fruit 102
    vegetable crops 42, 49, 50, 76, 78, 79, 80
microgreens 59
midges see specific types (e.g., pear midge)
mildew see downy mildews;
    powdery mildews
mint rust 63, 186
mites see specific types (e.g., spider mites)
mizuna 59–63
moles & molehills 175, 177
moss 175, 176
moths see specific types (e.g., codling moth)
mold see gray mold; sooty mold
mulching 13, 25, 30, 89, 114, 116, 131

N

narcissus basal rot 167, 169, 184
narcissus bulb flies 115, 167, 184
narcissus eelworm 167, 168
nectarines 90, 92–7
nematodes 27
netting pest prevention 26
    fruit 85, 89, 92, 101, 102
    seedlings 41
    vegetables 53, 56, 64, 66, 68, 69
nitrogen deficiency 13, 66, 184
nutrient deficiencies 13, 22, 184
    fruit 94, 95, 102, 180
    garden trees & shrubs 122, 125, 132
    vegetables 49, 50, 51, 66

O

onion downy mildew 73, 75
onion flies 73, 74, 184
onion thrips 73, 184
onion white rot 73, 74, 184
onions & onion family 45, 70, 72–5
organic gardening 24–7
ornamentals, growing 110–16 see also specific
    types (e.g., bedding plants)
overwintering 158, 165, 166, 169

P

parsnip canker 56, 184
parsnips 40, 53–7
patio plants 18, 19, 112, 113–14, 158–63
pea & bean weevils 79, 81, 184
pea moth 76, 78, 80, 184
peach leaf curl 22, 89, 93, 96, 184
peaches 22, 85, 87, 89, 90, 92–7
pear canker, apple & 92, 96, 180
pear midge 92, 96, 184
pear scab, apple & 92, 96, 180
pears 33, 87, 91–8
peas 42, 45, 76, 78–81
peony wilt 156, 184
peppers 38, 40, 44, 46, 48–51
perennials 16, 17, 111, 112, 113–14, 116, 150–7
    see also climbers; tender perennials
pestalotiopsis 126, 185
pesticides 23, 27, 28
pests 20, 22–9, 32–3, 180–7 see also plant types
    affected (e.g., garden greens); specific pests
    (e.g., aphids)
pH testing 13, 110
phytophthora root rot 123, 132, 185
pigeons see bird pests
pip fruit 27, 33, 84–9, 91–8
plant reproduction 10, 11, 21, 134, 164
    propagating perennials 150, 153, 155, 158
    see also pollination; seeds & sowing
planting & spacing
    fruit 84, 86–8, 123
    garden trees & shrubs 112, 120, 133
    ornamentals 112–13, 143, 159, 164–8
    replanting 110, 185
    seedlings 41, 42
    vegetables 55, 64, 65, 66, 70, 72, 77
plum moth caterpillars 89, 92, 97, 181, 185
plum sawflies 92, 186
plums 87, 89, 90, 92–7, 98, 99
pod crops 38, 39, 40, 42, 43, 45, 76–81
pollarding 128

pollen beetles 33
pollination 11
    beneficial insects 24–5, 29, 31
    fruit trees 84, 90, 91, 93, 94
    fruiting crops 44, 46, 47, 48, 50
    garden shrubs 134
    pod crops 45, 78, 81
    soft fruit 84, 100, 101, 103, 105
pot-bound plants 20, 111, 160
potassium deficiency 184
potato blackleg 185
potato blight 54, 56, 185
potato scab, common 55, 57, 182
potato spraing 57
potato wireworm 55, 57
potatoes 44, 52, 54–7
potting mix
    for containers 88, 114
powdery mildews 185
    climbers 115, 142, 145
    fruit 96, 105, 180
    garden trees & shrubs 115, 127, 133
    patio & bedding plants 161, 163
    perennials 150, 153, 157
    vegetables 49, 60, 78
propagating perennials 16, 150, 153, 155, 158
pruning
    climbers 15, 140, 143, 144, 145, 146–7
    fruit trees 88, 89, 90, 93, 95, 98–9
    garden shrubs 14, 116, 130, 131, 133, 134, 137, 138–9
    garden trees 14, 116, 122, 123, 125, 128–9
    perennials 16
    soft fruit 89, 101, 103, 106–7
    training 85, 87–8, 90, 91, 99

Q R

quince 91
rabbits 28, 121, 132, 153, 155, 160, 182
radishes 42, 53–7
rain shadows 12, 113, 143
raised beds 39
raspberries 86, 87–8, 100, 102–5, 107
raspberry beetle 105, 185
raspberry cane blight 102, 185
raspberry cane spot 102, 104, 181
raspberry rust 102, 186
red currants 87, 101–5, 107
red thread 176, 185
repotting 42, 88, 115
rhizomes 17, 165–9
rhubarb 71–5

root aphids 61, 62, 160, 185
root crops 38, 39, 40, 43, 44, 52–7
root rot
    garden trees 120, 125
    patio & bedding plants 160, 162
    perennials 151, 152
    phytophthora 123, 132, 185
roots 10, 20, 23, 140, 150, 151, 164, 165
    taproots 38, 39, 40, 44, 53–7, 151
rootstocks 21, 84, 87, 88, 90, 91, 121
rose black spot 115, 136, 185
rose leaf-rolling sawflies 32, 135, 186
rose powdery mildew 185
rose replant disease 185
rose root aphids 185
rose rust 115, 136, 186
roses 32, 115, 135, 136, 138, 146
runner beans 40, 77–81
running to seed *see* bolting
rusts 153, 161, 167, 186 *see also* by specific plant
    affected (e.g., rose rust)
rutabagas 53–7

S

salad crops, leafy 45, 58–63
sawflies 28, 153, 155, 186 *see also* specific types
    (e.g., plum sawflies)
scab
    apple & pear 92, 96, 180
    common potato 55, 57, 182
scale insects 186
    climbers 142, 144
    garden trees & shrubs 115, 120, 123, 133, 136, 137
    patio & bedding plants 160
scorch 51, 124, 132, 135, 142, 145, 155, 161
seedlings, vegetable 41–2
seeds & sowing 10, 11
    annuals & biennials 159
    microgreens 59
    station sowing 40
    successional sowing 39, 58, 61
    vegetables 38–41 *see also* germination
        problems
shade problems
    lawns 19, 174, 175, 176, 179
    vegetable growing 38
shallots 70, 72–5
shelter 12
shield bugs 33
shothole 95, 115, 186
shrubs 14–15, 111, 112, 113–14, 116, 130–9
silver leaf 95, 99, 115, 186

site selection 12–13, 20, 38, 110, 114–15
slime mold 175, 176
slugs & snails 26, 28, 29, 186
    bulb & stem crops 71, 73
    climbers 142, 144
    fruiting crops 49
    garden bulbs 166, 167, 169
    garden greens 66, 67, 69
    leafy salads 58, 59, 60, 61, 62
    ornamentals 115
    patio & bedding plants 160
    perennials 151, 152, 153, 156
    pod crops 77, 78, 79
    root crops 54, 55
    seedlings 41, 42
soft fruit 27, 84–9, 100–7
soils 13
    acidic 13, 85, 88, 101
    improving 13, 24–5, 112, 140, 141, 142
    liming 39, 64
    manuring 13, 25, 39, 57, 79, 112
    no-dig cultivation 25, 31
    organic gardening 24–5
    pH testing 13, 110
    preparation 39, 85 *see also* nutrient deficiencies
Solomon's seal sawflies 155, 186
sooty mold 68, 95, 120, 133, 136, 186
spacing see planting & spacing
spider mites 49, 50, 132, 142, 152, 153, 160, 161, 185
spinach 59–63
spraing 57
spreading perennials 16, 116, 150, 152–7
sprouts, Brussels 64, 66–9
squashes 40, 47–51
squirrels 123, 132, 167, 169, 182
staking
    fruit trees 86, 87
    ornamentals 114, 116, 127, 165
stem & bulb crops 39, 45, 70–5
stems 11, 20, 131, 139, 140, 141, 150, 158
stone fruit 84–9, 90, 92–7, 99
strawberries 85, 86, 87, 88, 89, 101–5
strawberry leaf spot 102, 105, 183
structure, plant 10–11
suckering shoots 100, 121, 127, 131
supports
    climbers 15, 114, 116, 141, 144
    fruit 86, 87, 100, 106, 107
    fruiting crops 43, 46, 47
    garden greens 64, 65, 69
    ornamentals 114, 116, 127, 165
    perennials 11, 152, 154

pod crops 43, 45, 76, 77, 79, 80, 81
sweet corn 47, 50
sweet potatoes 52
Swiss chard 45, 59–63
symptoms, disease 20–3, 180–7 see also specific
    diseases (e.g., downy mildews)

T
taproots 38, 39, 40, 44, 53–7, 151
tarsonemid mites 186
temperature requirements
    bulb & stem crops 39, 74, 75
    fruit trees & bushes 85, 93, 103
    fruiting crops 38, 40, 42, 44, 46–51
    patio & bedding plants 159, 161
    pod crops 38, 39, 77, 78, 79, 81
tender perennials 18, 19, 158, 160–3
thatch 172, 175
thinning
    seedlings 41
    tree fruit 90, 94
thrips 63, 73, 153, 161, 163, 184, 186
toads & frogs 25, 26, 29
toadstools 23, 126, 177
tomato blight 49, 50, 185
tomato ghost spot 33
tomato moth 186
tomatoes & tomato family 33, 38, 40, 42, 44, 46–51
tortrix moth, carnation 181
training, fruit trees & bushes 85, 87–8, 90, 91, 99
traps 26–7
tree ties 86, 87, 116, 127
trees see fruit trees; garden trees
tubers

ornamentals 17, 165–9
    tuber crops 44, 52, 54–7
tulip fire 167, 186
tulip gray bulb rot 167, 168, 186–7
turnips 53–7

U V
urine, animal 174, 179
variegated shrubs reverting 134
vegetable growing 26, 38–43
verticillium wilt 123, 132, 187
viburnum beetle 115, 132, 137, 187
vine weevils 187
    climbers 145
    garden bulbs 115, 167
    garden shrubs 132, 137
    patio & bedding plants 159, 160, 162
    perennials 151, 152, 157
viruses 23, 187
    garden bulbs 167, 168
    garden shrubs 132, 133
    ornamentals 115
    patio & bedding crops 161
    perennials 153, 154, 157
    soft fruit 22, 85, 89, 104, 105
    vegetables 47, 49, 51, 57, 67, 78

W Z
wasps 27, 29, 92, 97, 102, 187
water shoots 15
watering 10
    containers 43, 88, 115, 135
    seedlings 41, 42 see also specific plant types
waterlogging see drainage & waterlogging

weather problems 12, 38, 39
    bulb & stem crops 72, 73
    climbers 141, 142, 145
    fruit trees 85, 92, 93, 94
    fruiting crops 48, 49, 50, 51
    garden bulbs 167
    garden greens 67, 68, 69
    garden shrubs 130, 132, 134–7
    garden trees 122, 124, 126
    lawns 178
    leafy greens 40, 61, 63
    ornamentals 113
    patio & bedding plants 158, 159, 160, 161, 162
    perennials 151, 153, 154, 155
    pod crops 77, 78, 79, 81
    root crops 54, 55, 56
    soft fruit 85, 100, 102, 103
    see also cold damage; temperature
        requirements
weeds & weeding 30–1, 39, 43, 89, 111, 117, 173
    weed killers 23, 31, 133, 153, 155, 173
weevils see pea & bean weevils; vine weevils
white currants 87, 101–5, 107
white rot, onion 73, 74
whiteflies 48, 67, 68, 115, 187
wilting 10, 20, 51, 58, 61, 63
    patio & bedding plants 159
    perennials 151, 152, 154
winter moth 89, 92, 94, 124, 132, 187
wireworms 42, 55, 57, 187
wisteria 15, 144, 146
worm casts 175, 177
wound paint 98
zucchini 38, 42, 44, 47–51

Acknowledgments

Picture credits
The publisher would like thank the following for
kind permission to reproduce their photographs:

(key: b-below/bottom; c-center; l-left; r-right;
t-top)
Blackmore Nursery 90br, 96cl. **DT Brown Seeds**
64bcl. **Dobies of Devon** 100tr. **Fothergill Seeds**
67br. **Sutton Seeds** 53cb, cbr, 71tr. **Victoriana
Nursery** 84–85 tc. **Dorling Kindersley: Alan
Buckingham** 13cb, 20tl, 21c, cr, 22l, 30tr, bl, br,
31tl, tc, tr, bl, br, 33tr, 35br, 46cr, 50bl, 53bc, 54l,
55l, 56l, 58tl, 59tl, cl. bl, cr, 64bl, cr, r, 65b, 70ctl,
71b, 72l, 73bl, 74l, cr, br, 75cl, bl, 76tl, cl, bl, 77r, br,

78l, 80cl, cr, 81br, 82tl, ct, cb, 83tr, 84b, 86bl, bc, br,
87tc, tr, 89b, 90bl, tr, cr, 91tr, cr, br, 92l, br, 93br,
94c, bl, br, 95cl, cr, ct, 96tl, tr, c, cr, 97tr, tcr, cr, tl,
cbr, 100l, cr, 101br, 102l, c, br, 104cr, 105cl, 109c,
123br, 124cb, br, 135 tl. **Lucy Claxton** 9br, 17br,
25r, 29tc. **Emma Firth** 177cr. **Barrie Watts
Collection** 48br. **Igor Zhorov (c) Alamy** 10c.

Dorling Kindersley would like to thank:
Jo Whittingham, Chauney Dunford, Alison
Shackleton, Caroline Reed, Collette Sadler, Esther
Ripley, Elaine Hewson, Verne Crawford, and
Veronica Peerless for additional photography.
All other images copyright **DK Images**

Proofreader Constance Novice
Index Susan Bosanko

Author's acknowledgments
Many thanks are due to Chauney Dunford,
Alison Shackleton, and the team at Dorling
Kindersley for their contributions at every stage
of this project. I'm enormously grateful to
Malcolm Dodds for the loan of his camera and
tireless support. Thanks also to Judy and Paul
Whittingham, Alma and John Dodds, and all
others who allowed me to poke around their
gardens to photograph their sickly plants. And
to Evan, thanks for eating what I grow with gusto!